D1413357

UNION STATION

ALSO BY JOE FIORITO

NON-FICTION
The Closer We Are to Dying
Comfort Me With Apples
Tango on the Main

FICTION
The Song Beneath the Ice

UNION STATION

LOVE, MADNESS, SEX AND SURVIVAL
ON THE STREETS OF THE NEW TORONTO

JOE FIORITO

McCLELLAND & STEWART

Some of the material in this book has appeared previously, in a different form, in the *National Post*, the *Globe and Mail* and the *Toronto Star*.

Library and Archives Canada Cataloguing in Publication

Fiorito, Joe, 1948-
Union station : Love, madness, sex and survival
on the streets of the new Toronto

ISBN 13: 978-0-7710-4760-2
ISBN 10: 0-7710-4760-6

1. Toronto (Ont.). 2. Toronto (Ont.) – Description and travel.
3. Toronto (Ont.) – Social life and customs – 21st century. I. Title.

FC3097.4.F56 2006   971.3'541   C2005-905967-2

The epigraph on p. 18 is from "Brown Grass." Music and lyrics by Rita MacNeil. Published by Skinners Pond Music.

The epigraph on p. 101 is from "Multicultural Blues" by Pier Giorgio Di Cicco. Reprinted by permission of the author.

Every effort has been made to reach the copyright holders of material excerpted in this book.

We acknowledge the financial support of the Government of Canada through the Book Publishing Industry Development Program and that of the Government of Ontario through the Ontario Media Development Corporation's Ontario Book Initiative. We further acknowledge the support of the Canada Council for the Arts and the Ontario Arts Council for our publishing program.

Typeset in Janson by M&S, Toronto
Printed and bound in Canada

McClelland & Stewart Ltd.
75 Sherbourne Street
Toronto, Ontario
M5A 2P9
www.mcclelland.com

1 2 3 4 5   10 09 08 07 06

For Susan

UNION STATION

I never knew Toronto was disliked so much.

– J.B. PRIESTLEY, *Liberty*, August 1956

Nobody likes a winner.

This is a distinctly Canadian thing. Toronto won all the marbles a long time ago, at least the ones that matter most. How you feel about that, and how you feel about us, is the least of our worries. We don't have time to care. We have to go to work.

That's us, according to our reputation.

We are smug, aloof and in a hurry. I say "we" because I live here now, in a city that is, pound for pound, the richest, meanest, poorest, coldest, cheapest, most diverse in the world, among people who have the softest, smuggest, hardest, biggest hearts.

You don't like us? You are not alone.

Brendan Behan said it better than J.B. Priestley: "Toronto is barbaric without being picturesque. Toronto will be a fine town when it is finished." Consider the source: Behan was a dribbling old tosspot, and he had a grudge; on top of which he couldn't insult us once and get it right, he had to take two runs at it.

He lived in my neighbourhood for a time. According to the cartoonist Aislin, a.k.a. Terry Mosher, who went to school and learned to rebel at Parkdale Collegiate, Behan stayed in rooms down the street and around the corner from where I live now.

Terry told me that the Irishman came to his school a time or two. Such is life around here that the local barbarians scarcely paid him any mind. He would have fit in rather nicely: blotto all the while, except for the time he clocked a cop, and we locked him up in order to dry him out and teach him the error of his ways; perhaps that was the source of his grudge.

For that, too, is our reputation: Toronto the good, the sober, the minder of other people's business. Alas, not much has changed. Behan would recognize the neighbourhood if he fell in the gutter today, although he'd be more likely to step on a used needle than to trip over an empty bottle. We still have no good answer for the junkies or the drunks, just as we had no answer for him. But Brendan got it wrong. Most people get it wrong. Toronto will not be a fine town when it is finished.

It is a fine town because it is unfinished.

Cold, prim, smug, hard and harried: we endure such slights with patience. Our patience is not a virtue; rather, it is a tactic born of necessity. We don't have the time to stop.

I have been poking around the edges of this city for a long time. I think the people who hate Toronto do not know us, nor do they know the kind of lives we lead.

This place is being made and remade every day by layers and waves of immigration; roughly 160,000 newcomers come here every year, and every year roughly 100,000 residents leave here on the bounce, the rebound or the skip. That's a lot of coming and going, and it is a net gain of 60,000 people every year from all the countries of the world.

Nearly half the people who live here were born in other countries.

Can you speak Tagalog? We speak it here.

Men and women come to Toronto from all the countries of the world because they want what we have – relative peace, steady work, schools for the kids, an absence of automatic weapons, and the chance to vote without being blown up.

Check your race and creed at the door.

If you can't make it here . . .

The city – and I think this holds true of yours as well as mine, but it is more true of Toronto by virtue of its sheer size – is not the same today as it was yesterday, and it will be different tomorrow.

Toronto is a work in progress, a bird in flight, a swollen stream in springtime; it is a mural in spray paint on a wall that reaches to the horizon; it is . . . you get the drift. Who we are today is a function of who came here yesterday.

Our high-rises are filled with the poor, the tired and the hungry, the huddled masses yearning to breathe free; ours is a hybrid strength; newcomers are what makes us strong.

Immigrants arrive, settle down, look around, and you know happens next: Korean girls marry the Portuguese boys next door. Jamaicans open shops and sell cowfoot and salt fish to their neighbours. A Somali girl who, on a cold spring morning wearing sandals and a summer dress, crossed the Peace Bridge alone now sets her alarm and rises early to attend nursing school, and if we are lucky, she will tend us when we are old. The truth is this:

The lives we lead here are the same as your lives.

And if there is a comparison to be made it is not with Montreal or Chicago or any other city of the present age. To live here now is how I imagine it was to live in New York City in 1900, its doors open to the world.

You might not like our bankers or our business leaders or our hip taste-makers. Here's news: We don't like them, either. The wrong people have all the money in Toronto, just as they do where you live.

I am not interested in those people, or where they came from, although I have a hunch they came here from some small town; perhaps yours. There is no helping the ambitious. Let them be. They know how to help themselves. I'm interested in everyone else.

This is a contemporary history of us.

ONE

I think one of the biggest mistakes made in this country was that it was so tough about immigration. We should have another 30 million people here.

– MORDECAI RICHLER, quoted in *Quill & Quire*, 1989

The best time of day for students of English is first thing in the morning, before the lesson begins, before the teacher arrives, before the plastic-lidded paper cups of takeout coffee can cool off.

This is the time of day when simple words flow freely and there is no possibility of being right or wrong or misunderstood; pure pleasure reigns. Grazyna greets Elzbieta – although, because this is a language class, they try on their English names as if they were new coats, to see if they fit. And so Grace greets Elizabeth with a heartfelt "Hello! How are you?" The standard answer will do. "I am fine. How are you?"

By way of nothing more than the pure joy of living, the Polish nun Sister Leopolda – she is the class live wire – points out the window, past the forest of power poles, past the cars and the streetcars to the blue sky beyond and says, "Today, the sun to shine on all of us."

Yes, dear Sister, the sun to shine on us.

By us, she means the men and women in this room, the ones who have left their sunny homes in Poland, Sri Lanka, Korea,

Italy, Russia and Ukraine. Sister and her fellows have left the familiar slant of light on familiar streets; they have left familiar faces, familiar birdsong, the familiar scent of the air they first breathed; and they have also left the graves of their parents to be tended by others forever.

They have come to make a new life here.

And so they spend their days in a room above a drugstore at the foot of Roncesvalles Avenue, attending language classes at the Sunnyside Adult Learning Centre.

This is an unlikely place – one of hundreds of unlikely places – to forge the future of a nation. But you can bet that the children and grandchildren of these men and women are going to run the country.

In the old days, there was an implicit notion: the first to arrive were a sacrificial generation; newcomers with few skills and not much language who were willing to set their own lives aside for the sake of their children. These days, we keep the unskilled out. Apart from certain classes of refugees, we restrict immigration to the richest and the best educated from the other countries of the world.

The enduring Toronto cliché is no longer the Rosedale matron or the prim and pinstriped banker; those old stereotypes have been pushed aside by – drum roll, please – the cabbie with the Ph.D. in civil engineering. The first generation is still the sacrificial generation. Because they do not have Canadian experience.

Before they can get it, Grazyna and all the others must first nail down English as a Second Language. Although, in many instances, it ought to be called English as a Third or Fourth Language.

Sister Leopolda and her fellow classmates are keen to learn, but they still speak in hesitant, slow-motion rhythms. Here is what they have learned to say so far:

"I have been in Toronto since October."

"I have been to Mississauga many times."

"I have been in Wonderland for ten hours."

With a broadly theatrical gesture, Sister Leopolda adds, "I have ridden on the train that goes around. Oh!" She says, "train," but she means roller coaster. She says, "Oh," but she means "Buster, once was enough!"

They learn by asking and answering, and so they interview each other, and they take written notes. They ask: Have you ever been on a blind date? Dreamed in English? Eaten raw fish? Sister Leopolda rolls her eyes at that one and says, "Every day raw fish, ha, ha!" She means "Buster, once would be too much!"

The comedy cuts the tension.

It's hard to breathe when you're learning to speak. A word that won't come is a weight on your chest. Malini is Tamil. She says she has met the president of Sri Lanka. Father Teodoro is a Franciscan. He says he has met the Pope. But because they speak slowly, or because they hesitate, clerks in stores and drivers on streetcars sometimes ignore them.

Maria has a degree in health and physical education. She struggles with simple sentences, but in the time she has been here she has learned this very complex one: "I was working as a physiotherapist, but I lost my job due to government cutbacks." These words flow freely. The loss of her job has been an expensive lesson.

Grazyna – oops, this is ESL, let's remember to call her Grace – packs up her books and quietly slips out of class. She's leaving early. Where are you going? "I am working in a doughnut shop." What was your job before you came to Canada? "I was a layout artist in a printing plant."

There is a lesson in her graceful exit: It isn't what you do, it's how you do it.

Taped on the wall of the classroom are these bright sentences, which are the remnant of an earlier exercise:

Fall is a beautiful season.

Pick up lots of apples.

Children go to school.

Animals get fat.

Winter is coming. Yes, and the days are getting shorter, and soon there will be snow – snow! – on the ground; and classes will continue, and by the time spring arrives, you hope the sun will shine on Sister Leopolda and the others.

And sometimes it is necessary for the rest of us to study what it is that immigrants need to know outside of school.

A handful of young guys were hanging around the College Street offices of the Centro Organizzativo Scuole Tecniche Italiane, COSTI, founded in 1961 to provide social services support for Italian immigrants; now it helps immigrants from all over the world.

These young guys are in the prime of life. They are new here. They have come prepared to talk to a social worker about what it's like to be a single man – a single immigrant man – in Toronto. What they say will be used to prepare a booklet to help future single immigrant men adjust to life in the Big Smoke.

The meeting is late in starting because the single immigrant women are still together behind closed doors, talking about their new lives. The women are meeting separately because their needs are different; also because if you put lonely mixed singles together, the talk takes on another level of meaning. There are needs, and then there are desires.

Also, as women talk more easily in the company of other women, so do men talk more freely with other men.

But the men are getting restless as they wait in the hall. A late-coming newcomer, a Kurd, strolls in carrying a paper bag. Someone says, "What's that?" He brandishes a pair of rubber boots. He says, "For working."

"How much?"

"Twelve dollars."

The men nod their approval: that is a good price, and the boots have steel toes and they are a sign that there is work for a man with boots. And right away I figure that single immigrant men in Toronto need to know where to get such fine boots at such reasonable prices, and also jobs, and I am about to say so when the single women emerge from their meeting. It is an electric moment.

Handsome single women from a dozen different countries pass before the row of strong single men, who are also from a dozen different countries. The men smile broadly, and they stand up straight and the women cast their eyes downward, modestly. There is silence until one of the men says, "Hey, I'm looking for a girlfriend." Another ups the ante and says, "Hey, will you marry me?" The women laugh, and I had forgotten that the laughter of single women could be shy and hearty at the same time.

The men take their places in the newly vacated room. The smell of the women is like a scarf floating in the breeze – perfume and longing. Seated at the table is the interviewer who will ask questions in order to compile data. Just to make sure she says, "Everyone here is single, right?" One of the men says, "Unfortunately!" And I had forgotten that the laughter of single men could also be shy and hearty.

The questions begin.

"Where are you from, and what do you like about Canada?"

I am from Iran, I like the variety of people here. I am from Colombia, this is a safe place to live. I am from Chile, it's about jobs. I am from Turkey, I'm here to be free. I am from Venezuela, this is a multicultural place where people are free to develop their possibilities. I am from Romania, I like it that Canadian people respect the laws.

"How do you make friends?"

It's hard. It's not easy to make friends. You are scared talking for the first time. I go to Latin bars. I think all of us know someone from our own country who is here now.

"What do you do to make yourself feel better?"

I go to the Skydome, I like to watch baseball. Me, I can easily get friends. I go to the library, you ask something, you start conversation. It takes time.

"How do you pull yourself together when you are feeling down?"

I call my family. I go to the mall. Latin people are going to dances. I sing a song to myself.

"What do you do when your dreams seem far away?"

You have to remember this is a process, you have to go through it and be exposed to many things. You feel alone, you have to be patient. Canadian speakers have no patience with you if you don't speak well; they think you could be a terrorist or something.

"How will you make it through the holidays?"

There are a lot of Latins here, you can easily get with somebody. It's very different. It's very difficult. Me, I know some Iranian people, they're not Christians but they put up trees and have a party, ha, ha!

"Where do you go to meet girlfriends?"

Most women are looking for men with jobs or houses, they're not interested in us. The difficult thing is to break the ice. Most of the women don't come to this country alone, but most men do come alone; it's very hard. Me, I go to Latin dances. Oh, you Latin guys, you're lucky, you know how to salsa! Oh, well, you can come with us, we will teach you to dance, ha, ha!

"Do you cook?"

I go to McDonald's every day, ha, ha! Spaghetti every day, ha, ha! It's terrible, it takes too much time, ha, ha!

"Any final thoughts?"

If you go for a job they say, "Do you have Canadian experience?" What is the secret of Canadian experience? Many of us are professionals, yet Canada does not know how to use our brains. You have a degree, you work as a waiter, it's not your plan. We have to understand that this is a different country, different system – keep trying. If we were happy at home, we would not be in Canada.

If the social workers really wanted the newcomers to be happy, they would scrap the notion of a booklet and organize some dances.

What is Canadian experience?

Looking for work is work, and that is the most frequent Canadian experience, and sometimes work consists of staring at the Job Bank computer in the Dufferin Mall.

I drop by now and then because sometimes my job is watching people look for work. The Job Bank computer resembles a one-armed bandit minus the critical limb. It is as easy to operate: You press a number on a keypad, and a job listing pops up on-screen. If you are interested in the job, you press another key and the computer spits out a job description and a phone number on a scrap of paper.

There were 135 jobs listed the last time I was there: floral designer, computer data-entry clerk, baker, screw-machine operator, stocker, welder, waiter. These are the wages we pay:

Receptionist, $8.00/hr.

Barmaid, minimum wages plus tips.

Mover/driver, $12.00/hr. Must be able to lift household furniture, pianos, appliances.

Tandoori cook, $12.00/hr. Must have one year's experience at the clay oven called the tandoor. And oh, it is so like the Ministry to spell that one out.

And these are the people who are looking for work:

Linda is married with two children. She's been without a job since 1997. She is a CPA from the Philippines. She was a financial analyst there, and then she came here and her son had to have an operation on his ear. She quit her job to look after him.

Now the boy is on the mend and she reads the classifieds every day and she comes to the Job Bank twice a week. This is a hard town. Stand still and you get trampled. Move too slowly and you get run over. She knows she must keep moving. There is nothing for her today.

Donny is a truck driver. He is thirty-five years old. Married? "Used to be," he said with a sheepish grin. He has big, bright eyes, an easy manner, and a Class "A" driver's licence. He has a seasonal, part-time job, but it's layoff season soon; he'd like something permanent.

Come here often?

"Man, I'm out every day looking."

Lec is from Albania. He is thirty-seven years old. He has a master's degree in art history and massive wrestler's shoulders.

He arrived in Toronto three weeks ago with his wife and child; he's already working in a factory, making ducts. "It's a good job. I work from 5 p.m. to 5 a.m. I make as much in one day as one month in Albania."

But he misses his work in the arts. "I am a very good mural painter. I can do graphic design on magazines. I am not trained for this job market. I need training on computers." He looks determined. You figure he'll get his training. There was a deep fresh red scratch on his arm, running from the back of his wrist to his elbow; well, that's duct work.

He went home to sleep.

The others keep coming all morning: the teenaged girl with a turquoise scrunchy on her ponytail; the labourer, originally from Khartoum; the middle-aged man in the cheap suit with the briefcase in his hand and runners on his feet. And there is Mary.

She is twenty-seven, forthright, confident. Her three-year-old son licked a morning Popsicle, orange. She is a health-care aide who lost her job two weeks ago when the woman she was caring for died of Parkinson's disease. "It was like a death in the family," said Mary. They'd been together seven years. She'll find someone else to care for.

And then, a minor miracle:

A young man bellied up to the computer. He has a master's degree in electronic engineering, with a specialty in tele-communications. He used to design hardware and software for an automobile manufacturer in Nanjing, China. He has a wife and a son.

"I come here because it's better for my boy."

His jeans were new. His sportcoat was tailored. His manner was eager. He still had some of the money he brought with him from China. He has been here a scant few months. He looked at several listings, and he left ten minutes too soon.

Because, ten minutes later, a young woman arrived and spent half an hour at the computer. She had excellent posture, and by the time she was done, she had a sheaf of twenty job printouts in hand. "I am looking for work as a receptionist. I want to go to university, perhaps to study human resources or international trading."

How long has she been in Toronto? "I came a few months ago." Where is she from? "I come from Nanjing, China."

Sometimes my instincts are faintly ridiculous.

I have lost track of the number of times when people in Europe have asked, on hearing that I come from Toronto and have lived in Montreal, "So, do you know my cousin Tony?" But I refuse to let that stop me.

"Wait a minute," I said. "You wouldn't happen to know a certain engineer, a man from Nanjing, his name is W—?" She draws a breath. "A short man?" I nod. She gives me a neat description. I nod again. "Yes, I know him. We worked for the same company. He's here?"

I told her what he told me, that he comes to the Job Bank most mornings, around this time. She sighed. And I wondered to myself if they might have shared noodles and tea on their lunch breaks in Nanjing.

It is a small world.

No, it is a very big world.

It's a wonder, the way we get around.

Salma Adam walked into this country.

She was nineteen years old; she came here from Somalia. She is alone; no brothers or sisters. Her parents died in the Somali civil war. Her future did not look as if it included school. She was most likely going to become the youngest of several wives of the headman of her village, some grizzled old man with many cows. But her uncle paid an agent to get her out of the country and escort her to the United States. Her escape cost several thousand dollars. The agent dropped her off in Miami, bought her a bus ticket and wished her luck.

Salma made her way north to Buffalo, and she came across the border into Canada on a cold spring night. Imagine your teenaged daughter doing that in reverse: leaving here, landing alone and making her away across the border into Somalia in the middle of the night.

Salma said, "At eight o'clock in the evening I walked across the Peace Bridge from Buffalo. It was very cold. I was wearing a brown summer dress and sandals." She shivered at the memory.

"I went to Canadian Immigration. They said they were closed. They said I had to come back in the morning, so I walked back. U.S. officials stopped me when I returned. They kept me late. They asked me a lot of questions. They took photographs. They said I had to see a judge because I had entered the United States illegally. They told me I had to go to stay at Vive La Casa, a place for refugees in Buffalo. The officials asked if I had any money. No, I had none. I left U.S. Immigration at 3:00 a.m.

"I was dragging my bag in the darkness. A police officer saw me and said, 'What are you doing, young lady?' I told him. He said those officials were inhuman. He took me in his car to Vive La Casa."

The next day she made her way across the bridge a second time, alone in the world, with no one to lean on, unsure of what might happen. This time, she was allowed in. And when she arrived in Toronto, she set out to become one of us.

She enrolled in Emery Adult Learning Centre. And you may study immigration patterns all your life to learn what sort of city Toronto is, but you need go no farther than Emery. Here is where the new Toronto is being made.

In short order, Salma earned enough credits to allow her to attend college in order to study nursing. I spoke with her on the day of her graduation. In addition to her diploma, she had been awarded a prize for proficiency in English, and she was nominated by her classmates to be the valedictorian.

Salma said, "The hardest thing for me? This is such a multi-cultural city. The cities of Somalia are not multicultural. I find it very challenging to socialize openly with people. But I try to put myself in the shoes of others. My mind is open. I try to take the best values from each culture." She sounded like us on a good day.

She said, "I have been through so much, but I can still see the beauty. I want to be useful. I think nursing is a good way to go."

As she talked, she folded and unfolded a few sheets of paper; she was stealing glances at her valedictory speech.

"Last night I stayed up late. I wrote straight from my heart. I am very emotional. It is so hard for me to express what I feel. They have helped me so much at Emery.

"I don't have any family here. When I'm coming to school, I am so happy. When I'm leaving, it's so hard. The people here are part of my family now. That's something I haven't found in any other place."

Salma got a big round of applause as she walked to the podium. Her classmates were from Argentina, China, Ghana, Nigeria, Korea, all the countries of the world. They wore burkas or saris or suits or jeans. Some of them had taken time off work to come for their diplomas. Their children were happy and rest-less or they were thirsty and cranky, and their cameras flashed and everyone seemed eager to hear what Salma had to say:

"This is a day that I wish I was a poet. If I were a poet I would find a lot of adjectives to describe the efforts performed by Emery staff. But since I don't have a choice, I will just be con-tented with dropping some miserable tears."

Well, a single tear is worth any number of adjectives.

To her teachers she said, "You have taught us the value of patience, the value of understanding, the value of resilience, the value of wisdom, the value of sharing, the value of listening and the value of honesty."

She spoke with her head held high. She gripped the podium with her right hand and punctuated her sentences with stabs of her left, and at times her voice broke with emotion, and she had to stop and steady herself; at times, her teachers also dabbed their eyes with handkerchiefs.

To her classmates Salma said, "The good Thomas Edison wrote, 'Many of life's failures are people who did not realize how close they were to success when they gave up.' I hope that you will not be the one to give up due to the burden and the challenges of life when you would have been successful had you stuck to your dreams a little bit longer."

The students answered with applause.

A Montreal friend, Matt Radz, was born in Poland. Matt is smart, funny, urbane, culturally literate and perhaps the best-read guy I know. He told me once that, when he was growing up, whenever someone moved to his town from another country, that person was instantly popular with all the other kids; everyone sought the stranger out, eager to breathe the scent of the exotic, curious about clothing and habits and manners, anxious to find favour, popularity or perhaps even love. And so young Matt was looking forward to coming to Toronto. He was in his teens at the time and, based on his experience, he figured he would be an instant hit with all the girls at his new school simply because he was an exotic foreigner.

Imagine his surprise . . .

TWO

I've only circled back to find
Many changes made by time,
And many changes in my mind.
I was looking for a place called home.

– RITA MACNEIL, "Brown Grass"

I live in Parkdale, a west-end, working-class part of Toronto, although the class has been changing in recent years, as has the nature of the work: there are fewer lunch buckets and more laptops.

The price of houses is also rising. The old, retired European couples are moving out, and there are more young dot-com families moving in every week. The baby carriages may not be so numerous as they were a generation ago, but they are more plush and they have better suspension and wider wheel-bases, and the young mothers like to push them as they jog in the morning.

Toronto is a city of neighbourhoods. That is supposed to be our saving grace: the neighbourhood as village. But you can live in your neighbourhood all your life and never see the city, just as you can live on Vancouver Island and never see the ocean. It rains in Rosedale and Parkdale alike, but in Rosedale they stay dry.

One day, as I was walking home from work, I noticed an old

Polish lady rooting around on a neighbour's lawn. She was hobbled by age and arthritis. She was bent over, picking up horse chestnuts from under a tree and stuffing them into a plastic sack. I stopped and asked her what she was going to do with all those nuts.

She said she was going to take them home and put them in a pot and boil them up, and then she was going to mash them. She moved her hands as she talked, miming a pot in one hand and a potato masher in the other, the gestures familiar to us both.

I asked her if she was going to eat the chestnut mash. She said no, it was not for eating; she was going to put the hot mash on her ankles like a poultice. She said she had arthritis very bad, it was hard for her to walk, the doctors gave her pills but the pills didn't help, and she hurt all the time; hurt in her ankles, hurt in her knees. I could see how badly her legs were swollen. She said there was no use sitting around doing nothing.

There, right there. That's us.

I picked up a chestnut, still slick from having just popped out of its casing, and put it in her sack. I asked if the hot-mashed horse-chestnut poultice was an old Polish remedy. She said no, it was Russian.

I wanted to know more, but I was in some vague hurry. I wished her well and went on my way, hoping I'd run into her a little later so I could find out if the poultice had worked. I had a proprietary curiosity. My knees, my shoulder. But I never saw her again that fall. The snow fell.

A year went by.

Déjà vu.

This time she was wearing a head scarf, a zippered sweater, a heavy skirt, and a pair of sturdy shoes with orthopaedic stockings. She was bent over another lawn, stuffing more nuts in a sack. She looked a little older, a little slower, a little more tired.

I introduced myself and reminded her that we'd talked a year or so ago about the poultice, the hot horse-chestnut mash. She straightened stiffly, narrowed her eyes and sized me up. I took a nut from the lawn and put it in her bag, just like I'd done the year before; that's when she remembered. I asked if she was going to boil those nuts again.

This time she said no, she was going to soak them in alcohol.

I supposed the poultice hadn't worked. I mimed a gesture, as if knocking back a shot. "Horse-chestnut vodka?"

She said, "Not to drink." She told me she was going to rub it on her ankles. "Here, you want to see my ankles? I'll show you." She leaned against the tree, slipped off her shoe and rolled down one of her stockings. Her ankle was spongy and swollen, worse than I imagined, the pale skin netted with spidery veins. It hurt to look. I said I hoped the alcohol helped.

She pursed her lips and shrugged. I said using the alcohol as a rub was probably a good idea, because horse chestnuts aren't good to eat, and so probably no good to drink.

She said, "I ate."

Which stopped me cold; horse chestnuts are impossibly bitter. I asked her when she'd eaten them. "During the war." How did she prepare them? "You grind them up. You make flour for bread." I said horse-chestnut bread didn't sound very good. She touched her belly with the palm of her hand.

"When you're hungry, you eat."

I asked where she'd spent the war.

"Siberia; the Russians came through Poland. They rounded us up. Then they made us march all the way. I worked as a miner in a gold mine. Standing in cold water, always cold, hungry all the time."

And the way the Russians rounded up the Poles was not dissimilar to the way the Germans rounded up the Poles: they came down the streets in armoured cars, they blocked off the streets at the corners and they searched the houses, taking the men if there were any, taking the women, taking the older kids, taking any children, boys or girls, who looked big enough to work.

I looked at her hands. Her palms were rough and square. Her fingers were thicker than mine, curled and gnarled and knotted. She rolled her stocking up and stepped into her shoe, and as she did, she talked.

She said she lost four children during the war.

When she came to Canada, she did all kinds of work in factories and on farms, picking tobacco, doing whatever she could to make some money, because she had three more children, because life goes on.

She'd got this arthritis from working in the mine, and she hurt all the time now, and the doctors were no help, useless, and now the kids were all grown, live in the suburbs, out of town, lives of their own, always busy.

And she shrugged and went back to work picking up chestnuts.

I walked home. I can't imagine her life in the war. Her life here was no picnic. Now she is old and stiff and tired. These days I get a little stiff myself. I don't complain.

I haven't see her since.

There are smug wags who refer to my neighbourhood as Heil Park for the simple reason that it happens to be near High Park – oh, how witty – and for the darker reason that on at least one occasion in the past some minor war criminal was found hiding here.

The insinuation is that it is easy to hide here; the Poles, don't you know. This is an insult to those of my neighbours who survived the Holocaust, it is a slap in the face to the old woman with the chestnuts and it is a slander on the rest of us.

Two blocks west of my place, if you do not look too closely, you might think you were in some other Poland, unsacked, unburned, not hardened by all those centuries of war. I don't mean that the architecture is lovely. I mean that the shops are full of smoked fish, rye bread, ham hocks, sour pickles, strings of cured sausages, loaves of soft bread and bland, sweet jam-filled buns; a more practical loveliness.

It is of such a richness that when the Poles came here from the old country during the years of collective farms and Soviet domination, they saw in the windows of the shops on this street the kind of food they had only heard about from their grandparents.

You can get by in my neighbourhood speaking nothing but Polish.

At Christmas there are live fish flopping helplessly in blue plastic barrels, and frozen fish on cardboard trays, and salted fish as white as pocket handkerchiefs laid out in small wooden boxes stacked on the sidewalks outside the delis; this, too, is a loveliness.

There is a statue of the Polish pope in front of the Polish credit union. The statue, a good likeness, is of burnished gold; an apt colour, considering the location.

The streets were blocked by mourners when John Paul – no, Jan Pavel – died; mourners waved red and white Polish flags, yellow and white papal flags, and a single Solidarnoscz flag. There were ethereal hymns and tears. There were thousands of flowers and candles in front of the statue. The flowers stayed fresh; no miracle, this – some were in planters, and all were replaced before they could wilt.

We bought a house in this neighbourhood because we had seen far too many houses that cost too much money in too many other parts of town. The last house was not affordable so much as it was closest to what we could afford: a Victorian semi, more than a hundred years old, sixteen feet wide, with a postage-stamp backyard on the corner of a street named for an Anglican bishop of Toronto.

It was late in the day at the end of the week when we made the decision. We were tired of talking about bloated mortgages for quarter-million-dollar rat-traps. We were walking down Roncesvalles Avenue, dazed and hungry, and the butcher shops were still open; a good sign. I bought some smoked pork tenderloin, the meat still warm from the smoker; it was salty and sweet and that decided the matter.

The character of the old women in my part of town? Look no farther than the woman with the chestnut poultice. The character of the old men in my part of town? Let me tell you a story.

There is a home for the elderly near a busy intersection where the young girls work the curb. One day, an old man in this building had his throat cut by a hooker. Here's what happened: Every month, when the government cheques were delivered, the old men would stand on their balconies and drop their keys to the girls waiting below on the lawn. Perhaps he refused to pay, and things got out of hand. Afterward, the people who manage the building put a stop to girls on the lawn, and a stop to the dropping of the keys. But I somehow like the idea of those old men's flames flickering in the face of death; and the music of those keys dropping down on the grass.

On the corner down the block from the butcher shop . . . oh, that is a useless direction, there are so many butcher shops on Roncesvalles. Let me try again:

On the corner, north or just south of any number of butcher shops, there are two small Asian fruit markets. The markets are

side by side. The owners put their produce on adjacent sidewalk stands. Lemons, cherries, radishes, all the same; prices, all
the same. I don't know how they make a living. Maybe there's
only one living to be made, and they share that, too. The prox-
imity of the markets is a dilemma.

I do what others do. I spread my custom; tomatoes here
today, lettuce there tomorrow. I lived for a year in Toronto
when I was a young man. I thought then that the presence of
fruit stalls on the street was the height of sophistication, a
product of Southern Ontario's bounty, and a function of milder
weather – you can't put fruit out on the sidewalks in the winter
in the north because it will freeze.

Now I think they put the fruit on the sidewalks here not just
for display, but because the shops are so small and the rents are
so high that it is impossible to keep everything inside all the
time, out of the weather.

The greengrocers smile at me in both markets because
they recognize my custom. Let me be clear: I don't get a
valued-customer smile. I get what everyone gets, a smile of
desperation.

I'm sure if I were loyal to one store over the other, I'd get a
real smile here and a hard glare there. But then, if I were loyal,
I'd have to duck under one set of awnings and slink past one set
of fruit stands. I'm not prepared to duck and slink for lemons.

There are subtle differences between the two stores if you
want to look for them. One carries dried nuts, and the lettuce
usually looks a little fresher, and they have a larger supply of
ramen. I won't eat ramen, and I don't care if millions of Asians
and thousands of university students swear by the stuff; it tastes
fake to me. But I like to know it's there.

The ramen store is where the guy behind the counter tried
to cheat a woman out of a quarter; that's what the woman

thought. It was hot that day, and maybe he wasn't paying attention; in any case, he punched the wrong price into the cash register, and the woman noticed and made a sharp remark, and the man had to weigh her fruit all over again. There, there, you see, she said, I told you so and you didn't listen, and she saved herself a few cents, and she pursed her lips in triumph and walked out.

Behind the counter, the man's face was set impassively. But there was high colour in his cheeks, and the colour remained until everybody who'd seen the little exchange had left the store.

This is a two-bit town.

He's never tried to shortchange me.

The other store carries less ramen, and sometimes their lettuce is not as good as I'd like, but the fruit looks slightly better, and they sell flowers and bedding plants in the spring.

Here is where I saw the old man who was acting like a goat.

This store is set on the corner; the shelves out front are L-shaped. There is enough room on the long side of the L to set out pots of herbs and other plants, protected by a chain-link fence.

One afternoon I saw an old man standing with his face pressed against the fence. He had scrawny ribs and skinny arms. He was wearing a dirty T-shirt and a pair of baggy pants with a necktie pulled through the belt loops as a belt. No shoes or socks on his feet. His hair was white, and there were billy-goat whiskers on his chinny-chin-chin.

I recognized him right away. I'd seen him earlier in the summer, standing on the street with a can of Lysol in his hand and a smile on his face, his bare feet in a puddle of his own piss, his eyes closed as he stood there, wrapped in a fog of disinfected, deodorized bliss.

There was a pot of dill at eye level on the top shelf inside the fence. It was an end-of-season pot, brown and wilted; some of the fronds were poking through some of the links. The old man stood there with his hands at his sides. His eyes were closed. He nibbled like a goat.

The young man stocking fruit paid the old man no mind. He just kept sorting apples and piling the lemons into pyramids. And if you forced me to choose between one store and the other, I'd choose this one, even if the dill is nibbled.

South of my house the streets are lined, not with schoolchildren in the morning and shoppers in the afternoon, but with confused men and women all day long; refugees of a sort, they are the psych patients we turned loose years ago. They live in rooming houses; there is one of these just down the street from me, big, pink-bricked.

We rarely see these neighbours on the block, although sometimes they sit on their tiny porch smoking cigarettes in the fresh air; sunlight and nicotine, the vitamins of the dispossessed.

They are shy, they don't say much and they look away when you look at them. One morning there was an ambulance parked in front of the house, and there were police cars and strings of caution tape from the porch to the tree in the front yard.

Tie a yellow ribbon.

None of the other neighbours knew what had happened. I couldn't bring myself to knock on the front door. A few days later a company that specializes in the clean-up of blood and other biological waste sent a truck, and the workers parked out front and spent the day inside.

Eventually, there was word: one of the men from the pink house had stabbed another man who'd been lying in bed;

some imaginary threat, and then some vicious retaliation with a kitchen knife.

And while you might be able to make the case that neither man knew what was really happening, I'll bet the man who was stabbed in his bed knew he was bleeding to death.

So has my neighbourhood changed.

There is implicit danger.

Yes, junkies do get shot a few blocks away on Queen Street; yes, people leap to their deaths from the balconies of the apartment buildings nearby; yes, there are hookers on the corner down the block; and yes, I hear sirens all night long. But this is my street, and on my street is a house in which a man was stabbed to death.

A walk to the corner is now a walk past a tombstone.

We are young and old, feminists and misogynists, immigrants, drunks, cranks, kids with Down's syndrome, shrieking brats and people who are mostly just trying to get along. If you are lucky, you live as lightly with your neighbours.

There is a public school a few streets over. The residents' association uses the auditorium at nights for public meetings. There is a bulletin board in the corridor. I am a snoop. Here are the bulletins:

It's possible that sports teams will shortly be charged for the use of the school fields. The carpet is up and the new floor is down in room 109. The door at the front of the school will probably not be painted, at least not all at once, because of the price. There are now walkie-talkies available for teachers on yard duty. The gardening committee reports that the city chopped down the linden tree by mistake, and they have been asked to replace it with a sapling. Njacko Backo is giving after-school drumming workshops. Mieke is selling a double stroller, $350 or best offer. Jenni is offering to provide "babysitng."

Someone should check Jenni's spelng. I have a hunch one of my neighbours will offer to help.

As it goes with us, so it goes with you.

We wear toques and knitted sweaters when it's cold. We sweep our walks in the summer, we rake our leaves when the weather turns, and we shovel our walks when it snows. And you know without being told that the best sidewalk sweepers are also the best leaf rakers and best snow shovellers. Here is our news:

Bruce is stepping down after having chaired the neighbour-hood association for the past eight years. It's time, he says, to step aside. Maggie, who takes the minutes and has done so for longer than anyone can remember, is also stepping down.

Our city councillor came to the meeting with a citation, which he flourished: "On behalf of the mayor, we congratulate Maggie on fifteen years of service." Maggie laughed modestly and said, It's only been twelve years. Our councillor said, "Well, um, on behalf of the 2.5 million people of Toronto, we thank you; signed, the Mayor." And our councillor offered to retrieve the citation and have it redone, but Maggie wouldn't let it out of her hands, and there was much applause.

And so Maggie read the minutes of the last meeting for the last time, and they were adopted, as they always are, and the treasurer reported that we had enough money for recent expenditures on posters and gifts. Gifts? By way of thanks for their hard work, we gave Bruce a fanny pack and a Swiss Army knife, and we gave Maggie a silver pen which she brandished with a smile, and Bruce said he would not brandish his knife, and we smiled at that, too.

In other news, it was noted to general approval that the rail-line bike path now had a website, and there were weeds in the storm-water pond in the park, and there seemed to be a rise in the number of prostitutes working Queen Street and this required further vigilance.

It does, it does. But the room was warm and smelled of wool, and my mind wandered; it's hard to be vigilant after supper. I remembered a morning when I had to go to work early, and at the foot of the street I saw a girl skipping barefoot in and out of traffic. Her hair was the colour of the morning light. She was – there's only one word – gay.

She was also high as a kite, and she was leaning her pretty head into open car windows and asking the shift workers one by one if they wanted to party. She was so pretty and so stoned. Her teeth were white and her skin was alive, almost succulent. She also asked me if I wanted to party. I declined with a smile and a wave. Her disappointment was the merest flicker, and then she ran over to another car and flirted with the driver.

I saw her once or twice after that, and then I never saw her again until a year or so later. And I had to look twice. Instead of twenty, she looked forty. Her skin was grey. She'd lost a front tooth. Her hair was dirty. Her clothes were filthy. Her lips were chapped. There was no light in her eyes. Crack works that fast; it's always a short sweet party in my neighbourhood. She was no longer hooking. She was begging.

And then someone called the meeting back to order and asked those who wanted to take positions on the executive of the association to stand up and give us their reasons for running.

Kathy wanted to be a role model for her children. Peter has lived in the neighbourhood for thirty years. Michael loves the rail-line bike path. Roman wants to help in any way he can. And Carolyn wants to work on affordable housing. We elected them all. You'd have done so, too.

And when the meeting adjourned, we lingered together; the talk centred on George Bush and the axis of evil, and the evils of a war for oil, and also the evils of the sport-utility vehicle as a reason for the war.

I wondered whether the families of the Kurds who'd been gassed by Saddam think Bush is so evil, and I wondered if the average SUV has an axle of evil, and I thought that an SUV would probably be a good thing on the high roads of Kurdistan. But I kept my mouth shut because these are my neighbours, and I have to live here.

As I drifted away, I saw an old man wandering the halls of the school by himself. You can never tell about old men wandering in schools. I tailed him out of curiosity. He peered at a list of those men who had gone to that school and who had volunteered to serve in the First World War.

He finished reading, and he clasped his hands behind his back. I know he didn't see me because he farted as he walked along. One fart for every two steps. I was sorry I'd followed him.

He is my neighbour. And this is where I live.

I used to see a woman take a daily position in the sun on Roncesvalles in the summer, soaking up the heat near the south wall of the corner drugstore. She was my age, more or less. Her hair, cut in a bob. Her legs, fat and scaly. Her cloth coat, buttoned at the throat, too heavy for the weather. She liked to watch the passersby.

As she stood watching us, she held one fist in front of her mouth, and she kept up a running commentary in Polish, *sotto voce*, as if her closed fist were a microphone and she were reporting live to some radio station in her mind.

I like to think she was a journalist in her day, in her town, when she was young and pretty and people listened to her. No one pays much attention to her now; maybe someone should.

She used to watch us mailing our letters and buying our ice cream.

That is the real news.

I don't see her any more. That is also news.

I used to see a man in a rocker, sitting on his porch singing the same damn song every day. "De dang, de dang, de dang-dang-dang." An Italian folk tune. There was a "For Sale" sign on his lawn. I thought he was quite far off the rocker he was sitting on, and that the house was being sold out from under him. Now and then I'd nod at him, and he'd nod back.

Once, on my way to market, I saw him nail a small photograph to one of the railings on his porch, and then he picked up a small camera and took a photograph of the photo. I did not bother to ask why.

And then one day, just like that, the house was sold and he wasn't there any more. I thought perhaps he'd been scooped up and dropped off into a nursing home, one of those piss-soaked silos filled with elderly husks. Turns out he was utterly compos mentis.

One of the neighbours said he had been in mourning for his wife who had died the year before. He wasn't interested in talking to anyone but her. When the house was sold, he took the money, gave a forwarding address to the people who wrote his pension cheques and went back to live as a widower in his village in Italy. De-dang-dang-dang.

Crazy? Like a fox. He, too, is who we are here.

And this is what our lives are like.

THREE

Human beings have been my maps.

– FOLA ADEKEYE, NIGERIAN JOURNALIST

Welcome to Toronto.

Our kids aren't doing so well at school, our parents are getting old, our plaster walls are crumbling, our jobs are not much fun, our cars need work, things change too fast for us, but we can't slow down because we fear we will lose ground. Our lives are harder than we expected, somehow. It wasn't supposed to turn out like this. Most days we yearn for something which is just beyond our grasp. Most nights we hope for a decent sleep.

The people who live down the block have come here from away. They don't want trouble. They just want to get along. They're just like us.

We all came here from some other place. We had to come. We had no choice. We needed the work, or there was war or famine, or we wanted a better life for the kids. And some of us wanted to play on a bigger field.

Hate us, hate yourself.

An old newspaper man – I doubt he was apocryphal – said that not every man has a story. They don't say that in newsrooms any more, but plenty of people still think it. Here's the more modern truth:

If you get up in the morning and you make it to the end of

the day, that's a story – how you got up, went off to work and came back home again is the story of what life is like here. There is a corollary.

If you get up in the morning and you do not make it through the day, that, too, is a story. If you read this and you still think we are jerks in Muddy York, then you loathe life.

I repeat the most radical notion of all:

We are who you are.

And one day, coming home on the Queen streetcar, I got lost in a daydream. It happens all the time. A crowded streetcar makes for an inward journey, swaddled in white noise and the warm comfort of the crowd, although perhaps it is not always a comfort.

There are days when I don't like other people as much as I like the idea of other people. These are rude days, with too many empty coffee cups on the floor and too much noise leaking out of all those earphones; and I have, on occasion, taken a seat without looking and have sat on wetness.

I was riding with my eyes closed. And then for some reason I shivered and shook myself into the present tense. I glanced out the window of the streetcar and into the window of a neighbourhood tap. Frank and Voula's Place.

You know Frank and Voula's even if you don't: a few men leaning on the bar, chins in hands, staring idly at those of us who were staring in; a few others nodding off, or watching the bubbles rise in their beer, or keeping an eye on the television on the shelf above the cash register; so many sweet things to do while nursing a drink in the early afternoon.

The streetcar passed by slowly.

I like the idea of beer all afternoon. Where I grew up, the men in the bar would have been bush workers, mechanics or millwrights, some retired, some laid off, some injured and passing the time drinking their compensation cheques, and some would have been just too fed up with life or themselves to face the day at work, or the afternoon at home.

The same men here, although there is no bush.

I wanted to be with them. I could almost taste the dry smoke of their cigarettes. I breathed in the remembered smells of sour beer and stale urine. I could see the heaps of tangled onions on the salty griddle. And I could very nearly hear the soft song of those casual conversations, the hacking coughs and low cackles of old men laughing at old jokes.

You can laugh, but you can't smoke there or anywhere now.

I wonder all the time about Voula: Is she still there, or does only her perfect name remain? Was she big and tall and wide through the hips when she was young, and did she have long hair and warm hands and an attractive, off-centre smile? Was Frank strong and hard and dark and good-looking? And did they dream of making a kind of life with Voula's burgers on the grill, and Frank standing over there by the draft spigot, reading the daily papers with a cup of coffee?

The streetcar rolled along and I could not stop thinking about them, and the dream continued and I missed my stop. Not in the usual way. I woke up startled, and got off a stop too soon.

Ah, well, then. I walked along Queen Street, smiling idly, past the flower shop, past the shop that sells big underwear and lucky candles, past the stoners, past the solitary men who mutter to themselves, highstepping as if they were walking up a flight of stairs and trying not to step on the butterflies. And then, in front of the drugstore, there was a flurry. Two men, struggling. I knew what was happening in an instant.

A security guard – compact and powerful, his face impassive and his head close-shaved – was holding what seemed to be a small white jar of beauty cream. With his other hand, he gripped the elbow of a small brown man. The small brown man was holding on to a backpack. They were linked together, a slow-motion frieze of misery.

I thought, if he hurts the small brown man . . .

Because I tend to be twitchy about cops, all cops, any cops, uniforms make me nervous. I am even twitchier about security guards. Their powers and my view of their powers do not ever coincide. And I don't ever want to test the limits of that lack of coincidence.

But if he hurt this little man . . .

The security guard held on firmly, and I heard him say, "Come with me." The small man said, "Please, sir, forgive!" They struggled some more, but the security guard was stronger and the smaller man slumped into submission, as if the heart for struggle had gone out of him as I passed by; he just gave up. A relief. No harm done. I didn't have to intervene.

The stronger man dragged the smaller one back into the store. A simple case of shoplifting. No big deal. I kept on walking. I took four more steps and . . . wait a minute.

Something was about to happen here which may have been routine for the security guard and which might have been no big deal for the druggist, but it was going to change the life of the little man in some big way.

I stopped. I turned. I went into the store. I interrupted the druggist in mid-prescription and gave him a short fast spiel: there is a lot of shoplifting in this town; we all pay the price in higher prices; everybody knows that, but nobody knows what happens when someone is caught because we never see the consequences; could I watch?

He pointed me downstairs and said if it was okay with the security guard . . . and so I did my song and dance again downstairs. The security guard weighed the request and took a chance.

I never know why anybody trusts me.

The small brown man sat on a folding chair. The security guard was writing a report. The jar of cosmetics had been placed on the table, along with the rest of the contents of the backpack, including a jar of pills, several empty plastic shopping bags, two Hindi videocassettes, and a new universal remote control, still in its package, with a legitimate receipt.

The room was claustrophobic; low ceiling, and the shelves overflowing with boxes of toiletries, a first-aid kit, old flyers with best price discounts, a microwave, packets of noodles, junk.

The small brown man could not comprehend my presence. He had a particular expression on his face, as if he wouldn't have been surprised if I'd hit him. He looked so low, one more blow would not have mattered. I thought for a moment that he might have been relieved if I did hit him; at least then he'd have been on familiar ground.

I sat. I watched. I kept my mouth shut and took notes.

The security guard asked for the man's identification. No reply. He asked again and got the same answer. He asked a third time, and the small man said, "This will spoil my whole thing."

I supposed that it would. Too late for that now. The security guard said, "The police will get your name if you don't give it to me." The small man's thing was spoiling fast, the whole of it. He smiled wanly.

"Please, forgive."

"I want to see your ID. I'm allowed to grab it off you if I want. I'm being nice." The security guard looked hard and bored. There was a flicker of insight in the eyes of the small man, and a quick calculation from me: the security guard restraining himself because I was there. The small man glanced at me, and he took another stab.

"Please, forgive."

The guard said, "There's nothing you can do. I caught you. If you're not charged, this goes nowhere. Give me your ID."

The small man sighed. He had no choice. He'd lost the battle, and it was just one in a long line of battles lost. He fished his wallet from his jeans and opened it, his gestures clumsy, as if he was unused to having a wallet, or jeans, or anything to put in them. His identification consisted of some bits of paper in a small plastic sleeve. He also gave the security guard his address and his phone number; these, he'd been carrying around with him, written on a piece of paper.

The serious questions started.

"You're not working?"

"No, sir."

"On welfare?"

"I am a refugee. I am waiting for a work permit."

"Do you have any money?"

A key question, a Jean Valjean thing: if you steal and you have no money, that's a certain kind of crime; if you steal and you have money to pay for what you stole, that's another kind of crime.

"I have this."

The small man reached into his pocket and knelt on the floor and showed his money – three Canadian five-dollar bills, nine American singles and a twenty-rupee note.

It was easy to see what he was thinking as he knelt with his hands out and the money held up like a gift: perhaps this man will take my money and let me walk away; I have done this before; this is what I know to do on occasions such as this.

The security guard took the money and counted it and put it on the table. He told the small man to sit down in his chair, hard pity in his voice. The small man sat back down with the same sad smile. The security guard completed his report.

He listed the stolen items: one jar of anti-cellulite pills, and one jar of Fade-Out, a kind of cream for bleaching liver spots. It seemed peculiar to me. Cellulite would have been a foreign notion for this skinny man. Not in his lifetime would he have seen cellulite, unless he had a big fat girl back home; nor would liver spots have shown on his skin. Did he have a girlfriend? Were these things for his mother?

Total value? Thirty-five dollars.

According to the security guard, the small man selected the products, walked around the store idly, removed the jars from the boxes, dropped the jars in his backpack and then put the empty boxes back on the shelves. And then he had tried to leave.

And he got nabbed on the sidewalk in front of the store, and I came along and saw what happened next. Now it was a matter of waiting for the police. I had a few questions of my own for the small man.

"Where are you from?"

"Tibet. Please forgive."

It was not my place to forgive, but the story suddenly got larger. A few months earlier, some two hundred Tibetans seeking refuge had been kicked out of the United States. They landed here in Toronto; was he one of them? I don't know much about the detention of refugees in the U.S.A. I know even less about jail in Tibet. But I know the little man was terrified.

"Are you a Buddhist?"

"Yes."

"Buddhists don't steal."

He smiled at my naïveté. "Not everyone is the same, sir."

"When did you come here?"

"Two months ago."

My hunch was right.

"Why did you come?"

"To escape the Chinese."

The security guard was listening, in spite of himself. These things were complications. What had happened was quite simple: the refugee had stolen, he'd been caught and the consequences were serious enough to spoil his whole thing. I pointed to the loot on the table.

"Do you know what cellulite is?"

No answer.

"Are you married?"

"No, sir."

"Please tell me, why did you take the cream?"

No answer.

"Why did you take the cream?"

"Please, forgive."

My forgiveness and a dollar would buy him a cup of bad coffee. I pressed him, even though I had no right.

"Yes, but why did you take the cream?"

He looked at me, pleadingly, as if he didn't want to say out loud what should have been obvious to all of us but was clear only to him. He touched his cheek with his hand.

"Because of this."

I didn't, I couldn't, I gaped, I gasped.

"What do you mean?"

"To make lighter."

Oh, Christ.

"Your skin?"

"It will be better for me here, sir."

He meant it would be better if he had lighter skin.

The police arrived then: a young constable, so tall he had to duck his head in the low room; he was corn-fed, butter-blond, hard as maple and highly amused. He took down the particulars. He went to the phone. He had questions for Immigration: was the little man here legally, were there outstanding charges, and so on. He hung up. We waited for some official to call back. The phone rang. The cop whispered and conferred. And then he had a private chat with the security guard.

The young cop looked down at the little man with a bright smile. "You understand you could go to jail for this?"

"Yes, sir."

"The store is going to be nice to you today. They're going to let you go." The small brown man opened his eyes wide for an instant. He couldn't believe what he had just heard.

"No jail?"

"Not this time."

He didn't move. They told him to stand. He wasn't sure. They led him up the stairs and through the store, and they led him out the door. They stood together on the sidewalk.

The security guard told the little Tibetan once again that he was banned from the store. "Don't come in here ever again." The small brown man heard. But he did not understand. He didn't move. He looked at the big blond cop. The cop said he was free to go. The small brown man hesitated.

"Go, go, go on, get out of here."

The small brown free man took three or four steps. He looked back. He was expecting a cruel trick: let's just pretend to let him go so we can say he was trying to escape, and then we can catch him and beat the snot out of him. Instead, they smiled and shooed him away. "Go, go."

He looked over his shoulder one more time, and then he disappeared. He hadn't known. He couldn't know.

Toronto has a lot of faults. We have the police force we deserve, and everything here costs too much, and our wages are too low, and many of us do not have enough of what we need, and most of us do not have enough of what we want. But there are very few places anywhere in the new world where it is better to be small and brown than here in Toronto.

The security guard?

I got to know Tom Doyle, briefly.

I called the drugstore a few days later to see if I could buy him a cup of coffee, maybe get him to tell me some stories about drugstore security. He said sure, come on over.

I like to think of myself as a fairly observant guy, but while I was waiting for Tom in the store, I reached for a paper at the magazine rack; it occurred to me, in a purely academic way, that it would be easy, if nobody were looking, to just stuff the magazine under my . . . yikes.

Like a puff of air, Tom Doyle was there.

When I told him why I'd just jumped, and what I had been thinking, he laughed. Over coffee he said the store had been losing roughly sixty thousand dollars a year to thieves; that's five thousand dollars walking out of the store every month. Which means the manager can't afford not to have a guy like Tom.

The most popular item?

"Shampoo gets ripped off the most. They'll take two hundred dollars' worth at a time, sweep it off the shelf and into a bag."

They?

"Junkies."

What does that do to store profits?

"Well, if somebody takes twenty shampoos at $5.49 a bottle, the store has to sell two hundred bottles to make up the cost."

I can't calculate as fast as that, but we'd all have to wash our hair a lot more than we do to even things up for the pharmacist.

Tom said, "I had one guy, a heroin addict, he'd take five hundred dollars' worth of stuff at a time. He wore a big green coat with slits in the lining. He'd drop stuff inside – Oil of Olay, Claritin, Reactin, perfume gift sets; he'd sell the stuff to a bargain store." Tom paused, considered his words carefully. "I think the bargain store was telling him what to go for."

I did a double take. I understand why a guy who's driven by a drug habit is driven to steal. But I hadn't realized that bargain-store owners, aware of what the junkies have to do in order to stoke their habits, are actually placing orders. A kind of bespoke theft; who knew?

Is it dangerous work? "One day I saw the guy with the green coat. He was carrying a big bag out of my store. He went into a bargain store. I followed him. As soon as he saw me, he attacked. He went wild. I got him down, but I let him up; a mistake. He ran to the back of the store and picked up a knife, so I picked up a broom. A broom; they had everything in this store. I whacked that guy so many times I broke the broom.

"He ran out the door. I chased him from Lansdowne to Dufferin. I finally got him, but it took three guys to hold him down; he was pretty strong for a heroin addict. He had full syringes in his pocket. He was ditching them as he ran. The cops had to retrace his steps and pick them up. I think he got three years."

What happened to the owner of the bargain store? "They closed him down, but I think he just opened up again under another name."

Tom said he has been threatened by men and propositioned by girls. He's also given money to people in need. He had a letter once from a guy who was grateful he'd been caught; and, yes, he nailed that letter-writing guy again – as soon as he got out of jail, he was back in Tom's store, trying to boost some Sudafed. Caution. Makes you drowsy.

Tom caught one guy, Vietnamese, took his particulars, called the cops. Next day, he caught another Vietnamese guy; hmm, same address. In all, he caught six guys from the same address. "I cleaned the place out," he said. Nah, those guys, they cleaned themselves out.

How do you like us now?

This is what I do for a living: I poke around town. I keep my ears open. I get paid to look and listen. I stumble over things. There are days when, if I retreat to a coffee shop, the coffee is the last and the least reason. I need the illusion of companion-ship, and the chance to eavesdrop.

I like the smells of civilization: sugar and cinnamon, the perfume of the blue smoke from cigarettes – although you can't get that smell any more, not here, unless you are on the street.

I go to coffee shops now for the spoken word and the laugh-ter of the regulars in the air. There isn't much of this that is unfamiliar to me, not any more. But I am not, nor have I ever been a regular. A paid observer ought never to be a regular; conflict of interest.

In any case, it is never about the coffee in this town.

We have created a miserable hierarchy, starting from the bottom. Galaxy Donuts, Coffee Time, Tim Hortons, the Second Cup, Timothy's, Starbucks. A second cup? Spare me. A double-double? That's not coffee. Frappuccino? *Va fa 'n culo.*

The coffee in Toronto is bad in a thin and sour way; it is pre-tentiously bad, and that is the worst kind of bad. It makes you want to apologize to the men and women who come here from the coffee countries. You can read the grimaces on their faces;

you can see them thinking the first time they try a cup of coffee in Toronto: "We worked the land so these people could make this piss?"

And anywhere you go to drink your coffee in this town, the cup you are given is not just a cup. It is a symbol of your class; the cup is almost always paper, and it is a reminder of how much mediocrity we will endure, and how rootless we are. We carry our paper cups of ersatz coffee on the street, in the subway, on the streetcar, in the shops.

I think there is a reason: we – not me; never me, I can't bear to – carry coffee with us wherever we go because we feel the need to suck something sweet and milky and warm through a plastic teat; an infant's habit. We won't grow up. We also tend to ditch our cups on the street; another infantile habit.

The woman wanted a cigarette with her coffee. You can tell this story is dated. She thought she'd put the touch on the men at the next table. She put a haughty look on her face: lips drawn down, eyelids half closed; a carapace of dignity.

I was not optimistic on her behalf.

She primped her hair out of habit as she approached the table.

"Do you mind if I borrow a smoke?"

The politeness of her cadge. She was ducking under her straitened circumstances like a nicotine-stained Wimpy; she would gladly pay them Tuesday for a cigarette today.

The men were slim and dark, five of them talking in confidence to each other and laughing in some hot-country language, a secret language in this place. They stopped talking and sized her up fast, and the calculations were made quickly: too old, too fat, too weird, no smokes. Plus, they hadn't come across the ocean to give cigarettes to beggars.

No, no, no, they shook their heads and looked away, and she looked into the distance toward the door. No harm in asking.

She pretended not to be hurt, but she had suffered the small harm of having been rejected in front of all of us. She went back to her table, sat for a minute so that everyone would know it was of no concern to her and then she tidied up the way a real lady would – but then, a real lady would not bother to tidy up – and then she left.

I didn't see her put the touch on the guy in the watch cap. I'm not saying she didn't try to put the touch on him as he came in, just at that moment when she passed him and he held the door for her as she was leaving. All I'm saying is I didn't hear her ask if she could borrow a smoke. Maybe she'd had her fill of coming up empty.

The man in the watch cap took a seat. He put his elbows on the table. He had plenty of cigarettes. He was holding one in his right hand. It was half finished, and he held it close to his ear, as if the cigarette had something to tell him. I don't know what a cigarette might say, but there was a whisper of white smoke around his head.

He had a frankly pleasant face with big round eyes and a wide and ready smile. He wore paint-stained jeans. He had come to join an old man who was there at the table, waiting.

The old man wore a topcoat, powder-blue pants and a pair of black runners. All old men wear runners. Not all; many. Because runners don't hurt the feet, and they provide the illusion of spring in one's step.

The old man had fine and sandy hair; in some places his hair was the colour of nicotine, and it was carefully wet-combed in a swirl around a bald spot; the swirl, water running down a drain. He wore a hearing aid in one ear.

The younger, paint-stained, watch-capped man was talking through the cloud of smoke. I picked up what he said in mid-conversation. It wasn't hard. In a voice of rising loudness: "She might have told you she loved you. I said, she might have told you she loved you. Are you going to take her to Winnipeg? I said, are you going to take her to Winnipeg?"

The old man shook his head, "No!"

They were talking, I thought, about the old man's wife. My guess is that the old man's wife had been to Winnipeg once before; the old man's people were there; maybe he and she had gone there once before to meet them; my guess is she hadn't liked it very much, neither the city nor his people, and his people had probably not liked her.

I thought then of Winnipeg. I have never had a bad time there, but I have never expected much from the place. At one time, a woman I wanted to marry, and a woman who had wanted to marry me and a woman I had married disastrously all lived there at the same time. When I went there, I felt like a haunted man. I spent most of my time looking over my shoulder. The thought of it made me smile.

The younger man sipped at his coffee and dragged on his smoke. He leaned forward, pointed at his ear and said, "You should get that fixed today. I said you should get it fixed today."

The old man said, "It needs a new motor."

A new motor? An old joke between them. Times change, old men know motors, who the hell but a kid knows circuitry?

Men with hearing aids talk low as a rule; they think everyone can hear everything they say, and they can't understand why people always look as if they're yelling. He touched the rim of his cup with his finger. He folded his hands on the table. He did not elaborate on his answer.

The younger man said, patiently, "You should get that done today. You know, take care of that today." The old man sipped his sweet cup. The younger man wasn't giving up. "Do you have to go far to get it done? I say, do you have to go far to get that done?"

The old man said, "Not far."

"You should take care of that today; it'll give you some structure in your day." I had the younger man pegged now. He was some sort of shirt-sleeved social worker, doing double duty with a paintbrush down the street at the community centre; he was pitching in, working at his trade even though he was on his break.

The old man looked like he had all the structure he needed right there in his cup on the table at the Coffee Time on Queen.

Me, I'd had enough bad coffee and enough eavesdropping. You can't sit in one spot forever, and you can't tell some old guys anything, whether they are from Winnipeg or not. It was no fun listening in any more. But then, as I was getting up, the younger man said, "Why don't you get that done; do that today?"

I perked up. Say what?

"Why don't you get that done, do that today. Get that done, do that today." That's exactly what he said. Not bop, not bebop; rebop.

I've been saying it to myself ever since.

Ba doo, ba-deet, do-deet, oo-dat, oo-day.

Pretty good advice, if you ask me.

I don't think I could live in Winnipeg, on the cusp of the prairie and the boggy north; too many mosquitoes, not enough bookstores, and the chief geographical reference points are those to the south.

A secret, perhaps big enough to make life bearable: somewhere southeast of Winnipeg and northeast of Minneapolis is the forlorn little Wabigoon Lake. If you think that did not influence Garrison Keillor – it's been a quiet week in Lake Woebegone – then you have no imagination.

My best memory of Winnipeg? I went there once to see Karen Kain. She was dancing with a French troupe. I took the bus, rented a cheap room, bought a front-row seat. I sat so close to the stage I could scarcely breathe. I saw her strain. I saw her leap and swirl. I saw her long thighs tremble. I heard her small feet hit the floor. And I got splashed in the face with a single drop of her sweat.

Such a lovely memory. But I could no more live in the 'Peg than I could dance a pas de deux. I live in Toronto now.

So does Karen Kain.

I grew up in Fort William. It is my home town. I left there because I never felt as if I was good enough to belong; the failing, only mine. I left Northern Ontario for Baffin Island, a much more northerly north, where I was always and only a southerner.

From there I moved to Regina, where all the solitudes come in twos: city versus country, left versus right, atheist versus bible thumper, sod buster versus carpetbagger; a place where you are expected to choose black or white; not easy to live there if, like me, you see the world in shades of grey.

Like I said, welcome to Toronto.

One afternoon I was walking along Front Street with my head down when I bumped into three guys from out of town. They'd stopped in the middle of the sidewalk. They were staring up. I'd been looking down. I said, "You gotta be careful where you stop." They said, "Sorry." I said, "Whatchya looking at?" They nodded toward the tall towers; up, way up. One of them said, "Nothing like that at home." Those men were right. We ought to stop and look.

Keeping it fresh isn't always easy.

Not long after, I happened to meet Fola Adekeye, a young journalist from Nigeria. He'd been staying at Massey College for some months on a fellowship, and was about to return to Lagos. We were chatting in the common room of Massey College.

I was curious to know what the city looked like to him, whose eyes were far fresher than mine.

He said, "When I arrived here, on the way in from the airport, my first impression was that Toronto is a city under construction. I saw much construction of roads, a lot of big projects. Later, I learned that Canada has a tradition of maintaining the city. It's not like that at home."

He thinks we keep things up. We think the place is falling apart. It's a matter of perspective. He said, "Toronto is also a very clean city, that's obvious to a Nigerian. You know, an elder statesman, someone who had been here before, said to me, 'Fola, you're going to Canada. Just one week there will change your life.'"

And did his life change?

"When I see that man at home, I'm going to ask him to join me in a campaign to make pedestrians kings. I was shocked – here, when a vehicle comes, the driver sees you and he stops! At home you will find the corpses of pedestrians on the roadside." He said this, and he didn't look like he was kidding.

His impressions of the university?

"This is an intellectual paradise for an African; the quality of the instructors and the equipment, and the books, many books. If an African enters the Robarts Library, he feels he is really somewhere! And the technique of conversation in class; here, there is dialogue. At home, it is monologue."

We refer to the Robarts Library as "Fort Book" because we think it looks ugly. Eye of the beholder. Thanks to Fola, I no longer think the place ought to be demolished.

So, what's home like?

Fola said, "We had military rule for a long time. We have been a democracy for only a few years. The military looted the country. We have roads which have not been improved since colonial days. We are oil-rich, but if you were to see us today, you would weep." And I have wept for this place; foolish tears, in comparison. I ought to get out more.

Unbidden, Fola also said, " Toronto is a dream of humanity; humanity has long dreamt of this city of culture. How are people able to behave in such a civilized way here? How did this city succeed in forging a place where everybody knows what is good?"

Aw, this old town?

We talked about this at length, and we agreed that people who come here tend to put their differences behind them when they arrive; no one comes to Canada to fight.

He was making the city look good, so I asked him about winter. He grimaced, and then smiled broadly. "When I got here, it was hot and humid, that's my kind of weather. And then I enjoyed the fall colours. One day, the master of the college said, 'Fola, I hope you are prepared for winter.' I said, 'But people tell me it will be mild.' He said, 'What is mild for a Canadian. . . .'

"And then when it came, the winter was criminal. It was more than my expectations. I thought God was against me. I had to wear so many clothes, I was a mobile library of clothing."

A mobile Robarts library . . .

His first impressions of snow? "We never dreamt of it. In class, at home, if someone used snow for a metaphor, we would ridicule him, saying, 'There's nothing like that here. You can't use snow, you must use dust!' And then when the snow came, it was like dust, dropping and falling. I could brush it off my clothing. It was wonderful. I sent many pictures of snow home. Everybody at home is discussing snow." We discuss it here, too, although we do not think of it so fondly.

So much for the reputation of our roads, our weather, our intellectual life; so much for our wealth, and the daily freedoms we take so much for granted. I was almost hesitant to ask what he thought of us; remember we are cold, mean and uncaring.

Fola said, "Toronto people are very friendly. They like visitors. Let me explain: as a journalist, I wanted to see many places. But I don't have a map. I just go out. I stop you and I ask, 'Please, can you show me the way to the CN Tower?' A Torontonian, even if he is in a hurry to go somewhere, will stop and bring out a map and circle where you should go. In the time I have been here, human beings have been my maps."

Mine, too, now that you mention it.

FOUR

My lover looked like an eagle from the distance, but alas!
When he came nearer I saw that he was nothing but a buzzard.

– BLACKFOOT POEM, "Song of a Maiden Disappointed in Love"

Yonge Street used to be our dirty little strip. Times change, and the strip has been swept clean; now it is awash in the neon antiseptic of advertising. There is not much sex for sale, unless it is used to sell perfume. The real action is on the side streets.

All those girls with long legs and short skirts, standing with their hips cocked and their lips pursed and their crack pipes in their purses. And all those cars passing by slowly, their bright tail lights receding in the distance. You saw *Pretty Woman*, right? I know a vice cop whose standard line is that no little six-year-old girl ever said that she wanted to grow up to suck cocks for a living. He is, of course and obviously, right.

The pretty-woman fantasy is a one-way street.

Meet Anita.

She and I were standing on the sidewalk just outside a little convenience market in Regent Park, a massive social housing complex on the verge of being redeveloped. She took the utility knife I'd bought for her. I'd paid for it with a twenty-dollar bill. She dropped the knife in her purse and asked shyly if I could spare ten dollars from the change. I said, "Sure, why not?"

She palmed the bill and tucked it in her purse, made a cute little face, wrinkled her nose and smiled, and asked if I could give her another five bucks. And I just smiled at her because it was funny. I'm a sap but I'm not stupid, at least not past a certain point.

And she smiled back, you know, like nothing ventured.

And then she took my hand and shook it, funny-formal, and we went our separate ways, me to my job and she to hers.

A few moments earlier we'd been sitting on a patch of grass south of Regent Park, the grass nothing more than a small square thatch of unused ground; she'd been smoking crack, and I asked her what she used to protect herself when she went on dates, and she looked at me like I really was stupid, or maybe I was the kind of guy who wanted to hear her talk dirty. She wasn't sure if she wanted to give it up for nothing. I could see her thinking maybe she should turn the meter on.

But then she inhaled, and her eyes got a bit heavy-lidded, and she coughed and said, "Condoms." As in, doesn't everybody use them?

And I said no, that's not what I meant. I said that she was dating creeps, and she was vulnerable, alone in cars parked in dark lanes, or on the docks at night, and what if a date went wrong?

Ah, she got it then. She said she usually carried a utility knife when she tricked, which is how she earns the money she spends on crack, and the knife keeps her safe from the worst of the men. Except she lent her knife to a girlfriend who needed it to cut some rock, and she never got it back, which meant she didn't have a blade on her right now at this very moment, and I said that's probably unsafe if you're going to work, and she said yes, but what are you going to do?

I took her to the store and bought her a knife.

She's prettyish, Anita, in her way, in spite of and perhaps because of the scar on her cheek; the scar, insouciant, not unlike those earned in duels. She had red pixie hair then, and skinny legs, and a comfortably big ass with black stretch pants stretched over it. She wore a tight black top and purple runners with thick white socks rolled down to her ankles.

A girl needs a look to get looked at.

And there was an air of alertness about her, although I have a hunch you wouldn't have noticed her except to say, Oh, look, there's a hooker. Because she was twenty-seven then, and she'd been at this for a while, and the smoking and tricking was starting to show.

We were sitting on the grass, where there was no splendour.

Before she told me about the lack of a knife in her life, she pulled out her crack pipe; not a pipe, really, just a little plastic bottle, like one of those little hotel-room shampoo bottles, with a Pyrex tube jammed in the top to hold the rock, and the hollow body of a skinny ballpoint pen poked in the bottom for a mouthpiece.

She fired up her lighter and sucked in a discreet lungful of smoke, and she held the smoke in her lungs until she coughed, and then she blew her nose in a tissue. I asked her how it felt.

She asked if I ever did grass, and I said well, you know, and she said, "Like that, only ten degrees lower, three times as fast."

I said I could see the attraction.

I could see it is a tricky thing. The first high is the best one. All it takes is one hit for some people to get hooked. No high afterward ever comes close. But every high afterward helps numb the pain a girl feels after she does what she has to do to get money for more.

Just before she'd lit up, she showed me her little chunk of

rock. It was yellow and jagged, the size and shape of my son's milk tooth, the one I keep in a little lacquered Russian box. I was thinking of that tooth when I asked her how she got the scar on her cheek. It's not a pretty story. She said her ex-husband shoved her head through a glass coffee table. I believed her.

I believe what most people tell me. I don't think I always get the truth, but I do think the lies people invent are another kind of truth. She hadn't hesitated. She hadn't reached for the story. She just said it the way you'd say, Nice day.

She said, "He grabbed my hair, and he pushed my head through a glass coffee table." I looked at her face and I saw that, under her makeup, she also had the merest shadow of a black eye, and I asked her about that.

She said a few days earlier a creep of her acquaintance saw her go off into an alley to turn a trick; when she came back from the blow job, the creep asked her to give him five bucks so he could take a cab somewhere, because he was on his way to rob someone.

See what I mean about the truth? If she had the wits to invent a guy who wanted five bucks from a hooker so he could take a cab to a robbery, then maybe she should be writing this and not me.

Anita told the creep he could not have her five bucks; after what she'd done to earn the money, she was keeping every penny.

By way of reply the creep punched her in the face and took the money; he just cold-cocked her, grabbed her purse, took the money, threw the purse at her and then he went to get a cab.

A few moments before she told me how the creep had hit her in the face, she was eating a roast-beef sandwich and drinking a cold chocolate milk with a certain delicacy, even though she clearly hadn't eaten for a while. I had offered to buy her the sandwich, in return for which she agreed to tell me how she spent last night.

She said she turned four tricks: a middle-aged guy, oral, in his car, for thirty bucks at 7:00 p.m. Another guy, half-and-half, for forty bucks an hour later. Then she got lucky and did a guy for a hundred, and never mind what she did for the money except it was painful and it hurt to sit down afterward, and I couldn't quite see how it was lucky. And finally, around 3:00 a.m., she did a cabbie in his cab for another thirty bucks.

That's two hundred dollars for the night. No taxes. If you made that kind of money five nights a week – and that's not much in her line of work – you'd clear a grand a week, which is fifty-two thousand a year, free and clear. Which is not bad for you or me.

She took her money home and bought a case of beer for the alkie who lets her crash at his place, and she paid a couple of debts, and she blew the rest on crack. Which is why she couldn't afford to eat. Which is why I bought her lunch.

I'd spent the afternoon walking aimlessly, just looking around the city, looking for whatever I happened to see. A few minutes before buying the sandwich, I had turned idly into Regent Park.

I knew a bit about the place. It is the first and was the biggest social housing experiment in the country. Cabbagetown was levelled to make way for it. It is about to be rebuilt. Hugh Garner would feel at home there now, and so would Morley Callaghan. It is a blast furnace of character, of hard lives lived in a state of grace, with the occasional echo of gunfire and the sporadic flashing of knives.

One evening I was there after some shooting or some public meeting when I saw two boys and a girl, teenaged kids, sitting around smoking joints. I walked up to them and gave the girl my card. "If you ever have anything to say to the people who read the papers, give me a call."

She took my card and held my gaze while she reached into her pocket, took out a cigarette lighter, lit the card and let it burn right before my eyes. She didn't blink. She didn't say a word. She just looked at me, and she let the flame die and she let the ashes fall. It was so cool, all I could do was smile at her. That's Regent Park.

It was a progressive, smartly designed social housing complex, back in the days when we were unafraid to spend money. For a million reasons, Regent Park went bad. Not totally bad, but it added up bad over time. A shooting here, a life gone wrong there, a reputation for gang violence, mostly undeserved. Not all bad; just bad enough.

When I realized where I'd been walking, I wasn't particularly worried. I always figure, whatever happens, there's a tale to tell; unless nothing happens. But something was about to happen.

I noticed two young men with cornrows, baggy pants, basketball jerseys, and the kind of muscles you normally associate with steroids; they had tattoos on their biceps, and they wore fake gold chains around their necks. And they saw me.

They rode up on bicycles, which is the preferred method of transportation for guys who deliver crack cocaine.

One of them came at me from ten o'clock and the other came at two o'clock, and they fenced me in as if I were a stray calf, a middle-aged white dogie, and they said, grinning idly, "Hey, man, where you going? You look like you lost."

I told them I wrote for the papers. I said I was just poking around looking for stories. And they were about to get loquacious when Anita walked up, all sleepy-faced in the afternoon, a hooker on her way to work; she butted right in and said she had some stories, and would I like to buy her lunch, and did I want to go sit in the park?

Which is where we went and why I bought her the sandwich and how I came to give her the knife. A word for those boys: I was not the one who was lost.

There was more to the conversation. Anita told me she used to have a son. She said she gave him up for adoption. She said giving him up was the hardest, but maybe the smartest, thing she's ever had to do. I guess it was hard. I hope it was smart. All I know is, girls who give up their babies always say it was the hardest thing they've ever done, but they keep having more babies and they keep giving them up.

At that time, just after we met, Anita was at the bottom of the sex-trade pecking order; she was working the curb. No fur coat to keep her warm, no escort-service thug to deliver her to a hotel room and wait for her to call with the room number and say the set-up looks okay; no driver to wait for her to turn the trick and wait to take her home when it was over.

For the girls who work the curb, the knife is cheap, reliable protection. I'd bought Anita one, and I'm only mildly troubled about that exchange. I still consider and reconsider every sharp inch of it. I'm not sure why, exactly. It's not like I was buying a gun for a bank robber. She was broke, her work is dangerous, I had money in my pocket and the blade cost a couple of bucks. I could do that for her. So I did. A snap decision, to buy a knife with snap-off blades.

If she met some pervert, and he drove her somewhere deserted and he hurt her . . . on the other hand, if she cut some john for nothing, or if she cut him for money . . .

I don't like what Anita was doing, and I don't like why she was doing it. There isn't a shred of romance in it, and there's nothing cool about tricking for crack. It's flat-out dangerous. I also knew that if she didn't lay off, it would kill her, fast or slow. So I bought her the knife, and I'd do it again, because a girl can't kick her habit if she's dead.

I also gave her my card. Because sometimes there's a next step in a new direction. I didn't hear from her for a long time. And then she called. She had not burned my card. She said she'd lost the knife.

If you want to get technical, she didn't really lose it; the cops took it from her when they scooped her up. In her line of work that happens; girls get scooped. But it wasn't like that this time. There was no raid, no sweeping of the streets.

Funny, the way it happened. She wasn't laughing.

She'd been sitting with a friend in Pigeon Park at Parliament and Gerrard. It was so hot, even the pigeons were just sort of standing around, not doing much of anything; too hot to peck.

That's this town, in the summer.

Anita's girlfriend was goofing around, splashing in the fountain like a little low-rent Anita Ekberg, out for some cheap daytime *dolce vita*; you take it where you find it. But someone must have complained – aw, fer chrissakes, there's hookers in the fountain – because the cops came along and busted the pair of them, Anita and her friend. They didn't find any drugs. They found her knife, and they tossed it in a garbage can.

Was it my knife?

She thought maybe it was.

And then the cops ran her name, and they came up with a handful of outstanding charges. Failure to appear. Assault. Theft under. They didn't take my card. She still had my number. She called me from the Metro West Detention Centre, and she left a message on my machine.

I went to see her.

You've never been to the Metro West Detention Centre, and I guess you won't ever have reason to go. It's near the airport. It looks like what it is: a warehouse with tawny brick walls, looking nice and new and anonymous from the street.

Inside, there are bored guards behind heavy glass, and curt words barked over the intercom, and every door is locked and meant to stay that way. I asked to see Anita. I was told to sign in. Relationship to the inmate? Friend.

The cold smirk of the guard. A hooker, and her friend. I was told to wait. I waited. I thought about what it was like for Anita in there. You could get used to it, but I wouldn't want to get used to it, not even for a minute. I sat on a metal bench. The bench was bolted down. There's nothing in there that isn't bolted down or locked up except the pen you have to sign in with. They must figure a pen is safe. Like, it's not a weapon. Not unless you use it to write a really harsh note.

Hey, that's rich; a harsh note.

As I waited, I read the sad rules posted on the wall.

– Do you have urgent information concerning an offender's Health, Safety, or Risk to himself? If so, ask to see the General Duty Sgt.

– Number of Visitors: 2, excluding children under the age of 6. Offender/young offender "split" visits; 2 persons for first half of visit and 2 persons for second half are not allowed.

– All visitors will line up, sign in, provide their address, relationship to offender/young offender and produce acceptable identification.

– All persons under 16 must be accompanied by an adult.

– No visits on day of admission and days of court appearance.

– Smoking: prohibited in waiting, interview and visiting rooms. Violation may result in your being asked to leave.

– No cameras. No radios.

– Any visitors under the influence of alcohol or drugs will not be granted access.

– Deportment: visitors are not permitted to engage in loud or rowdy behaviour.

– Dress: appropriate behaviour is required.

– Money: may be left with or without visiting during business or visiting hours for canteen purchases or fines.

– Clothing: once per 6 weeks with or without visiting.

– Bail: if you wish to post it.

The visitors' room is just like those you see on television in the cop shows – long and narrow, with a heavy glass partition; sad little plastic phones in front of sad little stalls. You sit on a low stool. And then you hear the rattle of a thick key in a cold metal lock.

She had a chastened smile on her face when the guard led her in. The guard eyed me; who's this? She sat down, picked up the receiver and we talked, or rather, we yelled.

Anita was wearing grey sweats, prison-issue, with a teal-coloured T-shirt under the sweatshirt and laceless blue runners, Adidas; no one gets laces or belts in jail.

Her face was plain and free of makeup; her hair was clean, and she looked healthy and relaxed, the way women do when they don't have to get dressed for men. We talked over the phones and across the glass. She said the charge was bogus.

Yeah, I know. They all say that. It was not exactly a lie. It was a claim. Too bad. I prefer lies to claims.

She said one night an old man got rolled on the street. She'd been working when the old man came along. He was bleeding from the face, he was reeling down the sidewalk, he was holding on to his wallet. Anita said she was going to get help when another guy came along, and he snatched the old man's wallet, and he rifled through it and he tossed it on the sidewalk; an ignorant thing to do, because it was obvious to anybody with half a brain that the old man had already been robbed.

The old man wailed and moaned and wept.

Anita picked up the wallet, and said she'd called an ambulance with her cellphone, and she took the old man's health card out for when the ambulance boys arrived, and that's how she got blood on her shirt, and the old man was still yelling, and the cops came, and they pegged her for it, and there's more to it than that; also less.

Fact is, she was charged. And she failed to appear. And that's why she was in jail, because her friend had been splashing in the fountain. And she said that, when she got her day in court, she'd be looking at a year if she was convicted.

What's it like inside? She said she was in a small cell, two bunks, but she was alone at the moment. The food was as you'd imagine. Last night, she had broccoli in soggy pastry with a side of box potatoes. Yum.

She knew some of the other girls. Funny, she said, when they're on the street, girls share drugs and clothes and sometimes tricks. Inside, nobody talks to anybody and nobody shares anything.

Even if Anita beat the charge, she knew she'd be in for a rough ride. She had no place to go and nothing to wear when she got out. She had left all her clothes at a guy's place, but he'd gone away; she said his landlord thought he was running girls, which he wasn't, but Anita was sure her clothes got thrown out. Not that they were worth much.

She shops at Goodwill and Value Village.

She didn't look frightened. She didn't seem worried. There was no self-pity in her eyes. She looked vaguely muscle-weary. She said it was nice to be off crack, but she was afraid she was going to head back to the street when she got out; she had no place else to go. And she knows the street, and she knows what to do when she's on the street, and crack will quell her fear and it will dull the memory of bad sex, just as it will numb the humiliation of submitting to men who don't bathe, who are afraid of sex, and who are angry at women as a result.

She looks good when she's not smoking rock: healthy, chipper, self-aware, bemused. Her birthday's in September. She's my son's age. She says she'd like to make a clean start on her birthday. Addicts often do that, talk about starting over on their birthdays. She said she'd be in court soon, and she'd let me know how it worked out. She was right about the birthday thing; life on the street is getting old.

I left her some money so she could buy smokes.

I cooled my heels at the bus stop on the street in front of the jail. I wanted to know what that felt like; the bus stops, the cars go by, the drivers look at you and you can see them thinking: There's a man whose son, whose daughter, whose father or mother or lover is doing time.

The bus is a bargain because the taxi fare is sixteen dollars to the nearest subway station, or thirty dollars to go downtown. I waited in the heat, a bargain waste of time. I was angry; it was too hot to be angry.

Come on, bus.

Snap out of it, Anita.

Jail sucks the life right out of you. Jail is stupid. Jail is bad luck. I was still a little shaky, waiting there, shaky the way I get in hospitals, the way I used to get in church. It could have been me locked up like that.

It gave me the creeps.

And the guards; they don't know who you are, and they don't care to know. A guard thinks, "Scum, or friend of scum; same thing."

There's no such thing as the benefit of a doubt when you go to jail, even if you're just visiting. You think, why'd that guard have to look at me like that? What does he know? Nothing. I didn't do anything wrong, at least, not today. The look on his face; forget about it.

I didn't like forgetting about it. I wanted to smack him, except he would have smacked me back, and I'd have been charged, and so it goes.

What's worse was the game the guard played when I was leaving. He waited until I reached for the door. I reached to pull it open, but it was locked. I pulled, I pushed, I stood there like a fool. And then I turned around.

The guard gave me a special little smirk, like I'm supposed to know I have to play Simon Says. And then he was Simon and he said, pressing the buzzer that unlocked the door; his little power-game, nothing better to do. I kept my mouth shut. I left.

Come on, bus. Hurry up and wait. I wanted to go home.

I killed some time reading the graffiti scratched into the bus shelter.

SUGAR WUZ HERE.

Duran + Christian 4 Life.

Blood Down.

KIM M. + ED.

Mrs. Young Sucks.

Kevin is free FOREVER.

Acute wuz here 8/o6/98.

Acute, but clearly not so acute that the cops couldn't catch him. And oh, Mrs. Young; I wondered who she was and if she sucked. And I wondered if Kevin was still free forever. I don't know about forever; forever doesn't always last too long. The bus came. I tried not to look guilty.

Months went by.

I got another call. Anita had just got out of jail and was staying in a room above an east-end strip club, Jilly's, and did I want to talk, and would I meet her there?

It isn't often I get a chance to get to know someone beyond the needs of this moment and that deadline; it is a luxury.

So the next day I was sitting in the peeler bar nursing a beer in the early afternoon, glancing at my watch and fending off the table-dancers.

You shy, sugar? Yeah, that's it.

I am shy. And Anita was late. Maybe she forgot or maybe she was stoned or maybe she had a date or maybe she slept in; whatever it is, I'm not used to nursing a beer and staring at naked women in the Day-Glo darkness.

They let old strippers dance at Jilly's when they are long past their prime, when they can't dance anywhere else. Jilly's is where the singer/poet/journalist Duke Redbird drinks his coffee and writes sweet poems to naked women. Jilly's is the sort of place where, if you're a regular, the old guy behind the bar has your drink waiting when you come in, as if you'd ordered it telepathically. I'm no regular. I've never been a regular. I'm afraid to be a regular.

Afraid I might like it too much and never leave.

I was about to leave when Anita pushed her way through the door, scanned the room, saw me, rushed over with a little laugh and said, "What are you doing here?" I suppose I must have looked straight and out of place. As if I'm not – couldn't possibly be – the sort of guy who drinks beer and watches strippers in the early afternoon. I was almost offended. I almost laughed.

"Yeah, well, I'm waiting for you. How's it going?"

"You got a car?"

"No."

"Okay, wait here. I gotta pick something up. I'll be back in ten."

She looked healthy enough. She'd been out of jail for a couple of weeks, and it was easy to see she'd lost all the weight she'd gained, which meant she was on the pipe again, which meant she was going off to score.

Ten minutes later she came back to the bar, gave me a brief hug and said, "Let's get out of here. We can talk in my room."

I followed her up a set of sagging stairs and down a stale hall, past the day manager. He eyed me dully; whatever this looked like to him, he wanted me to know it was none of his business.

A couple of plain young dykes fretted over each other in a doorway, touching each other's collars, stroking each other's hair; ignoring me showily, they kissed deeply.

Some poor woman who was off her medication stepped out of a room then, and she looked around, closed her door, tried the key, jiggled the handle, was satisfied it was locked, tucked away the key, ducked down the hall and disappeared. Who knows, who knows?

Anita had the room at the end of the corridor. She stepped inside, fell into a chair, searched her bag for a lighter, found three, flicked two uselessly, tossed them aside, lit her cigarette with the third one and gestured for me to begin. Like, what did I want to know?

"What happened when you got out? What's the first thing you did?"

Her hair was clean. The dye she used was red. She'd showered earlier. You could smell the shampoo under the cigarette smoke.

"I was straight for a day; then I did eight tricks to raise a week's rent for this room. I went for a stiff drink after, and then I cried for half an hour. I hate it, but I did it. And I know why I did it. I'm not going to do it the rest of my life."

The room had two chairs, two small tables and a coat rack; there was a single window; someone had kicked or punched a hole in one wall, and there was a small iron cot in a plywood loft overhead. The carpet was grey and stained with dribs and drabs of every wetness you can imagine. But it was a place to stay, and it was hers, however briefly, for $143.75 a week. If she did eight tricks for that kind of money and that kind of room, then she gave it away cheap. What she really meant was that she'd done eight tricks for crack.

She said, "Right now, I'm good for two weeks. Somebody – never mind who – put up the rent. So I've got a bit of breathing space. And no, I won't do dates in the room; not unless the money's really good."

The junkie's hedge: I won't do that, not unless the money's really good. And the working girl's security blanket: a sugar daddy. It doesn't get any better.

Scattered here and there were old newspapers, paper coffee cups and a patchwork wardrobe of Goodwill clothes and shoes.

"You were clean when they let you out of jail; how much are you smoking now?" She slumped in her chair. She wasn't worried about me. She knew I'd be good for something at the end of the story. "Right now, my habit costs fifty bucks a day, more or less; I keep it down with this." She lit a little joint.

On one of the two tables I noticed a bottle of Nyquil, a tube of toothpaste and a toothbrush, some shampoo and a jar of petroleum jelly, the tool kit of the working girl. She seemed chipper. I wasn't so sure.

"How's it going, really?"

She stopped smoking then and told me how a recent date went wrong; the guy grabbed her by the throat and started choking her. She fought him off and jumped out of the car, screaming for the cops; he drove off in a hurry. She was lucky he didn't pull a knife. And he was lucky she didn't pull a knife.

And then a passerby who'd seen the trouble sauntered over and asked her, then and there, for a date. That's what they call it, a date.

She shrugged, and she rolled her eyes. A guy sees a hooker get roughed up, and then asks her for a date; how low is that?

At the moment, as long as she was here in this safe place, she needed to take care of business – she needed to replace her ID, get a proof of address form filled out, pick up a personal needs allowance cheque from welfare, oh, and she needed to see a doctor.

"I have a lump on my breast. I had an appointment, but then I chickened out. They stick a big needle in you."

Curb life – rough dates, torn tights, bruised lips, stone-cold dealers and bad drugs – that doesn't worry her; biopsy needles do.

I asked her why she didn't strip downstairs; it seems the safer way to make a living. She grimaced. She leaned back in her chair and pulled her top out of her jeans. Her belly was white and soft and spongy, like over-risen bread dough. That's why I like her. No illusions.

She waved an idle hand. "When I'm ready, I'll quit. I want to get my own place with my own key, where I can walk on my own carpet with my bare feet." Later, maybe. At that moment, at three-thirty in the afternoon, she figured she'd better find her dealer and make another score, and then she'd better figure out where to start. I let myself out. The day manager looked at me, and then he looked away; none of his business.

Anita called again, some months later.

Women who live the life usually pick up and move on, or they finish with nothing left to pick up at all. I was pleased that she'd called. Most addicts lose things. She'd kept my card. She wanted to have coffee. There was something in her tone of voice. She tends to sound like she's in a hurry. Not this time. This time, it was hurry up and wait.

We met in a shawarma joint on Parliament Street, near the welfare office. She was clear-eyed, healthy-looking, quick to smile. Her clothes were neat, her hands were steady, her hair was shiny, short and clean.

Of course, she was also pissed off. That's to be expected. She'd just spent an hour in the welfare office; pissed-offedness is a natural by-product. She brought me up to date.

Not long after our last visit, she moved into Tent City.

Tent City was a free-form squat on the waterfront, an exercise in crackhead anarchy. The residents were a merry combination of psychotics, losers, loners, dogs, rats and people who could cope quite nicely with the fact that they couldn't cope at all.

Some of the houses thrown up there were snug and tidy, built with foraged material, including good windows and doors with working locks. Nice view, the best view of the city. See the harbour, the sailboats, and watch the tugs push Paul Martin's fleet of lakers into and out of their berths. Hookers took johns there for tricks. Cops took lowlifes there to beat the snot out of them. Anita didn't last long.

One night, somebody burned her tent while she was downtown working. A good thing she wasn't in her tent stoned and sleeping when it happened. Whoosh, like a torch. I didn't ask what she'd done to deserve a burnt tent, and she didn't offer. At that time, in that place, shit just happened. There was no anarchy. There was two-bit petty craziness. She lost everything she had. Not that she had much.

She moved into a motel on Kingston Road, in Scarborough, out where the immigrants live. She had a room. She shared it with two hookers and a cabbie. It was okay for a while. It was warmer than the tent. The cabbie worked days. The girls worked nights. It was a come-and-go arrangement. And then she said she cut her wrist.

She showed me the scar. A weak attempt at suicide. Not the first time she'd done that; there were other scars up and down her arm.

Now, she said, things were different.

Things are always different, which means they are always the same. I said nothing. I sat. I waited. I drank my coffee. I looked out the window. And when she was ready, she told me an old story.

She met a trick. His name was Kenny. He fell for her. She was skeptical. He was persistent. She pushed him away. He was married. His wife was pregnant; second child. A recipe for romance.

One night she and Kenny had a fight, and she ran off. Kenny was worried that she'd hurt herself. He went looking for her. He was cruising up and down. The cops stopped him because they thought he was trolling. He explained what he was doing. They took his word for it.

One of those Céline songs leaked out of the radio then and spilled over the tables and onto the floor of the shawarma joint, something about a heart going on. That's what those silly sad songs are for. The soothing of the hearts of those who will wallow in love. Her eyes got teary.

She said she hadn't used drugs for months. Kenny had helped

her kick crack. He took Anita and her girlfriend Helen to a little cottage on a lake up north. He left them with some groceries. Anita ate. She swam. She got some sun. She swatted some bugs. She and Helen giggled at night while listening for bears. They also hitchhiked to one of the little cottage-country villages for smokes, and weed when they could find it, and then they hitchhiked home.

She said, "I kept a diary." I didn't ask. She offered.

She reached into her bag when the song was over and she pushed a fat little notebook across the table, and she said I could keep it and read it and I could give it back to her when I was finished reading. She said she'd call me again. She gave me a little hug. I gave her twenty bucks.

Call me a john.

Her writing is rounded, girlish, lots of underlining, lots of words traced over again until they stand out, plump and blue. Some excerpts:

Oct. 18: I've been at the cottage six days now with little to no cravings. Maybe it is as easy as it was hard.

There is a man out on his boat fishing. Should I wave? Why not. Snob. He doesn't wave back. Oh, the man waved. God, my legs need shaving. He's coming over. His name is Walter. I'm going fishing.

He's had a bypass. He's 33 years old. It reminds me of how lucky I am. I hope Kenny doesn't get mad.

Well, I'm back. Didn't catch anything. Bummer.

Oct. 19: Today is a lax day. I'm doing pretty good with the withdrawals. Today though I've actually thought about using more than usual. I had to clean out the garbage can. We found two dead mice in the bottom. Ew!

Well, we walked to the corner store. Mind you, the corner store was 6 1/2 miles! I puked my guts out. I'm not used to so much excitement, I guess.

Oct. 20: I found out that Kenny doesn't like my nose ring. I'm going to take it out and if he doesn't notice in 1/2 hour I'm hitting him and putting it back. Speaking of K. he's supposed to come tonight. I hope so. So I can fall asleep in his arms. Well.

I'm making spaghetti for dinner. Hope it turns out. Bye.

Oct. 23: I'm starting to get nervous. I'm going to town for a couple of days. I don't want to relapse. I haven't had any more stupid thoughts of suicide. I want to live.

Oct. 27: I ended up using when I went to Toronto. I hurt K. I never want to do that again. After all, the plan is to live.

Nov. 5: He says not to wear sparkle gel to town it intrigues the townspeople.

Nov. 8: I've become "domesticated" as K. put it last night. It's amazing as an addict what you take for granted. The simplest thing like making a bed, forgetting what it's like to defrost the fridge and other household things. K. seemed distant tonight, almost like something is bothering him. Am I demanding too much?

Nov. 13: It rained all day again. I just lounged around doing nothing. The furnace still isn't working. I keep thinking about my family. In my dreams my mom is either very old or dead. K. and I visit her but she's at her old place and she's her old self, blaming me for everything. It doesn't matter, though, because I've got to see her, I want to see her and my sister and her kids. At least I think I do.

Nov. 16: K. showed up around midnight and scared the bejesus out of me. Helen was already scared. She has a grizzly fixation ever since I told her she got eaten by a bear in my dreams. She says she wouldn't have minded if it was the Chicago Bears. Ha Ha!

Nov. 20: After a particularly cold night I did it, I did it. I fixed the water. I was right. I had to pull the hose right out of the lake and throw it back in. Keeping my fingers crossed.

Nov. 20: The water went off again. I have to move the hose again. I'll wait until morning.

Nov. 25: After a day in Toronto I did it, I'm so proud of myself. I didn't use crack or even think of buying any. Nor did I go in crack zones. Well I went to the circle to buy weed that's it. When those guys asked me how much I want and telling them I don't smoke crack no more of course I got the usual. I'm glad I'm not into that lifestyle any more. I owe a big part of that to Kenny.

Dec. 1: We discussed my moving back to Toronto. Kenny asked me if I honestly think I can handle the pressure. I told him honestly no. I also said that I have to face it sooner or later. I don't know what to do.

Dec. 4: Final chapter. I am no longer at the cottage so my feelings and emotions have changed. I'm now fighting a battle against using every day in the city. I have someone who believes I can do it. Now it's time to believe in myself.

I don't know Kenny. I never met him. I don't want to meet him. His wife gave birth while Anita was at the cottage. He told Anita he'd leave his wife, but married guys never leave their wives, especially when their wives have new babies. There are tougher rows to hoe than this.

Yeah, name one.

Anita is not so different from the rest of us. She came here from someplace else. She made a mistake. She paid a higher price than most of us. There are plenty of girls like her on the street.

That's the kind of town this is.

The girls on the corner all come from someplace else. They all have their own reasons for coming. You can guess what they might be. We don't pay them any mind. We're too busy to look closely. We're afraid to look twice. Most of us pass the girls by and think, "There's another hooker." As if that word told the story. As if there was some romance. As if it had to do with sex. But the girl on the street is not just a hooker.

She is a woman, a girl, a sister, a daughter, an aunt.

The last I heard Anita was working behind the cash register in a convenience store somewhere outside Toronto; away from the life, free of drugs, taking it slow and steady.

I still think of her.

FIVE

Toronto, for all its sprawling size, has a small-town psychology.

– HUGH MACLENNAN, "If You Drop a Stone . . . ," 1978

There is an old brick building near the corner of Bloor and Lansdowne. It is a house divided: on one side is the Church of the Crusaders, and on the other side is Club Paradise.

The church is an evangelical congregation. They follow the message of the gospel. The club is a strip joint featuring Girls Girls Girls.

Sinners here, saints there.

Pastor Don Boyd takes it in stride. I sat with him one Wednesday afternoon as he led a small prayer meeting: five elderly people in a semicircle, eyes closed, hearts yearning for certainty.

Snatches of prayer washed over me:

"Wherever two or three are gathered in Your name, Lord, let us pray. Lord, let us be wise as serpents and harmless as doves. Lord, let us pray for the mayor and his council."

That had better be a powerful prayer.

Don Boyd had been pastor of the Crusaders for eighteen years when I met him. He is a slim man with grey hair, pinpoint eyes and an open manner. He looks more like a track coach than a preacher.

His parish once numbered some five hundred people, enough to fill every pew. He was down to a scant fifty when I sat in. But if it is a small group, it is an interesting one, including some old root-stock Ontarians, a few Vietnamese and some Tamils.

The congregation on the strip-club side of the wall consists of solitary old men with flagging libidos, casual young men with shaved heads and baggy clothes, and a stable of leggy strippers.

The Club Paradise was once known as the Bloor Hotel. It was renovated with a new façade, brighter lights, a flashier disco ball, a beefed-up sound system; the same old shimmy.

The Church of the Crusaders was once a garage. It is in constant need of renovation. The air is musty, the carpet ought to be replaced and the altar, nothing special, stands above a pit where, like the Blood of the Lamb, engine oil once drained.

The corner of Bloor and Lansdowne is as good a place as any to pray; it is a conjunction of the sacred and the profane. Across the street from the Crusaders there are Buddhists; down the block there are Hindus; nearby is a house where men can rent hourly companions.

Of the strip club next door, Pastor Boyd said, "Sometimes I get their mail by mistake. I take it over. I used to know a few of the people who lived in the apartments upstairs."

Here, along a fault line no wider than a brick, is where the tectonic plates of faith and morals collide: it sounds much like a popular song, one of those thump-and-bump anthems favoured by the strippers on the other side of the wall. When prayers are over, Eleanor, a white-haired, long-time congregant, says, "We've had the odd one from next door drop in under the influence. We always invite them in. One girl said, 'I can't come in, I'm a hooker.'" Hooker or not, she'd have been made welcome.

As for the behaviour of the men who come at night to drink and to watch women strip, Pastor Boyd turns the other cheek. It isn't easy: "Sometimes they use our front entrance for a toilet. Of course, there is other activity at the side entrance." You are free to imagine what he means by "other activity." Eleanor adds, "That's why we meet in the afternoons. We don't like to come here at night."

Over at Club Paradise, the man behind the bar tends to a cup of coffee. He appreciates the irony of the geography: "They're trying to save 'em; we're trying to corrupt 'em." The lights dim, a new song begins. It's the same old song. A naked woman rises from the darkness and strolls around the stage with a desultory jiggle. The spotlight follows her.

She, too, turns the other cheek.

One block east of my house is Fire Station 15, the biggest and busiest fire hall in the city. I fall asleep to the sound of sirens, and far too often sirens wake me in the middle of the night. Once, instead of fighting sleep, I wandered over and hung around on full alert with the crew of Pumper Truck 15.

The night shift began at 4 p.m. with the placement of boots in overalls. And then the placement of boots-in-overalls by trucks, a timesaver, this: you run to your truck, you step in your boots, you pull up your overalls and off you go. Mostly you don't go anywhere. Mostly you sit and wait.

On this evening, Shaw is the captain, Galante is the driver and Lacey and Stawarek are the crew of the big red pumper truck. They are thick-wristed, strong-armed, short-haired guys, as easy in each other's company as ballplayers between innings. They wait and they drink coffee. They eat sweet buns and watch TV. They read the paper, crack jokes and plan vacations. In the summer, they wash their cars. In winter, they pump a little iron. They check their equipment – hoses, oxygen tanks, fire axes – every day of the year.

They eat supper together in the station every night, alongside the crews of two other trucks. They are a dozen men in total. How do they decide who cooks? Those who can, do.

On this evening, Shaw made fettucine with red sauce: he used tomatoes, tomato paste, onions, garlic, mushrooms, hot sausage, green peppers, zucchini and, he said, Al Pacinos. Al Pacinos?

"We used to have a captain here who couldn't say 'jalapenos.'"

Before the red sauce could come to a boil, they heard the familiar scritch and whirr of a computer printer. An incoming call; the corner of Howard Park and College. Plates down, everybody out, the Linh Son Buddhist temple is burning. Shaw took an extra moment to shut off, and then to double-check, each burner; it wouldn't be the first time a stove was left on in a fire hall.

Let's go, let's go, let's go, lights flashing, sirens wailing, cop cars blocking traffic when we arrived; there was a crowd in the street, the sky was dark, the night was cold and the flames were shooting upward. It looked bad. Four of the firemen scampered up ladders.

On the street, a small crowd surrounded three Buddhist nuns. The nuns wore yellow robes. Their heads were shaved. A woman in the crowd put her arm around the oldest nun to keep her warm. By now, the police had all the traffic under control. I asked the littlest nun a question. She smiled; she doesn't speak English.

A man stepped forward. He said, "I can translate."

Okay, is anyone still in the building?

The little nun smiled broadly and said nothing. Did you see

anyone start the fire? Smiled broadly, said nothing. Did you call? Smiled broadly.

And then someone else stepped forward and whispered in the translator's ear. He turned to me. "This nun doesn't speak."

Oh, you mean she's mute? More whispering. "No, she's a Buddhist nun; she doesn't speak." Ah, I get it; she was mute for religious reasons. Which posed a koan: Who shouts "Fire!" in a Buddhist temple?

No one, apparently. In any case, there was no need: a couple of passersby noticed the flames and knocked on the door; when they got no answer, they ran into the building and made sure all the nuns escaped.

The Linh Son Buddhist temple is a gaudy red and yellow building; the flames which leapt from the roof were also red and yellow.

Temple and flame, is there a difference?

Not to a firefighter. The blaze seemed isolated to a metre-square black wooden box which housed an exhaust fan; the firefighters prised apart the wooden box and doused the flames.

White smoke, rising like an offering to the heavens.

The firefighters checked the temple from top to bottom, to make sure there was no more fire lurking. What's it like inside? "There's a little water damage to one of the ceiling tiles, but the only smoke in there is from incense." In other words, a good fire. Not much damage, not much danger, no lives lost, no men hurt; the building was saved, the nuns were smiling and the men were clear to head home for supper.

Fettucine with Al Pacinos.

The mood was good; the tension of the start of the shift had been released. Captain Shaw reheated his red sauce and boiled water for the fettucine. The sauce was sweet and thick, nippy from the jalapenos. Every man ate his fill. An old boy from the neighbourhood – he is in the habit of dropping by at supper-time – was sitting in the office. Shaw looked at him, and he mimed dishing up a serving. "Oh, well; if there's plenty, I won't say no." The old man got a big bowl, no questions asked.

And after supper the firefighters washed his dishes with their own. All twelve men lent a hand scrubbing pots, drying plates and wiping tables. Everything was done in unison; intuitive, masculine, efficient. The leftover red sauce went into the freezer for a future pot of chili.

"Let me fill your cup," said Lacey. The coffee was weakly offensive, as if someone had been painting a watercolour of coffee and had dipped the brushes in water and had served that to drink. I was about to fend off his generosity when every man froze in mid-gesture: the scritch of the printer again. Wait for it, wait for the call: 55 Rankin Crescent. Oh-oh, that's a high-rise.

Boots on, in the truck, out the door; go, go, go again, again, again. Galante drove, Shaw rode shotgun; Lacey and Stawarek sat in back. The siren was sharp as a knife and the streets ran red with flashing lights. The temple was a good fire. No one likes a high-rise.

Halfway there, the pumper yielded the right of way to a pair of trucks from another station. Galante muttered, "Yeah, yeah, yeah; but they know we were here first."

In the lobby of 55 Rankin, the building super, a skinny man in a T-shirt, shifted his weight from one foot to another. It was all he could do; he waited, and by his side a salaryman with a cellphone waited, and near the door a woman in a green dress waited.

The fire alarm was deafening.

The captains of all three trucks stood alert, poised for action. A pair of firefighters headed up the stairs for the fourth floor, armed with pry bars. They returned after a few minutes, strolling casually. A faulty smoke detector; no sign of smoke. The super reset the alarm.

The building was silent once more.

Back at the station, most of the men turned in before midnight but some sat up, cracking their knuckles, tapping their fingers, flipping the soft pages of yesterday's papers; waiting, waiting.

Station 15 has taken calls as terrible as the rooming-house fire on Dowling Avenue in which three people died; and calls as absurd as the flaming toilet on the corner of Lisgar and Queen.

You never know; you wait.

Nearly half the calls are medical emergencies. A fire truck can sometimes arrive on the scene faster than an ambulance, and while paramedics don't put out fires, every fireman knows how to use a defibrillator. Suddenly, three quick calls in succession:

1:25 a.m. A forty-year-old man in a rooming house, having trouble breathing. He was also smoking a cigarette; he smelled vaguely of solvents. He'll be fine; that is to say, he will be fine for a while.

2:44 a.m. An elderly woman with chest pains in a nursing home. She is little more than a whisper in a nightgown; she takes oxygen from an ambulance crew. She'll be fine; that, too, is a short-term call.

3:25 a.m. An alarm at the CNE. No traffic, no siren, no matter. Gremlins or raccoons have tripped a security panel; another false alarm. And so to bed.

Leaves blew past the station in the chill air, and weak sunlight began to leak onto the street. No more fires now, no false alarms. The day shift, smelling of cinnamon buns, rolled in. Shaw and Galante, Lacey and Stawarek went home to get some rest.

I have trouble sleeping at night because I live within earshot of Fire Station 15. Not true, not true. I sleep a little better.

Who are we if not our stories? Where are we if we aren't out for a walk? Down the street from my place is a supermarket, formerly Knob Hill Farms, the first of the superstores; it was the cornerstone of the empire of Steve Stavro, an owner of the Toronto Maple Leafs. Stavro had money trouble. He needed cash. He sold the Farm.

I walk by the place a couple of times a week on the way to my streetcar stop. After it closed, it stayed empty for a time. And then one day I saw open doors and a sign: Auction Today.

There were many trucks and cars parked in the lot. The supermarket was packed with scavengers who had come to pick over the remains. The remains consisted of fridges, freezers, fryers, fire extinguishers, filing cabinets, cash registers, carts, cutting boards, sinks and meat saws, rolling ladders, rolling carts, rolling scales, shelves, deli slicers, meat hooks, floor scrubbers and a bug zapper.

The building was impressively cold and empty. I paced the distances off between the piles of auction goods: 117 by 131 metres, more or less. You could have had two football games in there, one going north-south and the other east-west, and still have room enough for fans in stands.

At one time the building had been packed with huge bins of fresh fruit and vegetables, shelves of tinned peas, coolers filled with cut-up chickens, including the feet; also cleaning products and paper towels.

Now it was just empty, and there was an echo.

The men who were looking things over – and they were mostly men – had dirty clothes and dirty hands and heavy boots. I fell in with a younger fellow. "Whatcha looking for?"

He didn't want to tell me. He thought maybe I'd try to scoop him out of a deal. I assured him I wasn't there to buy.

He said, "A compressor."

"What for?"

"I repair refrigerators. I'm just looking for something, you know, I can fix it up and sell it for a profit." See, that's just plain good business. That's how capital is accumulated. That's the way guys make enough money to put their kids through school. But maybe you thought we don't know how to do our own repairs in the Big Smoke.

That guy is who we are here now.

I noticed a little girl with a big grey plastic owl. Carefully loud, and within earshot of her father – it doesn't do any more for a strange man to talk to a child without her parents' knowledge; that, too, is who we are here now – I said, "Where'd you get that?"

She looked over to her daddy.

He said, "It was over there on that pallet lifter." You know what a pallet lifter is – it's one of those hydraulic things on wheels, with a fork in front and a long handle at the back end, used for moving heavy pallets loaded with freight. He bought the pallet lifter for a hundred bucks.

The owl, no charge.

Like I said, that's just good business.

I heard the voice of the auctioneer across the room, singing that old auction poetry: "All right, gather in, gather round, bid a little forty dollars, bid a little forty, who will give me forty-five? Bid a little, will you give me fifty? Sold for forty-five."

And then I bumped into José Kafie.

He had a smile on his face, tight little tasselled loafers on his feet and a toque with earflaps on his head. It wasn't cold, but he was from a warm country, and he needed to stay warm.

He said he had just arrived from Honduras. I asked him what he was looking for. He didn't care who knew he was looking for a cooler. He said he had plans to open a corner store.

Why would anyone come to Canada to open a corner store?

He said, "I know a little about business. My family has a textile factory. In my hometown, San Pedro, I also had a business selling refrigerators, domestic and commercial.

"I rent a house north of here. My landlord told me about a location, a very good location for a store; it used to be a coffee shop. I walked around the neighbourhood knocking on doors. I asked the people if they needed a corner store around here. Everyone said yes. There's even parking so people can drive over."

So here he was, buying cheap, trying to get set up.

He said, "We'd been thinking of leaving Honduras for some time. There is a lot of violence. Three months before we left, my cousin was kidnapped. The ransom was over half a million dollars but something went wrong. Maybe my cousin put up some resistance. I don't know. When I saw the body, there was a mark on his neck. I think they strangled him, and then they shot him."

Bid a little forty, who will give me fifty, bid a little forty-five.

"Not long after that, someone called the house when I was at work. My daughter answered the phone. The caller said to her, 'This is your aunt, come outside, I'll take you to the movies, we'll have fun.' Fortunately, the housekeeper took the phone from her. The caller hung up. Ten minutes later the phone rang again. The person said, 'Melissa, come outside.' It was kidnappers. That's when we decided to leave.

"We had been to the United States, to Miami, Texas, Chicago, but everyone we knew said Canada is the best place in the world. I think it's true. Why? When we flew to Miami from San Pedro, the stewardess didn't speak good Spanish. But when we flew on Air Canada from Miami to Toronto, the stewardess spoke English, French and good Spanish."

He walked gingerly, lightly in his tiny loafers. He was a man about to open a shop. He was looking at the shelving and the cash registers like a kid in a candy store. "The stewardess said that she was from Montreal, and that her father is Italian and her mother is German. I think that's good. Also here you have access to public health, education, Internet. Canada is very modern. This is a safe place, maybe the safest place in the world."

Who will give me ninety, bid a little ninety-five.

"We rent a small house. Our kids are in school. My wife is a pharmacist. She had a pharmacy in Honduras. She has a licence to practise in the United States. Now she is working on getting her Canadian certification."

How did he like it here so far?

"In my country, you pay 28 to 30 per cent for a mortgage, Here, you put 5 per cent down, and you can have the house of your dreams. This is heaven."

Bid a little hundred-dollar bill.

He bought a digital scale for twenty bucks. Three months later he moved to Niagara Falls. That's how it is here.

We take refugees, and we help them get set up, and when they get some breathing room, they can see the lay of the land, and then if they can, they move up, or they move on.

There are nights I lie awake, not because of the sirens from the fire station. I am not thinking of José, nor the temptations of the redeemed, nor of pasta with Al Pacino. I am thinking of the wild old man of Roncesvalles.

He has a new winter coat. He wears it all year long. It won't be new next year. His old coat was ratty and smelly and torn.

The stuffing had leaked out. I don't know where he got the new coat, but we are a generous people. If you sleep on the street, we'll make sure you are clothed. Soon the new coat will be caked with dirt.

The wild old man does not shave or cut his hair or bathe. He wears his boots or shoes until they fall apart, and we give him new ones and they chafe his skin and make his ankles bleed. We are generous that way. He has new boots this year. You can tell by the way he limps.

He's been around for as long as I can remember. He walks slowly up and down the block. I gave him some ham sausage one Christmas. He seemed overwhelmed. I saw him stripping shreds of tobacco from discarded butts and rolling the shreds into smokes. I handed him twenty bucks and told him to buy some tobacco. Perhaps he did.

He could be me. He paces up and down. He stands and stares. His plastic bags are full of newspapers, flyers, bits of string, dead batteries, pencils. One of the men who habitually begs on the street says the wild old man was a child of the Holocaust. Maybe that's true. It's as good an explanation as any.

The old man's hands have begun to tremble lately. It's hard to live on the street. You couldn't do it. The last time I slept on a floor – don't ask – I hurt for days.

The last time I saw the wild old man, there was a thick black scar on the index finger of his left hand; he forgets what he's doing and his cigarettes burn down and they burn him, and he doesn't seem to feel the pain or if he does, he ignores it the way he ignores the cold, the heat, the hunger. I said, "Grandfather, are you okay?"

"I'm nobody's grandfather."

"Are you okay? You don't look well."

"Are you saying I'm crazy? Get out of here!"

And he lunged his head at me, as if he'd bite. He does that now. He shakes his fist, he lunges and shouts at anyone who looks. He wears his new winter coat in the summer; no shirt underneath the coat, his ribs showing, his skin filthy.

There are plenty of churches in my neighbourhood, but there is no one to care for the old man and there is nothing to be done, beyond a gift of a sausage, a coat or a pack of smokes. He will die on the street. He is a wild old man. We do not want to catch him. We don't know what we'd do if we caught him. This is a big town. He has the right not to be caught.

We'll catch him soon enough.

SIX

The alienated ones have a natural intuition of ecology, since they are the victims of its absence.

– MARSHALL MCLUHAN

You come into Thunder Bay from the east, off the lake. You see the sharp light on the water, and the low blue mountains and then you see how the land flattens out toward the west. This is my hometown.

I return to the south side – Fort William; more specifically, to the west end, known as Westfort – for funerals.

Friends who still live there see me when death clings like an odour. They pour drinks and listen, even when I have nothing to say. This is what friends do, especially those who saw me grow up, fall in love, act stupid, fuck up, get lucky, fall back; these are the ones who can look in my face and see the evidence of youth. How precious they are.

I go back less often now; fewer deaths in recent years, for the obvious reason that the old ones have mostly died out.

I have been away as long as that.

There have been a couple of sharp corrections: two brothers whose hearts burst in their chests; they clutched at death and died alone in rented rooms a couple of years apart; the youngest, then the oldest.

The shock is that they died so young.

My age, more or less.

The town has changed. I can't find my way around so easily there, which means I, too, have changed. I have to stop and think. Westfort born, Westfort bred; more strength in the back than brains in the head. Or something like that.

The most obvious difference is that there are more Ojibwa living off-reserve. I went to school with native kids. The orphanage was full of them. But we never saw them outside of school. That's changed.

My hometown is a native town.

Is Toronto?

The numbers are small and in dispute; perhaps twenty thousand aboriginal people live here. But they come and go so easily, and it's hard to count men and women who won't stand still.

They are here. The evidence is available if you look for it. This is a tough town. And all I have is anecdotal information. But stories come from everywhere. I know a guy whose apartment overlooks the city. Why live downtown if you don't have a view?

He said he could see two men, native guys, living in a little park near his place. He said he saw them every day when he looked out the window. He thought they had a story to tell. He meant he was curious. He hoped I would ask. I took my cue from him. And so, a day later, there were three men sitting on a park bench. Two men talking; them. And one man with big ears listening; me.

"I'm Blackfoot," said Chris.

He was whip-slim, whip-smart, wispily whiskered. He bent forward then and peeled back the tongue of his laceless sneaker. His foot was unwashed, filthy. Oh, I get it; a black foot.

His partner said his name was Little Pony; said he was Ojibwa; said, "I got an apartment." Meaning, he didn't have to live here. His voice was as thick as cough syrup. He had a buzz on.

He said, "I could live there. I like to live here."

Here, *en plein air*, outdoors, he was one of nature's princes.

And Chris said, "I got an apartment; Toronto."

They laughed at the joke. They shared a smoke. They sleep in the park, a patch of green between the University of Toronto's Faculty of Social Work, and the Ontario Institute for Studies in Education. Both buildings are full of social engineers who think they know it all, and who don't trust you or me to know much of anything.

Chris and Little Pony would be a living lab in either place if anyone cared to pay attention. They eat and sleep, drink and fuck, piss and shit behind the bushes here all the time, and they stem – panhandle – on the nearby sidewalk.

Chris said, "Every time I leave Toronto I say I'm not coming back. It's a fuckin' concrete jungle." It is all of that. But he always comes back.

Maybe because doing nothing here is better than doing nothing on the reserve. You can't do nothing on the reserve, depending on the reserve. Most people, no matter where you live, won't let you get away with doing nothing.

There is, by the estimate of Chris and Little Pony, a rough group of about forty princes of nature who do nothing in this park on a floating basis. Not all of them are native guys.

"We're not racial," said Little Pony. "Black, white, red, yellow, it don't matter to us." What does matter to them? Money, smokes, booze.

"We're not east or west boys, we're central boys," said Chris.

He pointed to the Faculty of Social Work. "People in there

give us pizzas." He didn't say they were leftover pizzas from social work lunches; I suppose it doesn't matter, since a slice is a slice, and a slice of life is still a slice, and it's more tangible than anything they'll get from the social workers once they graduate.

They leaned back. They stretched. They yawned. They scratched themselves. They sighed and eyed me slyly.

"We clean up the park every day."

"We eat here, sleep here. Why not be good?"

"We live a day at a time."

"Day to day."

"Thanks the Lord."

"Manitou."

"The great spirit."

"In the sky."

"We do what we can."

"You got some *giuniasse*?"

I can't vouch for the spelling, but they said that was Indian for money. They said it doesn't matter how it's spelled. They said it only matters how it spends.

Just then, a woman cut through the park on the diagonal. She was a native woman, dressed in neat blue slacks, a white blouse, and white sneakers, carrying a little white clutch purse.

She noted Chris and Little Pony; took them in with a glance. She was not an elder, but she was older and she was a woman. The two men sat up straight. She came close enough to be heard.

"Have you seen Jason?"

"Which Jason?"

"Jason S."

Chris jumped up off the bench and wiped his hands on his jeans. He approached the woman as if she were his mother. He knew that Jason was passed out in a park nearby. He took the woman by the elbow and escorted her with a certain tenderness.

Little Pony didn't say a word while he was gone. I watched the passersby on Bloor. Chris returned alone five minutes later.

Little Pony said, "I didn't know that was Jason's mom."

That word, *mom*. The two men talked of family then, the importance of and the need to get away from. Chris said he had five kids from five different mothers. He ticked off the names of the kids: "Amy, Monique, Justin, Marcel and Marcel, Jr." A future problem for Justin: this is my brother Marcel; and this is my other brother Marcel.

Little Pony grabbed his crotch and said, "I never had children, but I'm trying." He rolled his eyes, savouring his own delicious wit. He was trying, all right. Trouble is, you can't get that job done by hand.

And then Jason's mom retraced her steps. She looked like any other mother who had just found her son passed out in a downtown park at noon. Her face, blank. There was nothing she could do.

Chris and Little Pony straightened up again.

She said, "Tell Jason to phone me. I can't wake him up. I left him a note. I wrote it on his belly. Tell him to call me."

Chris said, for sure, for sure he would tell him.

Little Pony nodded.

They would look for Jason later. They would see him somewhere on the street, or they would see him at one of the shelters having supper, or they would see him in that park or this one, or they would see him stemming. They would tell him there was a kite – a letter – from his mom, written on his belly. It was a promise. You could count on it as much as you can count on anything. The men in the park are part of a brotherhood. They take care of each other as best they can.

I wondered if Jason's mother wrote the note upside down, so he'd be able to see it when he looked at his belly, if he looks at his belly, when he showered, if he showers. Chris would read it for him if it isn't written wrong-side up. Because it could be confusing.

MOM upside down is WOW.

Little Pony's buzz was wearing off. He was getting hungry. Most of the shelters and many of the churches and plenty of the community centres put on a good breakfast. There's no need to go hungry in this town; hadn't he had a bite to eat?

Little Pony said, "I don't eat breakfast. I just drink. Okay, Listerine. I had two bottles today. The brown stuff. I didn't boost it. I got money."

Chris got up off the bench a bit stiffly. He walked over to the sidewalk without a word and returned with four cigarette butts, good ones, long ones, not too crushed, lots of smoke left in them.

"It's an old Indian tradition." He crumbled the tobacco into a cigarette paper, rolled it, licked it, lit it and shared it with Little Pony. And then he put the question. "You got some *giuniasse*?"

What for? "I need a bag of potato chips. I didn't have no breakfast neither." I bought the chips.

The man who tipped me to their presence said there was going to be a tower built across the street in front of his building. He said it would rise high enough to spoil his view. He will leave the neighbourhood before Chris and Little Pony do.

Floyd Kuptana, an Inuk from Paulatuk or somewhere close enough to there, was carving at a workbench in a garage in the west end; so far in the west end as to be nearly off the city map. His signature piece, a swimming polar bear. He moved around it with a rasp, soothing and smoothing, talking as he worked. The bear, in mid-stroke, if mid-air were water. And then Floyd stopped carving and dusted himself off and lit a smoke.

He said, "How do you know Joe the Shoe?"

Hello, Joe, whaddya know.

Joe used to run the shoe repair shop in the theatre district, in a mall in the basement of Metro Hall. He is Italian, third generation like me. He did shoe repairs for all the musicals: *Phantom*, *Cats*, *The Lion King*.

Joe kept several Inuit carvings, including a remarkable swimming bear, in the window of his shop. I have lived in the north and am drawn to soapstone; bears are not what I am accustomed to seeing in the windows of shoe repair shops anywhere, let alone in Toronto. But I was passing by and saw the bear and stopped to look, and then to talk, and I learned that Joe the Shoe and Floyd the Carver were pals.

And while we were chatting, Floyd happened to come by. My good luck. Because one thing led to another and that's when I more or less invited myself to watch Floyd carve yet another swimming bear on a bench in a chilly garage in the west end of the city.

The garage was owned by a man who imported stone from all over the world, who knew plenty of carvers, and who reasoned that itinerant carvers need stone and studio space; he had tools, and he took his rent in bears and owls, seals and dogs.

An Inuk with a chisel in front of a bear is not a sight you see every day in Toronto; it is a sight you see often in Paulatuk.

He's a wiry guy, Floyd; hard muscles, hard worker, good carver. Dusty cap, dirty jeans, moustache and beard; denim shirt, open to mid-chest. He was carving and smoking. I kept my jacket on. Hard work keeps you warm. Smokes keep you warm. I was neither working nor smoking. There are days when Toronto is colder than Paulatuk.

Tattoos on Floyd's hands, his forearms, his chest: a crude blue ink anchor, a blue ink bunny, a blue ink heart; foremost of these, a blue ink cross on his forehead. How'd he get them?

He grinned sheepishly. "We were kids, eh? Nothing much to do in Paulatuk." If you've spent any time at all in a northern town, you know what he means: kick some gravel, get a pizza-pop at the Co-op, drink a coffee, go for smokes, not much else to do, get tattoos.

You use a needle, candle soot, the ink from a ballpoint pen; you jab it into and under the skin. I dug at my skin like that in grade school. I used a protractor. I can't draw worth a damn. Lucky for me no trace remains.

Floyd shaved the bear, smoothed it, ran his hand across its back it, blew away some dust; turned it, worked it with his file, took the stone away a whisper at a time.

The tips of his fingers were red and raw from rubbing, smoothing, filing, but it was coming along good, the work was going fast; and when he was done, he would have caught the bear in mid-gesture; an ursine water-strider.

The Inuit have an oral culture. I don't mean they are always eloquent, nor are they loquacious. I mean they tend not to write things down. "If I write it down, I might get it wrong," an old lady told me once; how right she was.

The Inuit have a visual culture. To see is to do. Floyd looked at the bear. It was all bear, essence of bear. He picked it up and he saw what he had yet to do, turned it over and the back paw snapped off in his hand. A flaw in the stone. Rotten as chalk. Floyd stood stock-still. Not a sound.

I held my breath.

And then.

He reached into a pile of broken stone at the edge of the bench, rummaged among the broken bits and plucked out the head of a bird which had snapped off a previous carving. *Taima*; it will do.

He filed the neck of the bird until it was smooth; he smoothed the ankle of the bear. He then drilled and pinned the bird-head to the bear-leg, glued it, smoothed it, carved some more; it was as if he'd planned it all along. The back leg of the bear was now a bird; shaman bear, bird-bear, swimming bear.

I wouldn't have believed it if I hadn't seen it for myself. He set the bear-bird on its spindle. Lit another smoke. And smiled.

He let the glue set, and then he bathed the stone bear with its bird-leg in warm water; he held it, he felt it, he let the stone drink up the heat of the water; when it was warm and clean and smooth, he dried the swimming bear with a towel, and he waxed it. Johnson's Floor Wax. *Taima*; done. This is a Toronto scene as surely as any I know.

Some have the great city thrust upon them.

Joe Kiloonik, Inuk elder from Taloyoak, NU, pop. 900. He is a master carver and a man of few words, none of which are English. We met during his first trip to Toronto.

He was brought here to demonstrate soapstone carving on the grounds of the McMichael Gallery, north of the city. He had come with his nephew, another master carver, Joseph Suqslak of Gjoa Haven.

They had already done a little sightseeing. They had been to that major attraction, Lee Valley Tools. "It was like being in a candy store," said Joseph. They bought files and rasps, hammers and hatchets, bits and burrs. They are practical men.

I'm always curious to know what this place looks like to fresh eyes, so I tagged along with the practical men when they came downtown.

We were standing at the base of the CN Tower. Joe took a narrow-eyed drag on his cigarette and looked up.

The tower – world's tallest freestanding, etc. – is way up, all the way up. Joe said something in Inuktitut to his nephew. The translation: "He said he is thinking it will sway. Just by looking at it, it's the only natural thing it will do. He says it should at least be anchored."

The only natural thing it will do.

Leave it to an Inuk, or an innate engineer, to find something natural in the world's most unnatural, etc.

I hate heights. All I have to do is look up, and my nuts rise in the same direction. I felt a kinship with this other Joe, not just because it had been a long time since I'd heard Inuktitut, but because I, too, think the tower needs anchoring, if for no other reason than to comfort the eyes, mine and his.

The two carvers were clear about wanting to go up, which meant the three of us were going to go up together.

The Joes and I had one more thing in common: neither one of us had been up to the observation deck before. I was praying that it would not sway. Next stop, Up There.

As we waited for the elevator, Joe leaned against a tower wall. He said, "I can feel the building shaking." He was not nervous. The Inuit are not a nervous people. He was merely observant. He was stating a fact. I, too, leaned. He was right.

I tried not to appear nervous.

Here's a spin on the old Eiffel Tower joke: Where is the best view of Toronto? From the top of the CN Tower. Why? Because, from up there, you can't see the tower.

The elevator is clad in glass to afford a view on the way up, if you can stand it. I kept an eye on the two men. They watched as the city fell away. Joseph laughed. Joe swallowed hard. Me, too.

And then the three Joes spilled out of the elevator. My knees were a bit wobbly. The older Joe looked around the observation deck like a hunter who'd pulled a trigger and, as he was looking for his fallen prey, he suddenly somehow found himself on unfamiliar ground.

"This room is bigger than I thought. To me, the floor looks like it's slanting a bit." Now that he mentioned it . . . and why the hell did he have to mention it? The two men headed for the windows.

They are Inuit; their eyes naturally seek the horizon. There are no skyscrapers in the north. "That's Buffalo," said Joseph to his uncle, who smiled tightly and gripped the railing, also tightly.

It was much easier going down.

On solid ground in the gift shop, Joe said, with the merest hint of relief, "I couldn't even think any more up there." Joseph, who lives in the Western Arctic, examined a Calgary Flames cap. He was surprised by the price tag: sixteen dollars. Too expensive?

Joseph said, "These cost twenty-six dollars back home."

Caps are not the only things which cost more; smokes were eight dollars a pack in the North at a time when they cost $5.50 in the south. Each man had two packs in his shirt pocket. You come south, you can't afford not to smoke.

And where do men from the top of the world eat after they've been to the top of the town? Planet Hollywood.

Under the saurian eyes of Sly and Demi, who leered at us from posters, Joe asked for a cup of coffee. His stomach was upset. I could have told him Toronto coffee was not likely to settle it. I did not. I talked instead to his nephew.

So, Joseph – what's the food like up north? What do you usually eat? I knew the answer – I have lived in the North – but I liked to hear him say it. "We get bearded seals, ring seals, caribou, and three kinds of fish: whitefish, char and trout. Also rabbit. And sik-sik, that's ground squirrel; we have them in the fall-time, when they're fat; we eat them boiled."

There are plenty of squirrels here, but I have a hunch if we ate them, they would make us sick, sick. Joe ordered a turkey club.

I resisted making a remark about clubbing turkeys; in any case, Inuit do not club seals, they shoot them, and then they eat the meat, all of it, and sometimes they eat the eyes, and they use the guts for cord and the hides for kamiks and sometimes, as in the old days, they use the hides for runners on their kamotiks; sleds to you.

And I lived in the North when Greenpeace launched its first successful anti-sealing campaign. At one time a pelt was worth forty-five dollars. Men used the money from the sales of skins to buy gas and bullets, and they used the seal meat to feed their families. Two weeks later, the price of a pelt was seven dollars.

Thanks, Greenpeace.

Joseph excused himself from the table and called home. He reported that his wife had said it was cold up there. I have had similar conversations with my beloved.

"When she says cold, she means twenty-five below."

I have been on Baffin Island in January, and I have also stood on the corner of Yonge and Eglinton when the wind cuts like a knife. You want the truth? Take your pick. And button up your overcoat.

After lunch, the two men shopped for camping gear in the downtown sporting goods stores. Joe examined a folding chair; the ground is hard and cold when you are of a certain age, and no one really likes to plunk his ass in a snowbank.

He passed on the chair and bought three aluminum cups instead, but what he really wanted to find was a pair of sun-glasses with yellow lenses, to cut the glare when he was out on the ice with his rifle.

The salesgirl wasn't quite sure what to make of this old man who wanted a pair of yellow sunglasses to improve the view when he was sighting down the barrel of his rifle, an old man who clearly knew more about camping than anyone else in the store. But she had no useful shades. She recommended he visit an optometrist's shop.

Here's looking at you, kid.

They went back to their bed and breakfast; Joe and Joseph needed a rest. City pavement is harder than tundra to walk on, there's too much noise and too many people, and there is no horizon in this town unless you happen to be up in that tower. Which looks as if it sways; it's the only natural thing it would do.

A final thought?

"You people in the south, you make things in a clever way."

That's us, all right.

SEVEN

They are building Rome in one day in Toronto, and it will disappear in the snows.

— Pier Giorgio Di Cicco, "Multicultural Blues"

Here is a short history of the Italians in Toronto.

We turned this town into a city by paving the roads, digging the subway tunnels, throwing up the high-rise towers, laying down the bricks, plastering the walls and pouring the cement.

Before us there was no wine, no garlic, no *sprezzatura*.

I simplify; but not much.

Toronto will not be a real city – we will not have come of age – until we have elected a black mayor, a Chinese mayor; we've done all right by our Jewish mayors. But why have we not had an Italian?

I put this question once to the late Johnny Lombardi. He was the esteemed *dottore* of CHIN Radio, the *professore* of ethnic broadcasting, the *conoscitore* of the *principessa* in high heels and a bikini at the annual CHIN picnic; he was the most venerable *commendatore* of *spaghettata*. We have nothing like him now. He was to Little Italy as Honest Ed still is to the entertainment district. The question made him frown.

I asked because my father used to stare off into the distance at the very mention of Toronto. Big cities scared him, in a way.

He was prone to get into trouble if he was left in a big town on his own. But he used to say that a quarter of the population of Toronto had Italian roots, implying that a man could feel at home there, it was a kind of paradise.

Ahead of his time, my old man.

If it was not paradise at one time, it is now, thanks largely to the Italians; it is as if our blood got into the roots of the city from the very underground.

Johnny Lombardi had an explanation. "You have to remember, Italians don't vote for other Italians just because they're Italian. Even today, those from the south view those from the north as if they were from another country." He's right. There and here, the old prejudices endure: northerners are cold, and southerners are lazy and criminal.

"We don't have anything like this in Canada except Quebec."

He was slightly wrong. We have Serbs and Croats, just as we have Ethiopians, Eritreans and Somalis; we have islanders and hill people and people of the plains from all around the world. Everyone comes with grievances, but we tend not to pursue them on arrival.

I didn't press the point.

He said, "There's something else. The first wave of Italian immigrants sponsored the second wave." He looked uncomfortable when he said this, as if the memory was still fresh. "There was some exploitation. The ones who came in the second wave took the jobs they were offered, they lived in basement apartments, they worked twelve-hour days for low wages. People – families – don't forget."

There is another memory. He wouldn't say it directly, but it's true. Some Italians never recovered from the old days when they were dagos, wops, DPs and worse; when three Italian men could not stand together on the street corner; no matter how much success they achieved, Italians were for the longest time excluded from the city's major social and political institutions. And so they turned their backs.

You don't want me, *madonna damigiana*, I don't want you.

The Italians turned away from the city, away from the downtown core, and they put their energies into their families, into their businesses; they moved from College Street to St. Clair, and from St. Clair to Woodbridge, an Italian suburb north of Toronto. They seized the main chance. They went into federal politics.

We are a poorer city for it.

Politicians come and go. Assunta Marino endures; hers is another chapter of the real history of the Italians in Toronto.

Assunta ran a little convenience store in a tiny strip mall in the north end of the city. When she closed up shop after forty years, her friends, her neighbours, her old customers came with a big red pizza and a big white cake, and they threw her a party with balloons.

Assunta didn't start out with the idea of selling candy and magazines and quarts of milk. She was a seamstress in Italy. She married a handsome tailor. They had a family, and they had plans.

Emilio came here first. He got a job. He saved his money. You know how the song goes: weather's good here in the fall. He sent her down the fare long before Ian Tyson thought of doing so in song.

Assunta brought the kids with her when she came. They started a new life. In the beginning she and Emilio worked in the rag-trade sweatshops; he played his trumpet in dance bands on the weekend, and she cooked in the kitchens of the banquet halls.

They wanted to open their own tailor shop: Emilio cutting, Assunta hemming, the two of them working side by side. But when the time came, and they thought they had enough money set aside, they couldn't get a mortgage from the bank. That's how the banks treated immigrants in those days. That was not so long ago; it is still like that now.

Assunta and Emilio did what they had to do, and immigrants still do. They borrowed money, not from any bank, but from their own kind.

That's how the city was really built.

Marino's Tailors opened in 1961 in a little strip mall on Dufferin, just south of Lawrence. How far north is that? Nobody wearing sunglasses goes up there at night to drink blue martinis.

All the stores were new in the mall then – a pizzeria, the first in the city; a butcher shop; a barbershop. There was hope in the air.

Emilio died suddenly.

Assunta was left with four boys, a mortgage and a broken heart. Who could have seen it coming? Her sister and brother-in-law had the cobbler's shop a few doors down. They helped as much as they could. There is no help for that kind of grief.

Assunta held her boys close to her, and she clothed her grief in work and she worked as hard as she could. She worked, and she kept on working. She turned the tailor shop into a convenience store.

She stocked it with milk and bread, shoelaces and aftershave, greeting cards and magazines. In those early days she earned ten cents on a quart of milk, and three cents when she sold a copy of the *Toronto Star*. She kept the store open all the time.

She never made a lot of money but she made enough to raise the boys. They lived above the shop. The boys took turns helping her before and after school, and on the weekends.

In time, she paid the mortgage off. In time, the boys grew up and started families of their own. Assunta kept on working every day from early morning until late at night. She worked on Christmas Day, on New Year's Day, on all the holidays.

She was robbed once, at gunpoint. After the robbery, her sons installed a buzzer under the counter by the cash register. They rigged it to go off in the butcher shop a few doors down; when the buzzer rang, the butchers from Macelleria White Lamb would come by to see if she was okay. The buzzer made her feel safe.

She sold below cost if you needed a break. She gave candy to all the kids who came in. She had a reputation for old-world wisdom. Women from the neighbourhood would come to her and say, "Oh, Assunta, I got trouble at home with my husband." Assunta would say, "What's the use of trouble? Make peace, go home, have a cup of coffee."

That's what they did.

Her sons gave her grandchildren. Patty was the first. Assunta taught Patty how to count the twenties, how to line them up facing the same way. She'd send little Patty to the bank across the street to make the deposit for her. She watched Patty out the window as she went. You couldn't send a child across that street today, certainly not alone, and never with a bag of money. But that is how you teach responsibility: by giving it.

Assunta may be the only woman in Toronto who has never seen the inside of a supermarket. She always got others to do her shopping for her. She didn't want to leave the store. And maybe she did not want to know how much the outside world had changed since the day her husband . . .

The only trip she ever took?

She went to Italy once, in 1968, to see Padre Pio. She brought one of her boys with her. The little priest blessed them both, and he heard Assunta's confession. I don't believe Assunta had anything to confess, except perhaps that she worked too hard.

I don't know what her confessor told her, but Assunta observed the mass and took communion, and afterward she put her jewellery back on, and she stopped wearing black. And the years slipped away.

Her grandson, a firefighter-photographer, took over the shop. He has plans to convert it into a photo studio. That's good. What starts in the family stays in the family.

Was she happy to retire?

She looked around the store. She pursed her lips and shrugged her shoulders. She put her hands together as if in prayer, and then she opened her palms and looked up to heaven. What are you going to do?

And she smiled, and she said everything else can go.

But she kept the cash register.

Because you never know.

Here is another chapter of the history of the Italians in Toronto:

Cora Graziano had a fruit and vegetable stall, the Golden Orchard, in the St. Lawrence Market. Everyone in the belly of the city – the bakers, the fishmongers, the cheese and olive men, the butchers, the other fruit-stand operators – knew she was the market's beating heart.

And then one day she missed a day of work, and everyone was worried. She had gone to the hospital. Her stomach was bothering her. They gave her the bad news there. Cancer. She caught her breath.

And then she came back to work. She was tiny, and she seemed frail, but her eyes shone hard; there was no quit in her. She said, "I'm not a crybaby. I'm a worker. What do I want to stay home for? I gotta take care of my business."

She was eighty-eight years old when I met her, and she'd been in business for more than sixty years. I'd heard that she'd been ill, and I knew her reputation. I introduced myself the next time I was at the Market, and I asked her how she was doing. She said she was fine. She asked how I was doing, as if that was more important. Her voice was musical.

She told me she moved into the Market thirty-two years ago with her husband. They had kept shop and raised a family together in the west end. Her husband died. Cora kept on working. She said, "The business gives you life. I still work hard. Some women are lazy. Not me. I gotta work. Today, I put out the strawberries."

Her day began at four-thirty that morning. Her son Murray may do all the heavy lifting, but everyone knew that Cora was the spiritual leader of the Market. And you know how it is with spiritual leaders:

It takes one to know one.

This is the story of Cora and the Dalai Lama.

She said, "I like to make pies. I make a lot of pies. A few years ago, I was making fifteen or twenty pies on a Monday. I'd have forty or fifty pies in my freezer. What are you going to do with all those pies? I started to give them away to customers. People would say, 'Hey, these pies are the best.'"

The guy who delivers the Market mail was passing by then, and he overheard her, and he stopped to ask her how she was, and he said he'd missed her, and he hoped she was feeling better, and he looked at me seriously and told me that her pies were the best.

She shrugged. "My pies have been all over the world. People take them back to Sri Lanka, to England, to Ireland. Apple travels the best, better than cherry or rhubarb."

That's useful information.

"My mother was a good cook. She taught me how to make pies. We had a farm in the country, on Brown's Line." There are no more farms anywhere near Brown's Line now. There are streets and houses and highway interchanges; but no farms, not any more, not for a long time.

"One day my mother was going out. We had a wood stove. She said don't light the fire. I was a little brat with curly long hair. I was seven or eight years old. I lit the stove. I made a pie." And I love a curly-haired, pie-making brat.

She said, "I made pies for a lot of famous people. I made one for that guy with the TV show, Emeril. I made one for that tall guy from the *Toronto Star*." She meant my old boss, John Honderich. She has also pied the rock group Rush; a beauty way to go.

"When the Dalai Lama was in town, his people were coming to me to buy fruit and vegetables. He eats organic. They spent a lot of good money here. I gave them a pie for him. I think it was strawberry and rhubarb." An excellent choice for a Tibetan exile.

"They took him the pie. And then I got an invitation to meet him at the Royal York. He wanted to say thanks. He was waiting for me in the lobby at six-thirty in the morning. But there was a mix-up. I went to the wrong hotel, the King Edward, so I didn't get to meet him. The next morning, I got sick and I had to go to the hospital. I had to have some tests. I was thinking it was nothing."

That's when she learned about the cancer. The doctor told her that she didn't have much time left. She looked frightened when she told me that. But then she brightened. She said, "While I was in the hospital, the drapes were open a little bit. Three little men came by. I recognized them. They were his bodyguards. They noticed me. They all bowed. They were real nice. And then he came."

He, of course, was Tenzing Gyatso, 14th Dalai Lama, also known as Yeshe Norbu, the Wish-Fulfilling Gem. Sometimes he is called, simply, Kundun, or the Presence. He is namesake to a thousand little Tenzings in Toronto and all around the world. He was at the hospital because of his teeth.

Cora said, "He had to have some work done, some kind of dental surgery. It was all done quiet. He's an important man. He smiled at me, and he said to his people to tell me he was so happy about the pie, he said it was the best pie he ever tasted." Of that I have no doubt.

And one of the cheese men passed by then, and he smiled at her and took her hand, and he said he was glad she was back at work, and without being asked he also told me she made the best pies in the world.

Cora said, "I'm happy when I make my pies. I give them away. I also give away jars of my tomato sauce. I used to cook big meals at home. Now I have a housekeeper. She's Sri Lankan. She makes noodles, her kind of noodles. Sometimes I put some of my tomato sauce on them."

And that is the real fusion cuisine.

It was still early morning. Cora's grandson came by with her breakfast in a Styrofoam container. French toast, with a side of bacon. He said, "She's been telling you stories? Did she tell you she used to carry a mickey around in her purse? She used to say she never drank the whisky, it just evaporated."

Cora pursed her lips and shook her head no. She might have meant no, she didn't carry a mickey in her purse. Or maybe she meant no, the whisky didn't evaporate.

Her grandson said, "Did she tell you about the time she hit the guy who was stealing the tomatoes? She just walked up to him and socked him in the jaw." Cora chewed a piece of bacon thoughtfully. She wasn't remembering the guy she socked. She was remembering the taste of bacon. "This is the first time I've felt like eating in three months."

"Don't just eat the bacon," said her grandson. "Eat the French toast, too."

"I lost a lot of weight," said Cora.

Did she eat any pie when she was ill?

"I don't eat pies. I like cake."

A kind of enlightenment.

Cora died a few months later. Before she died, she gave me two pies, one after another; peach and blueberry, and then strawberry-rhubarb, a Dalai Lama pie. Everyone was right.

Best pies in the world.

And now the last chapter of the history of the Italians in Toronto:

Sometimes people tell you things that, suddenly, you think everyone should know. There's a little flower shop on St. Clair West, said a caller on the phone; you should go there and look at the photo of Frank Sinatra on the wall behind the cash register.

I am the sort of person who, when told about a photo of the Chairman of the Board, goes off to get the full picture. I know how many words a picture is worth. I headed for Little Italy. No, not College Street. I mean St. Clair, between Lansdowne and Christie, a few short city blocks. This is the part of town where I feel most at home, on those days when I need to feel like I have a home. I have been a migrant worker long enough that I can get by without a home, but I cannot get by without stopping at the Diana Grocery for my olive oil and prosciutto, and the nearby Tre Mari for my amaretti.

Home is where the heart is. The way to the heart is through the stomach. My belly leads my heart like a dog on a leash.

I walked along, looking in all the flower stores. The Italians cannot do without flowers, and so there are a lot of stores.

I looked, or rather I felt, like an idiot. Every time I stuck my nose into a rose-smelling shop and asked one of the flower sellers if they had a picture of Frank Sinatra, the woman behind the counter – always a woman – gave me that look.

What are you, some kind of wise guy?

No one quite said that. That's New York talk. Here, we are more polite. We might look like we want to say it, but we prefer to look away without a word; or we say no, no photo here, excuse me, I'm sorry.

And then I walked into Sina's.

Sina is a handsome woman, regal, but twinkling with self-possession. She was arranging flowers in the back. The photo was there, on the wall. There was a smile on the face of Sina in the photo, and there was a smile on the face of Frank. Sina saw me looking, and she wiped her hands dry as she walked to the front of the store. She said, "Can I help you?"

I nodded at the photo. "What's the story?"

She was happy to talk. That's why the photo is there, after all. It is a reminder, and it gives her a chance to tell the story again. Sina – her name is Vincenzina; Sina's easier – said:

"My husband, Tony, and I, we used to take our vacations in Atlantic City. I like to go to the casino. We walk along the boardwalk. We have a nice time. One night, I'm in the casino, playing the slots, and I hear a commotion. People's heads were turning, they were whispering. I thought it must be someone famous, so I looked."

It was somebody, all right. It was Ol' Blue Eyes with his entourage, heading for the crap tables. Sina and Tony joined the crowd. She picked up the story there:

"Frankie had the dice. He picked me out of the crowd, I don't know why. He introduced himself, and he said, 'What's your name?' I told him my name is Sina Rupolo, from Toronto. He said, 'Sina, what a beautiful name you've got. What do you do for a living?'

"I told him about the flower shop. He took my hand, and he said, 'Okay, Sina, you throw the dice for me like they were flowers.'"

You can see it: Hoboken Frankie, paying his respects to a woman who looked not unlike his mother: hardworking, honest, sure of herself and unafraid to tell the truth.

Sina said, "I take the dice. I throw a seven. I take the dice again. Again I throw a seven. It was the spookiest time of my life. All the time it comes up seven. I threw seven sevens. My husband says to me, 'You don't have a five in your mouth, you don't have a nine?' But I didn't. I threw sevens. Frankie, he gives me a great big hug. He made a lot of money, I don't know how much, it was more than thousands.

"He's got a man with him. The man's got a suitcase. He goes to the back and gets the money. Frank Sinatra says, 'Sina, I'm coming to the Skydome soon, I want you to come and see me.' Well, you know, he's a big man. He's not going to remember little me. I forget all about it.

"A few months later, the phone rings. I pick it up. A voice says, 'Sina? It's me, Frankie.' I say, 'What is this, some kind of joke?' I hang up the phone right away.

"A couple of minutes later the phone rings again. This time it's the manager of the Dome. He says, 'Sina, that was Frankie, you closed up the phone on him. He's got two chairs for you. He wants you to come and hear him sing.' It was no joke.

"I'm all excited. Later on, he comes to town. I bring my husband, Tony, my daughter and her husband. We had a nice supper with Frankie. He said seven wasn't lucky for him no more. He had champagne and a lot of hors d'oeuvres, salmon, little quiches, and they put out chairs for my daughter and her husband. It was a beautiful night."

It still is.

And Sina was still there, still listening to Frankie.

"A couple of months later, in the mail, I get this picture." She nodded to the picture by the cash register. "That's me, next to him. That's my husband, Tony. My daughter, she's pregnant there, and that's her husband." Sina beamed. She pointed a finger at the photo. "You see the look on his face? It's pure Frank, so nice, he's happy.

"My favourite song of his? I got a lot of them. I got tapes and CDs. 'New York, New York.' I love it. But 'My Way,' that's the best one."

It is the best one.

Frankie's way? Whoever rolled seven sevens in a row without a little help? But Sina did for Frankie, and that was his way, and maybe it was with his dice; well, what of it?

And then Sina's husband, Tony, came in. He'd been to the doctor for some tests, and they'd taken some of his blood. He still felt a little shaky. He had a package under his arm. He laid it on the table in the back of the flower store: some provolone and some prosciutto and also dried tomatoes in olive oil, and a stick of good fresh bread.

You feel shaky, you have to eat.

He said, "Wait here." He went to the cooler where the fresh flowers are kept, and he got a bottle of his own wine, and he laid out the cheese and the meat, and I had to have a sandwich, and I had to make mine first, that's the Italian way, and he poured a glass of wine, and we all drank the good cold blood-red wine.

Frankie would have liked that wine.

And it doesn't really matter if Frankie was being paid off in some way with those hot dice. What mattered was that Sina threw seven sevens in a row, and she threw them in good faith. And then Frankie came here, and he sang to her.

That is the history of the Italians in Toronto.

And this is my kind of town.

EIGHT

Too many people forget that people crawl across minefields to get here.

– IGNAT KANEFF in the *Toronto Star*, February 6, 1989

The United Bakers Dairy Restaurant, where I ate my hang-over latkes as a young man, is not on Spadina any longer; it hasn't been, not for years. It's in the north end of town now in, of all things, a mall. Spadina was never a mall. A bazaar, perhaps; never a mall.

But I can't stop thinking of that restaurant, on that street, in those days when I could drink all night without fear of the following morning, when I could get a plate of latkes with good thick plain sour cream, or some indifferent applesauce, and a cup of thin brown coffee to go along with the first cigarette of the day. Times change.

Where are you going, old man? Shut up, you punk. You never heard of the place.

On the block where the United Bakers used to be, most of the restaurants are Vietnamese, and if you can't find latkes on Spadina any more, there are plenty of places where you can get cha gio – spring rolls, deep fried or made of pale chewy wrappers and filled with bean sprouts, shredded pork, mint and shrimp – to go with a bowl of pho.

Who says things don't change for the better?

An old man in Montreal, a Vietnamese refugee, once explained the notion of Indochina to me. It had to do with influences. You could tell by the clothing. "The shirt like China. The pants like India." As if it were as simple as that. I suppose, for old men, it is.

And then he served me a bowl of soup – or rather he served me a chicken cube stirred into a pot of boiling water that he then poured over a nest of dried noodles, and he cracked a raw egg into the bowl, and he brought the plates to the table, and as he ate he said it was okay to bend low over the bowl and slurp.

A lesson that has served me well and has saved my shirts.

The old man did not bite his noodles off and let them fall back into the bowl the way I do. He slurped them into his mouth, no matter how long. The superstition has to do with long noodles, long life; or perhaps it is just what Asian women say to their babies.

In any case, he was old and he slurped noisily.

I ate with him but I wasn't there for the soup; lucky for me, there wasn't much of it, because it was not very good, and the egg did not cook at all, and raw egg makes me gag. But I ate it all.

I was there because the old man wanted to tell me a story of first love, a story of love lost and found again, a story seen through the cracked lens of a long hard dirty war, a story illustrated with the kind of human suffering most of us can't imagine.

He met a beauty when he was young.

Love at first sight on bicycles, for both of them. They managed to meet and they kept on meeting. They grew closer. So did the war. He proposed. Her family would not accept him.

Spies lurked, armies came, bombs fell, cafés blew up and families fled to safety and were separated. She feared he was dead. He feared she was dead. She married his rival. He came for her later, and he heard what she had done and his heart hardened and he married someone else. And so they were lost to each other.

They had separate lives and separate families and they came separately to Canada as refugees. They both outlived their spouses. One day, someone who'd known him, and had known them as a couple of young lovers, spotted her in a nursing home in Montreal.

The old man said, "She's here?"

By the time I met the old man and ate his soup, the couple had already met once, shyly, and they had wept, and they were considering moving in together.

Love stories are a dime a dozen; good soup is transformative.

Pho is the national dish of Vietnam, and that is what the old man was trying to approximate in his bachelor kitchen; the egg, a variation not to my taste. But pho might also be the national dish of Toronto.

Pho bo – beef soup – is the most traditional, but I prefer pho ga, or chicken soup: clear broth, noodles, shreds of poached chicken, bean sprouts, cilantro, fresh basil, a wedge of lime, and one of those little hot red devil peppers if I feel I have the strength to stand it.

The soup comes in a bowl big enough to drown in. It costs five bucks, plus or minus. It is not possible to eat better.

It is generally made southern-style here, with a bit of star anise in the broth; not surprising, since most of the Vietnamese who came here came from the south. It is very hard, in this town, to find indifferent pho. Try pronouncing it *feu*, as in the French *pot au feu*.

The pants like those worn in India, the shirt like those worn in China and the soup like that made by the French, who ruled Vietnam long enough to teach the people how to make broth.

Nguyen Dac Thoi is the owner of Pho Hung on Spadina. There is another branch of that restaurant with the same name on Bloor near Avenue Road. Pho Hung sets the pho standard in this town.

And if Thoi was not the first to make Vietnamese soup here, still all other bowls of pho in Toronto are measured against his. I won't bother you with my credentials. I will merely point out that I have eaten enough Vietnamese soup that whenever I see one of those signs, "24-Hour Photo," my first thought is, aha – an all-day soup joint.

Most of my bowls of soup have been eaten at Pho Hung.

One day I asked Thoi how he learned. He said, "I had a small farm in Vietnam." I put down my chopsticks and my spoon and listened.

He said, "The farm was about twenty hectares. I was growing jackfruit and mangosteen, rambutan, bananas. The communists came and took it. I had a store selling typewriters; they came and took it. I had a small factory sewing uniforms; they came and took it. I had some money in the bank; they took it and gave me a receipt for two hundred dollars."

He took a sip of tea. He paused to remember. And from the look on his face, you might be forgiven if you thought he was drinking something unbearably sour. Not far from his restaurant there are sidewalk stalls where, if he wanted to, he could buy jackfruit, mangosteen, rambutan, bananas; and while hardly anybody sells typewriters any more, up the street and around the corner there are plenty of computer shops. He has come here from far away, but he is familiar with the lay of the land.

"I had five kids and nothing left. I had to make a living. A friend of mine was making pho on the street. He taught me how to make the soup in a pot on a charcoal burner. I opened up a stall, and I was selling pho on the street." That's how it was then: broth, bowl, noodles, charcoal burner, everything fresh, you eat it on the go for breakfast, for lunch, or for supper. And this, too, is how it was there, then:

One day you are a man of property and you have money in the bank, and you have a small good farm, and a little factory and some workers who rely on you, and the next day you have a soup pot on a street corner.

Thoi said, "I decided to leave Vietnam. It was hard to get out. I had to change my name and pretend to be Chinese because they didn't want any Chinese in Vietnam. I left on a boat from Saigon. I went to Malaysia, to a refugee camp, then to Edmonton, and from there to Brantford.

"In Brantford, I was working as a roofer for Domtar. My wife was sewing for the Levi company. I was also picking dew worms at night. I was picking tomatoes and cucumbers on a farm. I was working day and night."

And do you recall that at one time we were worried in this country about the influx of so many refugees from Vietnam? We ought to have let more in.

Thoi said, "Once a week we would come to Toronto to pick up bags of clothes for my wife to sew. She was doing piecework. Also I was cleaning in a chicken factory, and my children delivered newspapers."

I tried to think about what I'd do if the shoe were on the other foot – if one day a gang of thugs seized Toronto and took everything from me, and in order to earn a living I had to learn to make and sell soup on the sidewalk; and I wondered what would it have been like if I had found a way to get on a boat with my family and land in Ho Chi Minh City?

Did I ever know how to work as hard as Thoi? Could I have learned a new language fast enough to be able to find enough small jobs to make one job? Thoi knew how to do these things. He also had help.

"My church, the ones who sponsored me, they co-signed a mortgage for me. I bought a duplex. I was living in one side and renting the other side. In five years, I owned the house. And then I decided to sell it and open a restaurant in Toronto. I was not the first to sell pho here. The first was Saigon Palace. I think I was the third. I called my restaurant Pho Hung." A big decision? A stupid question.

Of course it is a big decision to gamble everything you've earned in order to open a soup shop; to risk a roll of the dice again . . . but when you have already thrown the dice and risked your life . . .

The restaurant is never less than full.

Why did he call it Pho Hung?

"Hung is the name of my oldest son. He was a boy when we left. Now he is a man. He runs the restaurant on Bloor Street. That store up there has a bigger kitchen. All the spring rolls, they make there."

This is not a Vietnamese story any more than it is a Jewish story, an Italian story, a Portuguese story, a Chinese story, a Jamaican story, a Sri Lankan story; finally, it is a Toronto story.

For a time, I used to alternate between Pho Hung and Pho Tau Bay, which no longer exists. The woman who ran Pho Tau Bay was a stylish beauty of a certain age; she wore a long tight silver dress slashed at the thigh; high collar, high hair, high heels, carmine nails. She used to smile when I came in. I don't think I was special in her eyes; the smile was just good business, meant to greet a regular.

I don't recall how it came up, but I once asked if she'd seen the movie *Titanic*. She shuddered. "Mister, I spent three days on a boat in a storm escaping Vietnam. The boat, very crowded.

The storm, very bad. Many people die. Many people drown. Many friends of mine holding on to the side of the boat, holding on to ropes, they get tired in the water. They let go, and I don't see them any more. Why do I want to see a movie with many people on a boat, the boat sinks and they drown. No way I go."

What follows now is perhaps the essential Toronto story. In it you will find us at our best, us at our worst, us at our most combative, us at our most confused, us glorious in victory and aching in defeat.

Dan Tran Van owns a shop on St. Clair West: Danny's Vacuum Cleaner. This is not just the story of a man selling vacuums. This is the story of a war. Not the one you think.

One day I was alerted to the presence of a large number of vacuum cleaners lining the north sidewalk of St. Clair Avenue. I was told there was a feud. I was told that two shopkeepers – they had adjacent shops – were waging a pitched battle.

The Vacuum Cleaner War.

Who would not want to be a witness to such a war?

Danny invited me in. He wanted to talk. I could not stop him from talking. He said, "During the war . . ." He meant the other one. ". . . I joined the Vietnamese Air Force. I was very young. I was trained by the United States Air Force as a mechanic. I learned to fix anything – helicopters, F-4 and F-5 Phantom jets, C-130 Hercules. I can also fix tanks." And you know what happened to the Americans, so you know what happened to Danny's job.

But he was one of the lucky ones.

"I got out of Vietnam. I spent one month, three days on the ocean, hungry, thirsty, from Saigon to Hong Kong. I come to Canada in 1979. I got a job working for Electrolux. The manager was an Italian guy.

"He said to me, 'Do you know vacuums?' I said, 'In my country, we use brooms, but I can fix.' He gave me two vacuums. He wanted to see what I could do. I fix them in half an hour. He gives me something else to fix. I fix that, too. Pretty soon I fix everything in the store."

The boss saw something in the young man from Vietnam who could fix anything. And in a blazing act of generosity, he did something for Danny.

"He helped me open a store. He found a place for me. He paid the first month's rent, $300. He said, 'You pay me back when you make money.' The first month I made $450. The next month I made $500. Then I made $700, then $1,000. Every month, up, up, up. That Italian man, he helped me. That's the way Italians are."

And this is the way the Vietnamese are:

Danny built up a nice little business. His store is neat. He knows where everything is. His kids are studying hard at school. He said, "I am Catholic. We send money to my sister; my wife's sister, she is in Rome. We have two priests in my family. The Pope takes care of my sister, and I take care of the priests. I try to be nice to everybody. An old lady comes into the store. She says, 'Danny, I need a new motor.' I look at the motor. She just needs a new cord." He does not hose her. He fixes the cord.

And if an American F-4 Phantom jet made an emergency landing in front of his store, you can bet Danny could fix it just as fast and just as cheaply, and he would replace the cord, and he'd send the pilot quickly on his way.

At that time, there was a dollar store next door to Danny's. The man who owned the dollar store also had an air conditioning unit. It is ugly-hot in Toronto in the summer. We all need a little A/C.

Danny fixed the air conditioner for his neighbour. Shortly after, the man decided to get out of the dollar-store business. Danny bought the air-conditioning unit from him. And here is where the story turns.

A man called Amanuel signed a lease to rent the dollar store. He had come from one of the North African countries. He began to sell odds and ends at first – cheap perfume, toy cars, calling cards, sunglasses.

Time passed. Danny and Amanuel were not best friends, but here they were, strangers in a strange land on the same street. They'd had, vaguely, the same experience. And you'd think this was just another nice multicultural conjunction. Stop smiling now.

On a particularly muggy day, Amanuel asked Danny if he could buy the air-conditioning unit. Business is business. Danny offered him a price – what he'd paid for the unit, plus what it cost him to do the repairs; enough to make a small profit.

Amanuel misunderstood. He knew how much the owner of the store had sold the unit for. He knew what Danny was asking. He did some calculations, and he got the idea in his head that Danny was trying to screw him. As if Danny thought he was just off the boat.

It stuck in his throat.

Shortly afterward, the dollar store closed. Danny said he knew it would close. Who needs that dollar-store shit? There was a brief lull. But Amanuel was not done. The store next to Danny opened again.

Amanuel began selling vacuum cleaners.

He put up a sign, Ace of Vacuums; the name, poached from a well-known vacuum-cleaner dealership in another part of town. He then chained an upright vacuum to the front of his store, right there on the sidewalk, as a kind of advertisement.

People in the neighbourhood were confused.

They asked Amanuel if he was affiliated with Danny. Amanuel never denied it. Some people even asked him if his name was Danny. He never denied it.

Danny was outraged. In response, he put out two vacuums on the sidewalk. Amanuel took note of that the next day, and he put out three, and he also put up a sign much bigger than Danny's.

And then Danny put up an even bigger sign, and he put even more vacuums on his sidewalk. And then Amanuel's friends and relatives began sneaking into Danny's store on the sly and taking note of the prices, so that Amanuel could undercut him. Danny's sons noticed the spies. Hot words were exchanged.

Danny said, "How can he do this? I worked to build up my business. At first I open from 10 a.m. to 6 p.m. Before ten o'clock, I put flyers door to door. I built a strong business.

"When I opened, I had three people working for me; now I have five. He wants to steal my business from me. It's not fair. I have money. I have a lawyer. I don't have time for this. If a robber comes to your house, you protect your family. This is a free country, but I have older customers, and they go next door by mistake." And then he paused.

He said, "I pray for him."

Amanuel's store was empty of customers when I dropped by to get his side of the story. He seemed unconcerned, disinterested, bored. He had a few desultory vacuum cleaners lying around here and there. He also had some perfume in decorative bottles, and some toy cars in shrink-wrapped boxes, and some mirrored sunglasses, and various other things left over from the days of the dollar store.

He told me his side of the air-conditioner story. His account was more or less the same as Danny's, but he begged to differ about the rationale behind the price. He thought Danny was trying to fuck him.

I asked him why he closed the dollar store and started selling vacuums. He shrugged. "I could have opened any kind of store. TV, stereo repairs, VCRs, I even repair computers. But I opened a vacuum store. You want to buy a vacuum? I can give you a good price. You want to know why I open a vacuum store?" He looked at me with a piercing smile, as if he was trying to see what sort of man I was, as if he was waiting for me to figure it out. I kept my mouth shut.

"You want to know why I did it? I did it to fuck Danny."

Honi soit qui mal y pense.

With glowing hearts, we see thee rise to the bait.

Alas, Amanuel is no longer in business. And justice was seen to be done. When Amanuel moved out, Danny picked up the lease and opened the wall between the two stores, and he now uses Amanuel's shop as a showroom. Where is Amanuel? Danny said, "I don't know. I don't want to talk about him. I pray for him."

I think he says short hard sharp little prayers.

The kind that make God jump.

NINE

A nation like an individual to find itself must love itself in the service of others.

– Prime Minister W.L. Mackenzie King, Parliament Hill, July 1, 1927

We are famous for our homelessness. We tie ourselves in two different knots: We aren't doing enough, we should do more, it's the shame of the city. Or, let the bums fend for themselves; if they want to live on the street, that's their choice.

You choose your grate. I'll choose mine.

Our callous disregard? A lack of care? Our cold, cold hearts? We parcel out plenty of socks. We deliver hot coffee to the men in the ravines. And we open up church basements when the weather turns cold.

Many of those who sleep rough are not from here. They have run away from life in some small town. We have, for the most part, grown used to them. We don't interfere. We wouldn't think of taking away anybody's rights. You are free to sleep on our sidewalks if you will. And if there are no beds on our sidewalks, neither are there bedbugs.

Now and then someone will die in a dark cold corner, as if that, too, was a human right. A couple of years ago a homeless guy was killed by some roving punks simply because he was sleeping on the street. Not long after that another bum had his fingers chopped off while he was sleeping. And then there was a homeless woman who gave birth and abandoned her baby on the pavement by City Hall.

It is your right to die where you want. It is your right to have your fingers chopped off while you are dead to the world. It is your right to deliver your babies on the sidewalk.

We were vigilant for a while. We said we'd do something but didn't do much. We continued to wring our hands and beat our breasts and soothe our consciences with nightly deliveries of hot soup in the winter, bottles of water in the summer, and medicine doled out all year long by the charitable, the merciful and the teams of first-rate front-line nurses. But the man on the street is a thorn in our side.

Seaton House is a hostel for men.

You wince, we flinch, they grimace at the sound of that name in this town. The left knee jerks, and the right knee lashes out. "Isn't that where all those alkies and junkies live?"

And where would you have them live?

Seaton House is a shelter for men who can't kick their habits. It is a residence for old boozers, some of whom have been on the bottle so long they are past alcohol and well into Alzheimer's. It is a safe haven for old men who are dying. It is a refuge for those who have screwed up. It is most often a place of rest for those men who merely need a leg up for a week or two.

Seaton House is just off the Four Corners, east of Jarvis, north of Dundas, a part of town where the dealers and the junkies and the hookers buzz like flies, drawn by the presence of cheap Chinese food, fleabag hotels and crack dens. There is a strip club nearby; the marquee advertises lap dancing and face dancing and rooms for the night.

Seaton House was built in 1959. That's how long it took to figure out that some of the men who came back when the war was over in 1945 never really came back from the war at all.

I'm not sure we'd build anything like it again. We don't seem to have the vision. But we fixed the place up recently. The idea was not just to make it look nice, but to separate the old men from the young ones who sometimes preyed on them. Also to upgrade the clinic, and make room for a dentist, and so on.

Is this a small town? The architect of the renovations is my next-door neighbour. Is this a big town? My neighbour specializes in building shelter for the homeless.

If you want to fix your house, you move the kids and the dog into the spare room and everybody doubles up, and you make do. It isn't quite so easy when there are more than five hundred alkies and junkies to move, and there are no spare rooms available.

Men who are powerless get nervous about being shifted around, but the big day was coming, and there was a plan. I sat in on the discussions.

Boris Rosolak is the manager of Seaton House. He is an imposingly tall man with an acid glare and a shaven head. He is also a soft touch who is hard as nails. He likes a cigar now and then. He keeps an ironic, iconic statue of Chairman Mao on his desk.

Boris chaired the meeting about the move. I sat in the back and listened, along with two dozen gruff and grizzled old fellows who were busy sucking all the goodness they could from their cups of overly sweetened coffee. Men stink when they are nervous. There was funk and tension and the sound of coffee slurping in the air.

No one said much. Everybody waited. You could hear them thinking: How's it going to happen? When will it start? Where will I go? Will anything ever be the same once everything has changed?

Rosolak adopted an even open tone. He was firm and cheerful and reassuring. Before he had finished a few opening remarks, some little guy in the back of the room piped up, in a voice which was mixed two to one with panic and hope, "Change is scary, but change can be good, right?" He'd clearly spent some time with social workers.

Boris nodded in agreement, and another old boy called out, "When do we move?" And if he had an agenda, Boris threw it out the window now. He said, "Summer if we're lucky, fall if we're not."

Old Guy: "Fall it is, then!"

The laughter of the fallen.

Men drifted in and out of the meeting, the hairy and the hoary, picking up free muffins and stuffing them in their pockets for later and whispering to themselves. A guy who hadn't been listening asked, "When's the meeting going to start?" Someone replied, "As soon as Boris gets here." Boris smiled and said, "I'm Boris." The guy was not convinced. He asked, "Didn't Boris used to have a ponytail?"

Boris said, "That was when I had a head of hair." He also said he was looking for a temporary location for the shelter, maybe in the Moss Park Armoury, maybe at the old Downsview military base.

He wasn't sure how long it would take to finish the job. An old man said, "I used to work construction. One thing's for sure. It will take longer than you think, and it will cost a third more." He added: "It's okay, the mayor said I could come and stay in his spare room."

Laughs all around again.

Boris: "We're trying to get a hospital kitchen so we can continue to provide meals." Old Man: "Does that mean the food will improve?" Boris: "Hey, I eat here." Old Man: "Yeah, those steak-shapes are good." Boris: "Well, at least we don't serve liver any more." The old man had him trapped: "Yes, we do. Every three weeks, for lunch; excellent."

A scrawny runt with a yellow beard and a red shirt shook his pocket inhaler, sucked in a lungful and wheezed, "No offence to you, but I want to get out of here as quick as I can." He may get out quick. He may not.

One of the old boys Boris found a place for was James Bond.

James was one of the first men to move into Seaton House when it was built. He was one of the first men moved out during renovations; seniority, I guess. If anyone was going to be upset by the move, it would have been him. Old men take comfort in their habits.

I paid James a visit once he'd settled into his new place, a nursing home. James is short and slender, his skin is papery and his eyes are wet. He's hard of hearing, but his eyes are good enough. He broke his hip some eighteen months ago. Apart from the walker, you'd never know it. He was wearing a white suit. He'd gotten dressed for my sake. He has a trim white spade-shaped beard. He is bald, and he is one of those men who looks better without a head of hair. He owns the city record for time spent in shelters. It is a Toronto record, but I'd bet he could go national.

He said he didn't mind the move.

On the one hand, James is so old, he can't remember five minutes ago. On the other hand, he remembers some things very well. He remembers he likes to smoke cigars. He was smoking one as we talked. Now and then he forgot about the stogie in his hands. Now and then he jerked into alertness when his fingers began to burn, and then he remembered the cigar, and he filled his lungs with blue smoke, and he smacked his lips wetly as he exhaled. He was too damn old to stop now, and so he was indulged.

I said I was curious to know if he had any insight about shelter life, given the benefit of his long years. He looked at the fat cigar, cocked his head, dusted a bit of ash that had fallen on his chest and squinted hard at me. He meant no, he had no special insights.

Or maybe he forgot what I'd asked.

I took another tack. I thought I'd warm him up. "Do they ever call you 007?" I had to yell to get James Bond to hear. He heard fine. He glared at me. "They used to." The implication was clear. Don't fuck around or you'll regret it. He said he was born August 23, 1912, which means he was too old to waste his time on jokes he'd heard before that were never funny the first time. Fair enough. It also means he was forty-seven years old when he first went into the shelter. His trouble was that he drank long and hard in his day, and he had a very long day. The bottle killed two marriages.

"Do you have kids?"

"A couple."

"Do they come around?"

"Nope."

"Any other family?"

"Two sisters. Where they are, I don't know."

It did not sound as if he missed them.

"What did you do for a living?"

"I was a cabbie. I drove for whoever would give me a job."

The meaning was clear: there were times when no one would give him a job, because he drank himself out of jobs.

"Were you ever robbed behind the wheel?"

"Never."

"Why did you stop driving?"

"Couldn't make any money."

"Do you still take a drink?"

"I can, if I can get away with it."

"Did you get into trouble when you drank?"

His gaze sharpened. He sucked the wet end of his cigar. "I'm no angel." And he began to detect that I was leading him where he didn't want to go. "Say, if you don't like my gate, you don't have to swing on it."

An expression so old it is original.

"Were you in the army during the war?"

I knew this was a layered question. I risked it anyway. I wanted to know if James had ducked the service, or if he was rejected because he drank, and did he have any feelings about that; or was he one of those vets who went over and came back changed? He had the answer down pat, like he'd been waiting to be asked.

"They wouldn't take me; too ugly." If the army thought he was too ugly, the ladies liked him fine, and he still likes the ladies. A nurse looked in on us. She wore a uniform, or perhaps the uniform wore her. The sweet soft swish of her stockings when she moved. James smiled at her and licked his lips, and he waited for her to respond to the flicker of his tongue; she did not.

He said with a wicked, harmless leer, "They can't stop you from trying." She revealed no expression as she turned away. Oh, James, you've led a sheltered life in shelter. Girls have changed. They can stop you cold anytime they want.

"What was life like at Seaton House in the old days?"

"Not bad. The food was better than it is today. I like cheese."

And with that, he'd had enough. The questions tired him out. He got up and leaned into his walker and aimed himself in the direction of the elevator. He stabbed the button repeatedly, patiently, quizzically. He was sure he'd pressed it. Why the hell wouldn't the door open? "The elevator isn't working, James!" said an aide. He looked at her and quick as a wink he flashed her a smile.

"Neither am I!"

When he finally reached his room, he slipped out of his jacket, draped it over the back of a chair, took off his shoes, placed them neatly on his bedside table and curled up on the bed like a boy. Nap time. I noticed a tattoo on his forearm – a blue swallow, trailing a ribbon from its beak; the curl of the ribbon spelled "Alice."

"Who's Alice?"

"Don't remember."

"Good night, James." Too late. He did not hear. He was asleep.

What good are the shelters? The question is not rhetorical. If it weren't for Seaton House, James Bond would be dead. A better question: What's a life worth?

On any given night there are as many as five thousand homeless men, women and kids in Toronto. Not many of them are homeless by choice. Homelessness is sometimes an absence of choice, and sometimes it is an inability to choose where to live.

There are many reasons for homelessness. The reasons are not always the same: A man is homeless because he is gay and he could not hide in his little town any more, and so he lands here, and he lands hard. Or he got kicked off his reserve. Or he just got out of jail. Or he fell into the bottle. Or he got fired and he had no money put away and he lost his house. Or he stuck a needle in his arm and liked it so much he could not stop. Or he is a refugee. Or he hears voices and he sees things. Or his wife kicked him out and he has no other place to go.

Most of us are only three steps away: lose your job, lose your savings, lose your home. But some men will not go to shelters because shelters are too dangerous, and they are filled with lice and bedbugs, and the man in the next bunk is crazy. Which is why some men sleep outdoors.

I don't know which is worse – the guy on the grate under the blanket, or the guy in the suit with the briefcase stepping over him without a glance. I've had it up to here with trying to decide.

I tend to stop and ask a man if he needs help. If he doesn't respond, I call an ambulance. I'm no Samaritan, and I'm no doctor, but it is not up to me to guess if the body under the blanket is alive or dead, and it is not up to me to determine if the guy is stoned, or in a diabetic coma.

I do not want a dead guy on my conscience. I don't want to be the last guy who stepped over some bum; that's one small step. No, that's a step which makes you smaller.

James Bond is the exception. Most of the men at Seaton House are there for a few weeks. They are guys who just need to get their bearings. Some men stay for as long as a year; they just need time, and they need a leg up. Maybe sixty men at any given time are lifers like James.

Many of the lifers are drunks. I'm drawn to drunks, maybe because my old man was one, off and on, and maybe because my older brother was also one from the time he was old enough to buy his own booze. And I know I like to take a drink, and I know every glass I have is enough to make me want another one. So far, I know when I've had enough. But some guys never do, and they will always need a place to go.

The Seaton House drunks are also winemakers, only they don't call what they make wine. They call it pony piss because it's yellow and it packs a wallop. It is available in the shelter every day. You line up to get it by the eight-ounce cup, at hour-long intervals. No, the inmates are not running the asylum. Doctors vow to do no harm, and shelter workers know that booze does less harm than Lysol or Listerine or vanilla extract or Chinese cooking wine or gasoline or glue or anything else a man takes when he can't bear his pain, or any pain.

Pony piss is a lesser evil. It may be murky but its origins are clear. There was a time when you couldn't bring a bottle into a shelter. Guys who drink don't like to give up their bottles.

Every winter, a drunk or two would fall down, freeze to death. Or he would guzzle what he had left so he did not have a bottle to bring in, and he'd get ugly because he was drunk, and he'd get tossed back onto the street with the same result: drunksicle.

The staff at Seaton House are pragmatists. They began to store unfinished bottles in a lock-up.

But men still got thirsty. With no access to their booze, they'd take their bottles and leave. Hmm. And so the staff began to dole out drinks at intervals, with no moral judgments. They didn't ask permission from the city. They just did it. Because if you get a guy who needs help, it's a good idea to keep him around so you can, if you're lucky, manoeuvre him into a position where he can be helped. The only help you can give a dead guy is to dig his grave.

Things changed again. The men who were running the shelter began to buy wine from the liquor store. On the theory that if you have it, they will come. That was a decision which could have cost a couple of people their jobs. Instead, it saved a few lives. The workers hid the purchases in their budget. They called it "mineral water." There were signs in the shelter: "No mineral water before 8:00 a.m."

They don't do that any more. Now, they brew their own.

It costs fifty thousand dollars to ferment a year's worth of pony piss. It's cheaper than an ambulance. It's cheaper than a funeral. The men pay for their drinks with the money they get from their income supplements, their pension or their disability cheques. What they pay covers a third of the cost of the pro-gramme. They pay half a buck a cup.

Some of the men who drink this stuff have spent as many as one hundred nights in detox. Some guys, detox does not help; you might as well give them a drink. The maximum? Sixteen drinks a day, but nobody drinks the max.

I met a guy, Garry. His hair was lank, his eyes were leaking, he had the shakes and he'd missed the first pour. Garry locked onto Art Manuel. The pony-piss program was Art's idea. For which, Art ought to get the Order of Canada.

Garry pleaded. He told Art he was hurting. Garry is a man who hates to plead. You could tell he hates what pleading does to him. Art broke a rule and poured him a drink. Garry spilled as much as he drank. That's a common problem. There was a pool of pony piss on the floor outside the window where they pour the drinks. Garry's feet were bare. He made sticky noises as he stood and drank.

Nobody said this was pretty.

Garry levelled off a little when he'd drained the cup. He said, "My usual idea of a good time is a pack of smokes and two magnums of brown Listerine." Men like to drink the brown, because the blue stuff changes the colour of your shit; nobody likes to shit blue.

You can't get pony piss unless you are in the alkie program. Once you're in, they try to figure out what kind of help you need.

Let me tell you that, in addition to the bar, Seaton House runs a bank. Because a guy gets his disability cheque, he cashes it, he buys a bottle, he drinks it and he passes out, which means he's easy prey for the crack addicts. And a drunk who's been beaten and robbed of his bottle and his money will steal mouth-wash, rubbing alcohol, cans of aerosol.

Art said to Garry, "You want a job?" Garry flinched. Not at the question. He was tender, he was sore, he ached down to the roots of his hair. The sound of Art's voice flayed every nerve in his body.

Garry used to have a good job. He used to have a nice house. He used to have a wife and kids. Now he had the shakes, and the offer of this tiny bit of responsibility. "Sure," he said.

Art gave him a minute to clean up. Off they went in the van to Scarborough, to a brew-it-yourself winery tucked away in an industrial mall. Garry had done this before. He knew the routine. He sprinkled some yeast into several buckets of diluted grape concentrate. In a few days, he and Art would come back and pour the wine into a carboy, and after it gurgled and bubbled for a few days longer, they'd return and rack it off into stiff-sided plastic bags and bring it to the shelter. The men back at the house go through nine hundred litres a month. The vintage is never rare, but it is always precious.

Not long after the renovations were finished, and most of the men had moved back in, there was a quiet meeting on an upper floor at Seaton House. In attendance were the men and women responsible for running the city's major shelters.

The meeting was quiet because, as a rule, the people who run shelters tend to think before they speak; they have learned to look and listen, and they are professionally slow to form a fixed opinion.

They came from the Native Men's Residence, the Scott Mission, the Good Shepherd, the Salvation Army. Such meetings, held once a month, give them a chance to exchange notes, talk shop, make presentations, share information and provide each other with moral support.

The support is necessary. Our shelter operators did not create homelessness, but we have made them responsible for it. They care for those who have been cast aside, for those who can no longer cope, for those who could never cope and for those who have cut themselves loose from the moorings which are such a comfort to the rest of us.

Our shelters do not house only drunks. We have a problem with crack cocaine. Here are some of the remarks made during the meeting.

– The first stage of homelessness consists of people who need shelter once in their lives, usually for less than six weeks, usually as the result of a crisis, say, a house fire. These people do not get sucked into the black hole of homelessness. They have the motivation to get out. All they need is "three hots and a cot," and then they're gone.

– The second stage of homelessness consists of people who are familiar with the system; perhaps they've been released from jail, or from the hospital, or from a treatment centre. They tend to have the motivation to get out of the shelter, but they lack resources.

– The third stage of homelessness consists of lifers, people who have made a sad but very human accommodation: "This place isn't good, but if people like me are here, then it's okay for me to be here, too."

– Of the four thousand people who use Seaton House every year, 10% are lifers; 23% stay more than six weeks but less than a year; 67%, or the overwhelming majority, stay less than six weeks.

– If you focus your resources on homeless people in stage two, you can cut the number of people who reach stage three.

– Many lifers are crack addicts.

– Smoking crack gets you higher faster than shooting crack,

but the more you smoke, the more you have to smoke in order to get the same high.

– Crack kills brain cells, which is why addicts say they get stuck on stupid.

– To treat crack addicts, first you have to help them get clean; then you help them learn to use what's left of their brains. It is a bit like working with stroke patients. You have to train people to learn how to do routine tasks. We're still learning how to do this; it's unbroken ground.

Who knew?

And here are some comments made by the shelter operators after the presentation was over and they sat around talking:

– When mental health beds close up, we're the ones who pick up the slack. We get the addicts, the refugees, those who suffer spousal assault, people who have fallen through the cracks – and we're supposed to be experts in all these problems.

– This winter there were forty-six cold alerts; last year, there were four. How do you plan or budget for that?

– As the population ages, so do shelter users; old people have particular problems, but old crack addicts have even more particular problems. We're only just learning how complex those problems are.

– We don't choose our clients; people dump their clients on us. There was a man recently dropped off at Seaton House. He had a broken leg. He came by ambulance. The ambulance came from Montreal.

This last, a surprise to me, but not to the shelter operators. None of this is simple.

Jerzy was living at Seaton House when we met. Jerzy is from Poland, and that is not his real name. I was told I should meet Jerzy because he was one of those guys who ought not to have been in a shelter, who ought not to have been in an adult education class, who ought not to have been out looking for work. He ought to have been in a hospital.

He's trouble on the hoof.

Jerzy was in his teens when he came to Canada. You can bet the Poles were glad to see him go. If you think that sounds harsh, pay close attention:

Jerzy is short and he is short-tempered. He's hard and angry and cruel. He has lizard's eyes and an appetite for kicks. I'm not convinced he knows right from wrong. Oh, and he hears voices.

I don't know which language the voices speak, but they tell him to do things. There's trouble when he listens. He wasn't listening to much when we met. He was doped to the eyeballs. He takes fifteen different pills when he is under supervision, a cocktail of medication so strong he can barely stand up. The pills keep him from hurting himself.

Sort of, but not always. He shuffled into the room where I was waiting, and he slumped in a chair. If he'd tripped and fallen on the floor, he would not have been able to get up; he'd have nodded off in an instant. That's how strong his meds are. You can understand if he doesn't always take them. Here's how he got to Seaton House:

The police picked him up six months ago. They got a call from someone in a rooming house. He was out of control, hopped up on cocaine, morphine, horse tranquilizers, booze and who knows what else. He was threatening to kill himself.

The cops picked him up and dropped him off at the shelter for no other reason than he had been there before: here, you deal with him.

By the time I met him, Jerzy had racked up thirty notations on his file. You get a notation for unacceptable behaviour; he had variously harmed himself, bullied the staff, missed the curfew and abused other residents with and without the help of weapons. He was especially fond of picking on an old man in a wheelchair. The old man is in his eighties; he only has one leg. One leg or two, what's the difference to Jerzy?

Why is he at Seaton House? No one else would have him.

Can Seaton House handle him? They're doing their best, but the staff aren't trained to handle problems quite like this.

Jerzy has spent time with the Seaton House doctor. He was sent to a hospital for treatment and evaluation. It's clear he has some sort of personality disorder.

The hospital turned him loose.

Ask him to roll up his sleeve and, if he feels like it, he'll show you a collection of thick and rubbery scars, some fairly fresh, running up the inside of his left arm from wrist to elbow.

I can't tell you much about Jerzy – we weren't together very long; and he kept looking at me with his cold hard eyes like I was some lovely chunk of rotten meat that he might feast on – but I do know this: he's right-handed.

In addition to a dozen scars made by knives or razor blades or pieces of glass, his left forearm was dotted with forty additional scars that I could see, some fresher than others, all of them round as polka dots. Because Jerzy likes to stub lit cigarettes into his flesh; you've got to be right-handed to grind a smoke into your left arm.

Ask him why he does this, if you have the nerve; if he's feeling up to it, he'll give you a sidelong, heavy-lidded grin; pure menace.

He says he burns himself to stop the pain.

You assume that, at the worst of times, the best he can do is to short-circuit one kind of pain by replacing it with another; and so he grinds lit cigarettes into his arm.

I looked at him as he talked. I saw deep grooves running down both his cheeks. It was as if he had cried tears of acid. The truth is not so grimly poetic. He has, on occasion, clawed his face until he's bled. The voices tell him to do that. One pain masks another, but he's not sick enough for the hospital. The hell he isn't.

The last I heard, he swallowed a razor blade and had been taken to Emergency; they turned him loose as soon as they took his stitches out. He showed up at Seaton House. He didn't last long. They kicked him out. I don't know where he is now. I keep my eyes peeled. He's here somewhere.

Everyone's here somewhere.

At one time there were twelve hundred rooming houses in Toronto. There was a fire in one of the rooming houses some years ago; many men died. Most of those old rooming houses were hellholes. We didn't want more deaths. So we stopped issuing licences. Now there are some four hundred rooming houses. The loss of eight hundred rooming houses means that roughly four thousand rooms were taken out of the system. That's awfully close to the number of men and women sleeping in shelters.

The city is broke. We can't afford to inspect the remaining rooming houses very often. Some of the four hundred houses are still hellholes, crack dens, rat traps. Sometimes, all a man needs is a good safe room. In the absence of good safe rooms, there are shelters, there are church basements and there is the street. You'd think we'd build some good rooming houses, and beef up the system of inspections; but, no, that's too simple.

Just so you know, not all bums are bums.

There are men who live in shelters who also get up in the morning and go to work. You can see them on Cash Corner –

Queen and Sherbourne – in the morning. They have wet-combed hair, and they may be hungover, but for the most part they are loose and limber and in good humour, with their slow-burning, hand-rolled cigarettes and their heavy-lidded double-doubles from the Coffee Time.

They come to the corner to look for day labour. Or rather, they have come to wait where the work can come and look for them. Cash Corner is an informal, unorganized labour exchange, a place where men in cube vans drive by looking to hire men who are willing to work hard for cash. Abbas Khan comes here almost every day.

He lives in a men's residence. He is a carpenter by trade. He is forty-three years old. He has startling pale green eyes. He does not slouch. He stands up straight. He is reliable. He has been coming to Cash Corner, on and off, for ten years. "I do construction, mainly. That's what most of the guys here do. Moving, heavy lifting, roofing, labouring. It's usually ten dollars an hour, in cash at the end of the day. I need the money to get by."

He means he uses the money to buy drinks to get by. I don't know why. Neither does he. "The best job I got here? I helped a guy build his house the winter before last. We built it from the bottom up, four months' work. The worst job? That would be cleaning boilers in government buildings. The guy who hired us, he worked us until the inspectors shut us down. It was dirty; asbestos. He still owes me a couple of hundred bucks." Early light, soft wet streets, passing cars, the smoke from cigarettes, the smell of doughnuts in the air.

At one time there were dozens of men on this corner, and there were lots of jobs. This morning, there were perhaps twenty men and they had been here since first light, and no one had come with an offer of work and it was now 8 a.m.

"It used to be really good," said Abbas. "You could get work every day. But the last five years, when the drugs came here . . ." There are plenty of drugs in this part of town. A young man was shot to death there recently.

The presence of guns and drugs and addicts and hookers means that employers are often reluctant to drive by; because, if a man gets out of his truck, a crackhead might sneak in the back door and steal his tools. Or a girl might jump in the front seat high as a kite, and the police, who make regular patrols, might think the man is a john.

Abbas points to some bloodstains in a doorway. "An addict was caught smoking crack in the Coffee Time the other day. The woman who runs the place told him to get out, and he punched her in the face. The cops came by, and he resisted arrest and they beat the living snot out of him."

A guy named Al, a friend of Abbas, nods his head in agreement. "It's definitely getting worse." Al is a regular on the corner even though "I got a medical condition. I take pills for blood pressure and for my stomach. My doctor just told me I could work again."

He was phlegmatic about his chances to get picked. "I'm fifty-four, I'm overweight. If a guy knows me, he'll hire me. But there's a lot of young guys." As if on cue, a young guy came by.

He was wearing a basketball jersey with a tangle of cheap chains around his neck, a wave cap on his head and a cellphone in his ear; tattooed on the young man's bicep was a face. The face, vaguely and inexplicably familiar. And then it hit me.

It was the young man's own face on his bicep.

Abbas laughed. "It's as good as TV here."

If you didn't know Cash Corner, you might think these men were just killing time. But they want work as much as they need it. You might think these men look unreliable, but they come here early every day.

Al said, "I'm not going to go to the church drop-in and watch TV, eat coffee and doughnuts. Why would I want to be inside on a nice day? It's depressing to stand here if there's no work. But if I get depressed, I'll go for a walk." Just then, a cube van pulled up.

"Hi, Al."

"How are you?"

"Looking for work?"

Al panicked and blurted, "No."

The guy smiled gently. I don't know who he was, but he knew Al from before. He was aware of the dimensions of Al's panic. He said, "Easy job today. Moving some trees at the zoo. Couple of hours' work."

Al grinned. "Okay."

It was the first hire of the morning.

A man named Sonny watched Al leave. In his backpack, optimistically, Sonny had a sack lunch, a box of juice, a pair of shoes and a pair of shorts, a hammer, and pliers of all sizes.

Sonny is sixty-two years old. "I had two jobs yesterday. Taking a kitchen counter apart in the morning, and loading a truck in the afternoon. I made forty dollars. I got a small pension. I can't live on it. I do office packing, house packing. I pack the trucks, I let the young guys do the heavy stuff. I can't go up and down the stairs like I used to."

Who among us can?

Abbas and Sonny hung around, shooting the breeze until nine-thirty. A kind of display: two men who got along. Somebody might want two men. They were about to call it a day when a black van stopped at the corner. The driver nodded at

Abbas and said, "You want to move some drywall?" Abbas brightened. The man said, "Two-man job, half a day's work." Sonny stepped up smartly. Off they went in the van.

Half a day's work is better than no work at all.

It is a good break for two guys who want a bit of work today because they might not find any tomorrow. It is proof that not all men on the street are bums.

TEN

We eat before we talk.

— MARGARET ATWOOD, in *The CanLit Food Book*

If, over time and in spite of our celebrity-chef pretensions, you pay any attention to the food sections of the papers and the glossy magazines, then you might be forgiven for thinking Toronto is a poached salmon, boiled asparagus, rice pudding town; these are the foods that crop up with the most frequency.

Don't tell that to Ghassan Abu Ali Allam. He was putting on his chef's whites one morning when he noticed a woman staring in the window of his restaurant.

Antonetta had just come from morning mass. She wanted a cup of coffee and a nice breakfast. She has lived in Leslieville, in the east end of Toronto, all her life, but she had spent the last year on holiday in Australia. She was curious. Queen Pita used to be a little Chinese-Canadian greasy spoon. Ghassan unlocked the door and let her in. You could see Antonetta thinking: things have changed since I was away.

She sat down and said, "I want a nice breakfast."

Ghassan squinted and smiled at her. He said, "What kind of nice breakfast do you want?"

"Egg and toast."

"I don't have egg and toast."

"What kind of breakfast do you have?"

"Mediterranean breakfast."

Antonetta paused.

She said, "I often used to come here after church. There were Chinese people here in this place. They served a beautiful breakfast. Where are you from?"

"Lebanon."

"So, I've found you now."

"Very good."

"What is a Mediterranean breakfast?"

He recommended the spinach fetayer, a kind of savoury turnover. She had never had it before. He heated one for her. She said it was good. She said she would be back.

And you would know Ghassan was a chef even if he weren't wearing his whites – the giveaway is a ridge of callus along the inside of his right forefinger, the result of years of prep work with a knife.

He earned his calluses and his scars in the kitchens of the grand hotels of the Arab emirates. He has roasted lambs over open fires in the desert. He has cooked for royalty. He once fed seven thousand people at the Dubai air show. And now, on the eastern reaches of Queen Street, he makes shawarma and fetayer for the breakfast and lunch crowd. You have never had such hummus; and you haven't tasted lahim bil agin, a kind of Lebanese pizza, until you've tasted his.

As Ghassan watched Antonetta take her leave, he said, "I'm new here. I am in Canada six years, but only months in this place. I live in Newmarket. I am working fifteen hours a day by myself. The rent is good on this part of the street. But people in this neighbourhood don't know Mediterranean food. They are now learning.

"I had one guy try my falafel. He said, 'Very good falafel.'

Two days after, an old gentleman came; it was his father. He said, 'Can I try your falafel?' And yesterday he is bringing his wife. He said, 'I don't want egg and bacon any more.'"

Ghassan makes the falafel himself: chickpeas, fava beans, fresh ingredients; he does not use a mix. "Lebanese food – parsley, olive oil, lemon, garlic – it's good, it's fresh, it's healthy. Once people know it, suddenly they will come."

Ghassan is betting they will come. It is a serious bet.

He left Beirut and came to Canada with his family in order to get away from civil war. On arrival, he found work in a 250-seat Italian restaurant; when the owner wanted to expand, he asked Ghassan to open a 350-seat restaurant for him; the restaurant opened, but it failed.

Ghassan bought into a well-known franchise; it not only failed, it took every cent he had. "I made a mistake. Twenty-five years' savings, gone in two years."

And so now here he is at age fifty, making pita in Leslieville.

He chopped fresh salad. His knife was a blur on the cutting board. He told stories of the old days. "When I cooked for the seven thousand VIP people at the air show, I had big trucks to deliver the food; one for meat, one for fish, and so on. I served one thousand kilos of Iranian caviar.

"A truck driver said, 'I hear rich people eat caviar. I have never had it. Will you give me some?' I give him one hundred grams. I saw him an hour later. He was sick. He said, 'If you give me a million dollars, I won't eat that again.' It was too rich for him. He was not used to it."

He'd better hope the people in his neighbourhood get used to his kebabs. As he prepared to make shawarma, cutting bits of marinated chicken and putting them on a skewer, he said, "In Lebanon, I wanted to be an artist – painting, sculpting – but it was not practical. So I went to hotel school from 1969 to 1971.

I am trained in French cuisine. Without French cuisine, there is no kitchen."

But a good chef is worth any number of artists.

He looked up from his work and said, "I find if you cannot give, you cannot cook. Food, you give it from your feeling."

The grandest theme is the simplest: we leave home, we come here, we feel homesick all the time. The easiest way to keep the old country alive is to put it on the table and feed it to the kids.

The Porco brothers made sausage on College Street. They made the kind of sausage that, before I moved here, when I used to visit, I'd bring a hundred dollars' worth home on the plane in a box.

Salami, capicollo, pancetta and prosciutto.

The brothers came from the south of Italy in the fifties. They knew how to butcher hogs. Their knives were cold and sharp. They made a good living; more than that, they made a name.

I could never persuade them to let me watch them work. I used to think of them as artists of the flesh. They weren't sure what to think of me; a shrug of the shoulder, hands forward, palms up; "Kind sir, talk to my brother." Same shrug from the brother.

Maybe they thought I was after the recipe for the sausage.

A couple of years ago, the brothers reached a certain age: the cold of the meat locker made their bones ache; it was no longer easy to throw all those hogs' legs on the butcher's block. They called it quits.

This is the real story, or a chapter of it, and it may be the story Ghassan will tell when his time comes:

The Porco brothers had sons. The sons went to school. They did not want to work with meat and fat and bone. A butcher never goes hungry but these days a white collar, not a white apron, is the symbol of success.

The shop was too valuable for a young butcher to buy, and the brothers would not part with the recipe. Fratelli Porco became a drinks club; it is a meat market of another kind.

There is no more sausage, nothing like it.

I remain bereft.

But all is never lost here.

Matteo D'Agnello is a butcher. He works with the Masellis brothers. They run an Italian market on Danforth Avenue. In the back of the shop and in the basement, they also turn hogs' legs into prosciutto.

Prosciutto is to the hind leg of the hog as grappa is to grape juice. It is a distillation of patience. It is light cast on darkness, banishing despair. It may not be the word made flesh, but it is the flesh made poetical. Got the picture? Now get out of the way. Matteo has work to do.

He works the old-fashioned way. Let me be precise: There is and only ever has been one way.

He set the first leg on the butcher's block and seated it properly, so that it would not move around as he worked.

The meat was clean and red, the fat was the colour of cream, and the thick skin was the same shade as the inside of my forearm.

Matteo did not want his knife to slip; proof of this may be found in the long white scar on his left thumb. He honed his knife with a sharpening steel, and when the blade was like a razor, he made slick, deft cuts around the hip end of the leg.

This is a simple task which takes a few seconds, provided that you have done it thousands of times. Matteo – his last name means "lamb" – has done this hundreds of thousands of times.

He did not trim for tidiness, although that's part of it – the meat must be exposed to salt; and so, snick, snick, off came a ribbon of skin and fat, a little, not too much. "To make more round," he said.

Matteo paused and slapped the meat with the flat of his hand. He said, "This weighs ten kilos now. Next year, it will weigh six kilos."

You may think of this loss of weight as the merest result of salting, drying and aging; you may also think of the smile on the face of *La Giaconda* as the merest result of oils, a sable brush and . . . Forgive me, I do go on.

Matteo bent forward now, scraping intently with his knife, exposing a small flat bone – "This is the paletta." – at the top end of the leg. When the paletta was properly exposed, he snipped it off and tossed it aside.

He left the knob of the thigh bone protruding from the flesh. There are some modern butchers who take the thigh bone out; what they make is convenient to slice, but it is not prosciutto.

I do not know who invented prosciutto or how, and I do not care to know. I merely hope that, when my time has come, I have sufficient appetite for one last slice, the meat nutty and salty and sweet, and maybe there could also be a piece of *parmigiano*, a chunk of rough bread and a glass of new wine on the table.

When Matteo sent the first few legs downstairs, Costantino Masellis took over. Mario, his oldest brother, was upstairs stocking shelves. His youngest brother, Ambrogio – Andy to you – was off on deliveries. His father, Leonardo, the founder of this enterprise, was keeping an eye on things. This is why the old man came to Canada. To have sons. To make a life. To grow old, and to keep an eye on things.

Costa rubbed salt over the skin and into the flesh of the leg, and then he tossed it into a brick pit filled with hundreds of kilos of salt. "I use different salts. One is high-grade, fine. The other is coarse. And I also use a curing salt." How long has he been doing this? "Ever since I was a kid." He is twenty-nine years old. The air of the basement was cold and smelled clean, a white smell, almost like new snow.

He said, "I grew up down here."

I asked him the Fratelli Porco question: Why did he choose to work with his father and his brothers, tossing legs of pork into bins of salt in the basement of the family market, when it is the fashion for smart young men these days to find white-collar work?

He picked a fresh leg, and he took a fistful of salt. He said, "When I got out of school, I had a job lined up at King and Bay. I walked into that building with my resumé and I looked around. I decided I couldn't do that. I walked right out."

He grew up in the neighbourhood; his friends live nearby; this is the city as village. He threw another leg into the salt pit. "In about two weeks' time, we'll rotate these, put the top ones on the bottom so they get an equal amount of salt." And then? "I'll weigh them down to give them a flat shape. I'll wash them with vinegar, rub them with oil and add my seasonings."

His seasonings are black pepper, a lot, and red pepper, a little. He will eventually hang the legs on hooks, and the meat will finish drying in the cool basement air. "These will be ready in six months."

Time passes as slowly in my neighbourhood.

Once, after a week or two in Italy, during which I ate almost nothing but *pici* – a thick and comforting pasta, the specialty of Montalcino – I was faced with the prospect of an empty refrigerator at home; no prospect at all. I walked over to Roncesvalles Avenue intending to stock up on staples.

In my house, one of the staples is caraway rye, a kind of canvas with mustard as the primer, against which I apply – forgive me – pigments.

The Poles know at least as much about the uses of the pig as do the Italians. I aimed for the Polonia Meat Market. I wanted a foot-long krakowska, still warm from the smoker, pink and juicy under its taut mahogany skin. You may call this garlic sausage; you are wrong. It is ham sausage, redolent of mace and pepper, the pride of its namesake city, Krakow.

I also wanted a slab of smoked spareribs, the meat sweet on the bone, meant for a bed of sauerkraut, there to rest alongside some Vienna sausages, a handful of juniper berries, some grated apple, sliced onion, chopped garlic and a sufficiency of white wine; this, after a couple of hours in the oven, is the lazy man's *choucroute garnie*. I am such a lazy man.

I wanted a pound of lean bacon, because a house is not a home without a BLT. I needed a couple of smoked turkey thighs to chew on in idle moments. And no visit to the Polonia is complete without some pork loin. It is perfect for her sandwiches. Because she may be the one who scrambles my eggs, but every day I make her a bag lunch to take to work. I am nothing if not uxorious.

The doors of the Polonia were locked. The windows were masked with butcher paper. I stuck my head in a hurry into the deli next door. They said – smugly, I thought – that the Polonia had shut down and they didn't know where the butcher had gone. I walked home with nothing but bread.

Two days later, I gathered myself and hit the street again, in order to find out what happened. I did not have far to look.

At the Polonia, I noticed that the butcher paper had been stripped away from the windows. I peered inside. I saw a man standing in the back of the shop. A compact, white-haired man. Bob Korkus, butcher.

I tapped on the window. He shook his head. I tapped again and waved a hand. He put down a rag and came to the door.

"What happened?"

"The landlord upped the rent."

Bob said he didn't get much notice. He said he had no choice. He couldn't afford to stay. The landlord refused to cut him any slack. He had to shut up shop. Now, he was waiting for the man from the gas company to come and read the meter one last time.

He said it was a shame. How else could he say it but sadly?

Bob Korkus came to Canada from Poland around the same time as the Porco brothers came from Italy. He landed a job half an hour after his arrival. He worked hard, saved his money, then struck out on his own.

He had worked in this spot for twenty years; he could have afforded to retire in a couple more. His son and right-hand man, Adam, had already found another job. His son's wife, Anya – she worked the counter and handled the slicer – was still looking for work. They'll do okay.

Bob wasn't doing okay. He looked lost. He said, "For me, it's very hard. I get up at 1:00 a.m., I can't go back to sleep."

I shook his hand. I thanked him for feeding me so well. And I told him he was the reason I moved into Parkdale. He looked at me quizzically. I explained how we'd been looking at houses, and it had been a long day, and we were cranky, tired and hungry. The Polonia was open and so I ducked in, waited in line and bought some smoked tenderloin. One bite was all it took. Bob smiled. He understood.

All that's history now. He had dismantled the smoker and moved his grinder, his mixer, his stuffer and his slicers into his garage. He said he would recondition them over the winter. He said he'd take a breather. He said he'd only had two holidays in twenty years.

Will he open another shop?

He wasn't sure.

Not everyone can go out for groceries.

Not everyone can cook, or pay for cooking. Not everyone can get out of the damn bed. I got a call one night, late. A quavery voice: "I've fallen down. I think I broke my hip. Can you help me? The nurse won't come. I'm lying on the floor. I can't get up. I'm so tired."

I knew in an instant what had happened: some old woman in a nursing home was in need of help, and she'd found me. I couldn't quite imagine how. I had no idea who she was. She must have dialled a number in desperation, at random, hoping for the best.

I hurried to ask her the right questions: where are you, what's your address, what's the name of your nursing home, what's the number of your room, is there a nurse on duty, do you remember the phone number of the nursing home – those kind of questions.

I had no idea who she was. She had no idea who I was. She was on the floor, connected to the world by a flimsy telephone connection, talking to a stranger. She gave me a phone number. I kept her on the line, found my cellphone, called the nursing home, got an answer, told them what had happened; they said they'd call the nursing station.

I said I'd keep the old lady on the line.

We talked. She said she was ninety years old. She said she was in a lot of pain. And then I heard a knock on the door, and a nurse came in, took the phone and said everything was in good hands now.

I called the nursing home the next day. They said the old lady was fine. I felt like I'd saved a life.

A year later, late at night, the phone again.

That quavery voice. I knew it in an instant. I asked her all the same questions, got the same answers, found my cellphone, made the call, kept her on the line. I called the nursing home the next day, as I had done before, and they told me she often got confused.

This time, I called the old lady. I said I'd like to meet her. I intended to tell her that I wrote for the papers, and it wasn't every day that I saved a life. She was flustered, but she said I could drop by.

I was expecting to find her in some hellhole. The building was new and clean. The receptionist on duty looked crisp and properly suspicious. I asked for my new old friend. She pointed me to the dining room.

Fifty old people, milling around happily: some big-band swing music, playing low; the men wearing suits and ties, doddering along with the help of their canes; the women in long skirts and long-sleeved formal sweaters shot through with sparkly thread; fat white corsages; plenty of aluminum walkers; more women than men.

There were flowers on each table. I found my night caller. No evidence of a broken hip. She seemed bright-eyed and vaguely embarrassed; perhaps she was just vague. I wished her well. I let her be.

I asked the receptionist why the old lady would have called me, not once but twice; we put our heads together; turns out if you dial the number of the nursing station, and then you

JOE FIORITO

dial 9-1-1, you get my number. A wonder it doesn't happen more often.

I noticed the menu as I left. If this is hell, I want in: grilled salmon or beef tenderloin, new potatoes with dill, tomato salad, strawberry shortcake or profiteroles, white and red wine on each table.

I told you this was a salmon town.

Some years ago a man named Frank was standing in back of a restaurant with his waiter's apron on when a man from the kitchen came upon him from behind and caved his head in with a pot, or perhaps it was a frying pan.

Why did the man hit Frank on the head? Frank has no idea. One explanation is as good as another. Maybe the pot-swinger was a pearl diver with ambition – if there was an immediate vacancy in the ranks of the waiters, perhaps he could step up and fill it.

The blood was cleaned up, assault charges were filed, but nothing ever came of them. It seems odd; except for this one guy, everybody likes Frank. He's short and trim, with a clipped moustache and big brown eyes. He's light on his feet, and quick with a joke or a kind word. He's a guy who likes to get along.

His skull was badly fractured. He still has trouble with his ears, and for a time he had trouble with his speech. But you know how they say something good can sometimes come from something bad?

There's an old lady living in a ratty, musty house on a side street south of Dundas, near Ossington. A heap of crap on her porch: old furniture, bits of wood, junk that's been there for years. The old lady lives alone, she walks with a cane, she doesn't get around so good. As old as the lady who called me.

158 •

And in a funny kind of way, you could say the guy who smashed Frank's head in did her a favour: After the doctors saved Frank's life, he started to get seizures, he needed therapy and he went on meds; he knew he'd be on a disability pension for the rest of his life. A social worker asked him what he wanted to do when he got out of the hospital.

Frank said he'd been a waiter. He liked serving people. The social worker – they are not all numb and dumb – steered him into a Meals on Wheels program at St. Christopher House. You know how that works – hot food in thermal trays, volunteer drivers, and runners who deliver food to people who can't get out to get groceries, or who don't have the wits or the strength to cook. So Frank became a runner. Every day, he and his driver stack the trunk of a car with trays of food and off they go.

First stop of the day, Frank walked up the stairs of that old lady's house, the one with the junk on the porch. He knocked and then opened her door, gave her today's tray, asked her how she was doing. She said she was fine, more or less, and Frank picked up the mail from the floor, collected yesterday's tray, wished her well and then he was off to the next stop.

That old lady can't afford a nursing home with flowers on the table. She is better off in her house than an old-age warehouse. Nothing makes up for the time Frank spent in hospital, and nothing makes up for the seizures. But she needs him, and she needs the food he brings her.

So the guy who brained Frank did that old lady a favour.

Today's menu? Penne with red sauce, corn, an apple and a box of juice. The food is institutional. The pasta was mushy and the sauce was sweet as corn syrup. And who eats niblets with penne? At least it was hot.

Frank delivered the next tray to an old man on the top floor of a rooming house. This old man was always under the covers, even on the hottest days. Frank peeked in, said hello, put the food on the kitchen table and took the time to square the tray off neatly, with the main course right up front, so that when the old man gets up and comes to the table he won't have to reach. Less likely to drop food on the table or the floor, you see? No point in feeding the cockroaches or the mice.

That's Frank. Thoughtful.

And so it went, with a dozen stops between 11:30 a.m. and 1:00 p.m. Frank speaks Portuguese – he's from Venezuela – but when he looks in on an old Italian couple, he speaks to them in Italian, and he asks how they're doing, and maybe he's the only contact they have with the outside world all day. And if Frank notices that *nonna* can't get out of bed, or if he notices that *nonno* has been looking poorly a couple of days in a row, he tells the social worker when he finishes the route, and the social worker calls the family, or visits the house, or calls the doctor. It all fits together.

Frank's still a waiter.

I wish Meals on Wheels served better food. I wish they delivered flowers and wine with the meals. Just because you're old doesn't mean you've lost all sense of taste or love of life.

If you're cooking for everyone in general, you won't please anyone in particular. We ought to put Ghassan in charge. And Bob Korkus, and the Porco brothers, and Thoi Nguyen at Pho Hung. The Masellis family can deliver.

ELEVEN

If Toronto is a sort of amalgam of New York and Chicago, Montreal can be understood as the best of Boston and New Orleans, a combination of old-world charm and modern technology.

– ALAN F.J. ARTIBISE, "Canada as an Urban Nation"

I mean no disrespect to a certain leathery old Orillia choirboy, but the skyline of Toronto is not something you get onto.

Toronto is plain here and ugly there.

The way a city looks – its tall towers, the ornate links to its past and the mercantile richness of its downtown core – ought to be a metaphor for the lives and the hopes of the people who live there. If you pay taxes in a city, you ought to be able to draw nourishment from the cityscape. At the corner of Bloor and Yonge, you could die of starvation.

I ought not to be so critical; this is a Toronto habit, easily learned, and I suppose ought to know better. One day I fell in behind three guys from out of town. They had come to see the Hockey Hall of Fame at Front and Yonge. They were nice guys; weekend barbecue, mow the lawn, wash the car, share a beer over the backyard fence kind of guys.

They just stood and looked up at the skyscrapers.

"Nothing like this back home."

Damn right.

And yet we get it wrong.

The CBC building, that temple of Canadian culture, was designed by an American. I'm not an internationalist when it comes to this stuff. Were there no Canadian architects who could have . . . ?

Our best new building, the Ontario College of Art and Design, is a box propped on coloured stilts directly above another building. It is a jaw-dropper; you can't help but stare up and smile. At night, it seems to float in the air. It has the shape of a tissue box; its skin is a fresh crossword puzzle, all white and random black squares. It would have been multi-coloured but – this is so us – we ran out of money.

Alas, it is not quite unique. It was recycled from plans meant for another project by the English architect Will Alsop. As an aside, it is claustrophobic inside.

Our other good building is City Hall; oddly enough, it, too, is claustrophobic. As if we are too small for our own dreams.

The tall towers those out-of-towners were staring at? They kill hundreds of migrating birds each spring. The birds are confused by the bright lights at night. They smash into the windows and fall in fluttering, bright-feathered, bloody-billed heaps on the sidewalks below. We had a blackout a couple of years ago. We still haven't learned to turn out the lights.

Our Mies van der Rohe office blocks? They are identical to towers built in Chicago. They built theirs first, and they put big gaudy art in the front. And we put bronze cows in back of ours; lovely cows they are, but you can't quite see them and you don't know they are there.

We are a modest people. Doesn't do to show off.

Our modesty is not without merit. Here, we suffer for a lack of here. In part, this is because here is no one Toronto. There are as many Torontos as there are people who live here.

We say this is a city of neighbourhoods, as if this was our

particular glory, as if the notion of the neighbourhood was somehow our idea. Jane Jacobs lives in a neighbourhood, therefore neighbourhoods are good.

We think of neighbourhood identity as a virtue. But in a city this size, our neighbourhoods are a result of lateral growth – Toronto is as big as it is because it has gobbled up adjacent villages.

And the mere fact of our neighbourhoods means that we do not have to be divided before we are conquered. What does Rosedale know of Parkdale? No one from Rexdale plays road hockey in Mimico. York is numb to Agincourt. We identify with our neighbourhood first. Perhaps that is because the whole of the place is too awful to contemplate. Who is proudest of Toronto? People who live on the outskirts of town. When are they most proud? On vacation, when people ask where they are from.

The notion of neighbourhood makes some small sense to us as individuals. Everyone is famous in a small town, if fame means that the people who see you think they know who you are as soon as you come into view. And the butcher on the block knows your custom, as does the dry cleaner and the old woman who runs the corner store, and the waiter in the bar down the street remembers what you drink. We will settle for this sort of fame; it is reassuring.

Life in the village is a mirror in which your sense of self is twinned with the image others have of you. But just because you know your neighbourhood, or some of your neighbours, doesn't mean you know the town. There are snobs who think this is the case. They cling to the notion that what they know about the city – the club of the moment, or where they take their habitual coffee – is all there is to be known. These people are our provincials.

We like to pretend to a certain sophistication. We have opera and ballet. In truth, the community choir is more popular in Toronto than *Tosca*. We have pro sports, but our Leafs fill the stands in spite of their mediocrity, the Raptors do well at the ticket office even though they stink, and I don't know anyone who watches the Argos.

Our best team is our Triple-A baseball team, the Maple Leafs. They win with regularity. We pay them no mind.

Toronto is not a snooker town, it is an eight-ball and a nine-ball town. Cliff Thorburn was an aberration from the suburbs.

You can get a facelift here, but not a decent loaf of bread.

Toronto has a fair harbour. You cannot get near it.

Ontario is a huge freshwater lake. You would think we would have a long history of catching and eating fresh fish. You would think the shores would be lined, not with clam shacks, but with huts selling whitefish and chips, herring, smelts in cornmeal batter, lake trout, rainbow trout, speckled trout, splake, pike and, yes, salmon fresh or smoked. Not so. The water is polluted, and so are the fish.

Torontonians had, at the turn of the nineteenth century, a fair interest in hunting for wild ducks and fishing in the waters of the harbour. There is even a pert little canoe of local design with a wide bottom used by fishermen and hunters. An example used to hang from the rafters of the waterfront museum. We no longer have a waterfront museum.

You may come here from any country in the world but when you arrive there is precious little to tell you where here is.

We are a tolerant bunch. If you want to get married here, you can: boy on boy, girl on girl, come on down. We take our tolerance pretty seriously in these parts. Alas, we take ourselves so seriously that we didn't understand the grins on the faces of the men who came to tie the knot at City Hall when gay marriage was legalized.

Where is City Hall? On Queen Street. Ha, ha.

Oh, I get it: Queen Street.

We thought they were laughing from happiness.

One of our ways of death: Look out below.

The Bloor Street Viaduct crosses the Don Valley. There are sidewalks across the bridge. There were some four hundred jumpers since it was built in 1919, or roughly one every three weeks; that's fewer than the Golden Gate Bridge, but more than the Jacques Cartier, if you're keeping ghoulish score.

An Armenian teenager jumped; afterward, someone spray-painted his name and his dates on the footings down below, in that lovely cursive Armenian script which seems perfect for recording sadness.

The bridge was a magnet. It attracted, and it repelled.

A rumour: kids in a nearby school used to peer out the windows at the comings, in the hopes of seeing the goings.

A rumour: someone hailed a cab, stopped in the middle of the bridge, paid the driver, got out of the cab and jumped.

We put up a barrier to stop the jumpers. The barrier is made of metal rods which, seen from a distance, look not unlike the guts of a piano. We call it the Luminous Veil. Said the wag, I'd rather have voluminous ale than a luminous veil.

We jump elsewhere now.

The rods – there are some nine thousand of them – whisper in the high winds like an Aeolian harp. They were made, not across the bay in the steel mills of Hamilton, but around the world in Mumbai.

Signs at each end of the bridge advertise the telephone number of the suicide helpline. They take our calls in India when we need help with our computers, our printers, our electronic devices. Perhaps they ought to answer our suicide-prevention lines as well.

Certain comparisons are inevitable. I've lived in both cities. The real difference between Montreal and Toronto?

I bumped into Michael Goldbloom downtown one day. The former publisher of the Montreal *Gazette* had just taken over the *Toronto Star*. He was new here; he looked not lost, but not quite found.

We had the usual expatriate exchange.

"Michael, how are you?"

"Two words."

"Which ones?"

"Good bread."

He meant he was still looking. He sounded as if I was his last hope. I had to tell him there isn't any bread here. He took it like a man. He did not whimper. But he wanted to.

Montrealers take good bread for granted. Not quite true; they take for granted – Le Fromentier, *mon dieu* – that the best bread in the country is a right of citizenship.

There is "good" bread in Toronto. By which I mean Ace Bakery donates a portion of its profits to various worthy causes. But the baguette of Toronto is an approximation, as a poster is to a painting.

Other differences:

Toronto got the educated Jews of Europe, the ones with money and position. Montreal got the Jews of the working class. Montreal got the better deal; not just smoked meat, but Schwartz's and Ben's; not just bagels, but Fairmount and St. Urbain.

Wine costs more in Montreal; provincial tax collectors know which goose to pluck. If there are also more good small restos in Montreal, it is because rents are cheaper there, and the cost of the lease is reflected on the plate, and not because palates are somehow more refined.

In any case, the trend is upward in Toronto – we are becoming more sophisticated. And the trend in Montreal is up and down: as falls separatism, so rise rents; as rise rents, so rises the price of steak frites.

Toronto drivers are stupid. Montreal drivers are stylish, a synonym for psychotic. Toronto drivers are habitually and infuriatingly slow off the mark on a flashing green, as if promptness were rudeness. Montreal drivers make up the rules as they go along.

A driver in Montreal once ran a light and smacked someone. You know that moment: I'm going a bit too fast; is this a new orange or is it old? Can I make it through? Do those people see me coming?

Screech, crash, bang.

His defence: "I couldn't help myself?"

Oh, well, then.

I quit a good job and moved to Montreal to start over. I had no prospects there. I was forty-three years old. The people I met in Montreal said, "Oh, how wonderful, you're going to remake your life." The people I knew in Toronto said no such thing; from the looks on their faces, they were thinking, "What, are you nuts?"

The Metro is smoother, sleeker, runs quieter and the seats on board are lower. The Toronto subway system is older, the cars look like aluminum lunch pails and the wheels shriek on the rails.

Montreal is a small town; friends see each other often. Toronto is so vast, friends plan for weeks to venture outside the neighbourhood.

Montrealers take a little pleasure every day, even if that pleasure is no more than a slice of *jambon persillé* with a glass of wine, or a croissant and a cup of coffee; some little perfection. In Toronto, we are suspicious of both pleasure and perfection.

Montreal has the St. Jean Baptiste parade. Toronto has the Caribana and the Gay Pride parades. All three provoke a certain dramatic tension, but Toronto's parades are pluralist and Montreal's is not.

Toronto skinheads swaggered in force on the streets when the Roma refugees came here from Europe a few years ago. Montreal skinheads spray-painted "Englishit" on the walls of the city in the days before the referendum. Call it a draw.

Toronto's coldness?

In Toronto, it was British; class as a way to keep a distance between "us" and "others." It has changed, and yet it has not. A certain reserve is a useful strategy; it is hard to tell if the man you have met is Tamil or Sinhalese, Ethiopian or Eritrean, Serb or Croat; easier to say nothing than risk provocation.

In Montreal, there is a kind of coldness, stemming from the duality of languages: which do I offer to speak, English or French? And what if I guess wrong? Easier to say nothing.

A woman grew up in Toronto during the war. Her uncles and cousins were wiped out in the Holocaust. Her mother told her what happened, and how, and when, and to whom. The girl began to search through her neighbourhood in secret, keeping a list of places she and her mother could hide. I have a hunch children also did this in Montreal.

There was a storm of concern in Toronto about whether to allow diners to bring their own bottles of wine into a restaurant.

In the end, we made it permissible in all restaurants. We got it wrong.

No one brings wine to Toqué in Montreal.

In Montreal, you bring wine to the neighbourhood bistro, which is licensed so that the chef can spend on his cuisine and not his cellar.

You cannot get wine in a corner store in Toronto. You cannot get good wine in a dépanneur in Montreal.

A Montrealer walks proudly, as if in a crowd of a thousand there were a thousand centres to the universe. In Toronto, we walk with our eyes cast down.

We say, "Excuse me."

They say, "I excuse myself."

We eat on the streets; our restaurant lobby is weak. They have no chip trucks or hot dog carts; their resto lobby is strong.

I saw a Montrealaise with perfect *maquillage* walking her dog in the soft sweet morning on the grass in Parc Lafontaine. When her dog did what dogs do, she pulled on a surgical glove and picked it up and carried it away, the crap steaming in her hand.

In Toronto, we carry plastic sacks, and we drop the crap in other people's garbage cans.

I saw a woman leave Union Station in the morning on her way to work; she was perfectly made-up, wearing a well-cut trench coat, blouse and skirt, silk stockings and sneakers. Sneakers with nylons and a skirt? Never once in Montreal.

There, they kiss on both cheeks. Here, we don't.

When I lived in Montreal, we put our garbage on the curb twice a week; everything, all at once, no questions asked. In Toronto, we have green, grey and blue boxes. We wash our cans and rinse our bottles. We keep our refuse on our front porches; welcome home.

Montreal had wealth when there was good architecture.

Toronto had wealth when there was mediocre architecture.

Montreal has the second-largest collection of Victorian buildings on the continent, after San Francisco. Toronto has the largest collection of second-rate buildings on the continent.

We have no memory of our past: you can't tell where here is. Old Montreal is a living museum.

We had a famous snowstorm. Toronto was at a standstill, so the mayor called in the army. The country laughed at us, but the country is an idiot. When nothing is moving, the old and the ill are at risk: no fire trucks, no ambulances, no cop cars. Snow, a life or death matter.

My first snowstorm in Montreal: an army of trucks and graders invaded the streets, the truck drivers paid by the load. Sirens, flashing lights and front-end loaders wheeling, turning and biting into the white drifts in the night. A woman walked past as a truck was backing up in the darkness. She didn't make it. Snow, a life or death matter.

The province of Quebec is suspicious of Montreal. The province of Ontario is suspicious of Toronto.

Toronto wins if sheer power is the sole criterion. We will concede to you your daily joy, fashion sense and the perfection of your baguette.

Now excuse me, I have work to do.

TWELVE

Canada's very survival depends upon more massive immigration –
and on learning to construct a cohesive society out of many diverse
communities that rival each other in size and ambition.

– BRUCE HUTCHISON, *Maclean's*, July 11, 1988

The cabbie was a handsome man. His car was plush and silent.
I told him where I was headed. He pulled away without a word.

His shoulders strained against his tailored shirt. His posture
was good. He had an athlete's build. His bearing was regal. He
drove as if the street belonged to him alone, slipping in and out
of lanes, rushing up behind the slow movers. He let me know
that his job was to drive and mine was to sit back.

We were heading east. He took a shortcut. We got stuck in
traffic. His anger was visible, palpable, almost scented. He
snorted sharply, slumped in disgust, thumped the steering
wheel – it was plush and padded – with the heel of his hand. He
could not believe his bad luck.

I was the one who was going to pay the fare. His cellphone
rang. He took the call. We weren't going anywhere.

"Hello. Yes."

I was looking idly out the window and idly at my watch when
the conversation grew so loud it startled me.

"I don't believe it. You're kidding me. No, you're kidding
me. Tell me you are kidding. I told you it wasn't me. I told you,

and you didn't believe me that I didn't do it. Tell me where did you find it? You put it where? I don't believe it. Tell me again, where did you find it? You see, I told you. How did you find it? Next time you will believe me. Oh, yes. And next time, please do not put it there. I don't believe it. All right. Bye."

And then he was silent.

But the call had clearly lightened the driver's mood. He sat straighter in his seat, and he squared his shoulders and tapped the wheel with his forefinger, and the traffic opened up, and he stepped on the gas, and the big cab snorted and bucked away. Who could resist?

"What was that all about?"

"What do you mean?"

"The call."

"The call?"

As if he'd forgotten.

He said, "The man I was talking to, he is my boss. Last week I gave him a cheque. He said I didn't give it to him. Now he calls me to tell me he found it."

"Where was the cheque?"

"In the garbage."

"He threw your cheque in the garbage?"

"He thought I didn't give it to him, but I did. I gave it to him, all right. He put it with some papers – he is a busy man, he has many papers – and he threw some things in the garbage."

"Including the cheque?"

"Including the cheque."

He swerved around a little car, cutting it off. He tried to overtake a truck using half an inside lane; a cyclist appeared, the cabbie braked, he nosed back into place and cut the little car off a second time.

"A big cheque?"

"Fifteen hundred dollars."

"That's a lot of money."

"My payment for the cab. He is the owner. Every month I give him such a cheque."

"But he threw it out?"

"I knew I gave it to him."

"I guess he's happy now."

"Very happy now. I am an honest man. I wouldn't lie about a thing like that."

"Your owner a nice guy?"

"Very nice. I will tell you something else. That kind of money means nothing to him."

"Nothing to him?"

"He's very rich. But it is a lot of money to me." He drove the rest of the way like a man with a clear conscience who'd been delivered from a debt. He delivered me on time and I tipped him.

The city cliché: The cabbies in this town are engineers, doctors, physicists. But Leo Agwu is the grandson of a Nigerian chief.

I met him not long after the visit of the Pope. I had gone to Mass for the sake of my newspaper, the only reason I'd ever go to Mass. Leo picked me up afterward.

We talked about the Pope, and about religion.

I tend not to have much belief, except in the present tense, and in who we are together here. That did not worry Leo. He invited me to the summer picnic of the Onu-Ofu Cultural Association, which is how I found myself in Mary Amibor's kitchen early in the morning. I wanted to see how Nigerian cooking was done.

Mary's stovetop was crowded with gleaming, steaming pots and pans. The Onu-Ofu are Delta Ibo from Nigeria. This means the cooking must be done right, and for it to be properly right, there should be a lot of it. "I'm making egwusi soup," said Mary.

Egwusi soup is a traditional dish, eaten by itself or used as a kind of sauce and ladled over rice or potatoes or especially on heaping plates of pounded yam.

She said, "I already have my meat cooking. I have boiled the cow feet for forty minutes. The goat meat will take an hour or more. The beef meat will take twenty minutes. I'm seasoning with garlic, black pepper, thyme, onions, salt." She seasoned by hand. She did not need to measure. She has made this soup before.

"Egwusi?"

Mary lifted a lid, gave a stir, took a taste, then whirled and chopped and threw something else in the pot; her hand, quicker than my eye.

She said, "Egwusi is a creeping plant. It starts with a yellow flower and develops into a melon. We cut it open, ferment it for a week, strain and clean the seeds and spread them to dry in the sun. We grind them up and put them in this soup."

In addition to egwusi and meat, she uses tomatoes, palm oil, hot peppers, dried crayfish pulverized into powder and azuokpo, a kind of smoked, dried catfish; also fresh spinach, dried bitter-root and one or two other things I didn't recognize but which seemed optional and not important enough to mention.

Mary's niece, Grace Omelebele, stopped by to lend a hand. The two women worked side by side, blending, stirring, chopping, grinding, laughing. There was no surface in the small kitchen which did not have a pot, a plate, a pan, a bag, a box, a tin of ingredients. Mary mashed some garlic and massaged it into a bowl of okwukwu. What's that? Say it out loud. Okwukwu; chicken.

Mary mashed more garlic with her mother's akangwose, an

hourglass-shaped piece of wood whose flat ends are perfect for mashing, pounding or grinding.

There are thirty-two Nigerian social and cultural organizations in Toronto. And there is idozi-okwu. Emmanuel Amibor, Mary's husband, came in then with a bag of groceries, and he explained:

"We do family conflict resolution. We call this idozi-okwu. If a man and woman are having problems, we will hear about it. We would call you and set up a meeting. We would visit you and ask what's going on. You would be glad to talk to us. I would invite you to come to my home. We would listen to your story. It's a round table. We talk with both the husband and the wife. We would know who is wrong. We would say, 'Stop doing what you are doing.' We don't go to court or call a lawyer. You will never see the police at a Nigerian house. But we don't just use idozi-okwu to help with the problems of husband and wife. We solve many kinds of disputes, business disagreements, if you are looking for a job, and so on."

I understood this to be a non-Muslim variant of sharia.

Emmanuel added, "Leadership is determined by age, not by the one who talks the most or who has the most money."

Does idozi-okwu favour men over women?

Mary, who was listening from the kitchen, said no. Grace said yes. Emmanuel said it may not always be 50–50, perhaps it's 49–51, but it's the traditional way. It binds the community together.

How was the picnic?

Yams on the barbecue, music in the air, kids kicking soccer balls, young Nigerians flirting in the sun, elders talking things over seriously, men making jokes or talking business. The egwusi soup was good. Leo ate his fill. He did not look happy. He looked lonely. He kept to himself.

We stayed in touch after the picnic. He invited me to come with him on the day he became a citizen. He picked me up in his cab, and he drove north during the morning rush hour, taking a couple of zippy shortcuts here and there, up streets you couldn't find without a map and a magnifying glass. He said, "If I know anything, I know this city."

He was early, off-meter, making good time. But when he slowed to make a left at a busy intersection, the driver behind him honked his horn. Leo said, "What does he want me to do? Fly through the air?"

Leo was flying, in a way.

He was dressed in high Nigerian style. He wore his good black trousers and a silvery-purple caftan under a belted trench coat. On his head he wore a bright red felt hat – his okpu ododo.

He said, "This hat, this colour, is only worn by titled people. If I was back home, I couldn't wear it, but my mom is the first daughter of the King of Ewulu, and I'm wearing it because of this day."

Who could deny him?

Leo came to Canada in 1993. Why did he leave Nigeria? "Travelling is the biggest education you can think of. The main cause of my travelling is seeking peace of mind. Here, my mind can be at rest."

As good a reason as any. Maybe better than most.

He parked his cab and entered the Department of Citizenship and Immigration at 55 St. Clair East. He took the elevator to the room where the rites of citizenship take place. He was early.

The whole room was full of people who were early.

There were seventy-eight other men, women and children, from thirty-three countries, most of them waiting patiently. Some were nervous. One man read his newspaper as if he was sitting on the subway. More than a few looked wistful – there was no going back now. Leo looked dignified.

A clerk entered the room and said, "We'll be calling you by number. I will check your landing documents. My colleague will stamp, 'No Longer Permanent Resident.' If you have a blue resident card, you must surrender it. I know you paid fifty dollars for it, ha, ha, but it will be of no value because you will be a Canadian citizen."

Leo was sitting in the front row between two men, one old, one young. He removed his okpu ododo, and he helped the younger man put a small Canadian flag pin in his lapel.

Most people had come with relatives. Most relatives had come with cameras. The clerk said there would be no photos during the ceremony because the swearing of the oath was "a private moment between the individual and the government of Canada."

There would be time for photos after.

And then the room fell silent. As the silence grew longer it became solemn. And then the presiding officer, Professor Ezra Shabas, O.C., entered the room. We stood. He sat. We sat.

He said, "Welcome to the Canadian family." He reminded the newest members of the family that Canada was a democratic country where rights and freedoms are respected. He said along with rights come responsibilities. He said we must respect, help and understand one another. Then, phrase by phrase, in English and in French, he read the oath of citizenship, and phrase by phrase with right hands raised, the newest Canadians swore allegiance.

And then they sang the anthem sweetly.

Later, over his first breakfast as a Canadian, Leo said, "Professor Shabas is a special man. I've heard about him many times. They always mention his name on the radio. I studied music up to Grade Two in Nigeria. I like classical music. When I spoke to the professor, I thanked him for his contribution to the musical world. He laughed."

Leo tucked into a plate of French toast and talked about the citizenship test he had taken before the ceremony. "They asked me if I knew the provinces, if I knew the political system, if I knew who was the Queen's representative in Canada – that's the governor general."

He said, "I know I passed easily. And when I came home from taking the test, there was a letter from my wife."

He paused for effect.

Leo was married in Nigeria on December 23, 2001. His wife had been unable to get a visa. That's why he had been so sad at the picnic. He missed her. He had been lobbying hard on her behalf.

What did her letter say?

"She wrote to tell me she has been called for her interview. She must pass the medical, and there will be a police check – I know there will be no problems – and then she will come to Canada."

He did not dwell on his years of loneliness.

Leo put down his fork and knife and said, "I felt complete peace of mind during the ceremony. I was just thinking of the day I got off the plane. I still remember that day. September 22, 1993."

He verified the date by looking at the stamp in his old, green Nigerian passport. It is no longer useful to him, except as a souvenir.

And then he went home to change his clothes and go to work for the first time as a Canadian.

He called me a couple of months later with the good news. His wife, Joy, was coming to Canada. Did I want to meet her at the airport?

He picked me up in Parkdale. He drove in a careful hurry. He was keeping himself in check. But you could tell from the look on his face that the paperwork, the endless inquiries, the waiting and the sheer frustration, all this was fading into memory.

His cellphone rang insistently as he drove. He spoke more quickly than usual when he answered. A crowd of his friends and relatives were waiting for him at the airport. They were calling to check on his progress and to learn his whereabouts and to determine his estimated time of arrival. He signalled a lane change and said, "They're all getting mad at me because I'm not there yet. I know how long it takes. She has to clear protocol. It will take at least an hour." But Leo was driving on the cusp of time, and he knew it. The plane was due an hour ago.

He scanned the throng as he entered the airport, and he walked directly to the Flight Arrivals board. He stood still and stared at the long list of information. He blinked and frowned and blinked again. Oh, no, no.

Joy's flight, delayed six hours.

Leo held his breath. He did not move for a long instant. And then he turned and sought an airline agent, and he asked why Joy's flight had been delayed. The agent did not know.

Leo's friends stood near him then, they made small jokes to lighten his mood, they touched his forearm, they held his wrist. "You can feel his pulse," they laughed. Leo didn't crack a smile.

He adopted a philosophical manner, like a man pulling on an old, familiar overcoat; he shrugged into it. "Personally, this doesn't bother me. You have to take things as they are. I'm a bit disappointed. But she will come. She took off yesterday, travelling from Nigeria to Amsterdam to here. She's going to be exhausted."

He decided to drive back to his apartment on the western edge of the city and wait there. His apartment was filled with yet more family and friends and many elders, including Mary and Emmanuel Amibor. Leo explained to them about the delay. The atmosphere remained merry because everyone wanted to make sure Leo kept his spirits up.

He got a bottle of cold beer from a bucket and sat down in the kitchen. There was pepper soup on the stove, and also a pot of docanut soup, and another of egwusi soup, and there were big pots of joloff rice and fufu, and many bowls of chin-chin. No one would go hungry, no matter how long they had to wait.

Leo said, "I met Joy in Lagos almost four years ago. She came into her uncle's office in the bank. I was there to drop something off. Seeing her, I felt different. She was part of my life from when I first saw her. She greeted me nicely. I felt good. I asked her uncle, 'How can I meet her?' I got her number. I kept calling her on the phone. That's how it started."

How does a man court his beloved from afar?

He popped a couple of chin-chin in his mouth and left the kitchen wordlessly; chin-chin are small cubes of sweet, deep-fried pastry; they are very good with beer. He came back carrying a large cardboard box.

"You see," he said. And I saw that the box was filled to overflowing with used long-distance telephone cards. He looked at his watch again, and someone decided that every-one should eat.

Pepper soup is hot and rich and salty, made of beef and goat and chicken and much pepper. Egwusi soup was familiar from the picnic in the summer. But the fufu was new to me.

Fufu is a thick, snow-white starch. It is made of yam flour and dried potato flakes. It is both spoonful and spoon; that is to say, you take a piece of fufu with your fingertips, and you roll it into a ball, and when it is nicely rolled, you make an indentation with your thumb so that the ball becomes a kind of scoop, and you dip the scoop into the soup, and then you eat. It was dip and scoop, all night long.

Leo said, "When she arrives, I will take Joy to the CNE grounds. I love that place. And then to the CN Tower, because you see it on all the postcards. That's where I will take her." From up there, he knew Joy would see the clean streets of Toronto, the fall leaves and the silver light shining on the lake, so very different from Lagos.

And someone said, "She's going to get the shock of her life in the cold." And everyone in the room laughed because everyone had known that kind of shock, and one of the men laughed ruefully and looked away because he, too, was waiting for permission to bring his wife to the cold shock of Canada.

The music in the apartment was loud and getting louder. Everyone was cheerful. All ate heartily. Leo paced up and down. His friends admired him as he waited. He kept looking at his watch. And then it was time, and he slipped out of the apartment.

Once again Leo parked his car and strode into the terminal; once again he made his way through the late-night airport crowd; once again his friends smiled to see him, and they welcomed him and joked with him and clapped him on the back.

He walked over to the Flight Arrivals board. He read the information twice, just to be sure. The flight from Amsterdam had touched down. He tried to look calm, but his heart was racing. In a few minutes, everything in his life would change.

He waited patiently for his bride to clear Immigration. Soon, passengers from Joy's flight began to come through the gate. Leo's friends became excited as they craned to get a look. "Is this her?" They were not sure. They know Leo very well, but they had only seen photos of the bride. No, this was not her. Not her. Not her. There was no Joy.

Finally, Leo couldn't stand it any longer. He left the Arrivals area and walked down the corridor to Immigration. He knocked on the door. No answer. He turned and began to walk back, and just as he turned he saw a small hand waving from a distance, and he hesitated, uncertain, and then suddenly she was running toward him through the crowd, and she threw her arms around his neck. They clung to each other wordlessly.

And then everyone piled into various cars, and they all drove back to Leo's for the celebration. As we passed through the clean, well-lit, unfamiliar streets, Joy said, "Three hours out of Amsterdam, we had to turn back. Something was dropping from the plane. No one knew what it was. Finally, when I saw the lights of Toronto, I was very glad." She and Leo held hands all the way.

When Joy finally entered the apartment which was now her home, all the women who'd been waiting to meet her broke into a cheer, and they clapped their hands and began to sing.

Many of the women were wearing those bright and billowy African dresses. They stood hip to hip with Joy as they pulled her into the room, bumping hips with her and laughing all the way, and the song they sang was this: "Here is the new bride, we see her, we like her, everything she is wearing is appealing to us." And they also sang for Leo: "Here is the new husband, we see him, we like him, everything he is wearing is appealing to us." This is the traditional way.

And then the women pushed the couple together. Leo seemed hesitant. I was curious about this, since I knew how long he had waited. Emmanuel Amibor explained that the bridegroom's hesitation is also traditional. The couple was made to sit on chairs in the centre of the small apartment, and the blessings and the speeches began.

Emmanuel held up a small plate and said, "These are kola nuts. They are a symbol of unity. Whoever eats this receives a blessing of long life." Kola nuts are smooth, and their colour is dappled and various.

He also said, "And this is alligator pepper. If you eat this, it brings you fortune for the rest of your life. Anywhere you go, it brings success." And he passed the plate of nuts and pepper around the room.

Then he held up a bottle of the finest cognac. "This strong wine is a binding factor. It brings fear to this wife not to separate from this husband." He splashed some of the VSOP binding factor on the floor at the threshold of the apartment, and then he filled a glass for the bride and groom. To Joy he said, "When the husband talks, you should listen."

At this, all the women in the room piped up with one voice, and they said to Leo, "Yes, and when the wife talks, you should listen." And everyone laughed, and the bride and the groom shared a glass of cognac.

There were many more blessings and speeches, and everyone ate the kola nuts, which are meaty and crunchy, and everyone had some alligator peppers, which are much smaller than the peppercorns in your grinder, but just as hot and spicy. There seemed to be a lull. I asked Emmanuel what would happen next. He said "Merriment will ensue."

And there were more toasts from others in the room, and there was very much more laughter when one of the women said to Joy, "If you're good, you pound on your mortar. If you're bad, you pound on the ground. So, pound on your mortar."

That is a rough translation of what they said, and I'm not Ibo but I don't think it has very much to do with the pounding of yams in mortars.

Finally, Emmanuel Amibor said, "By this time next year, I will come here to bless a new baby." And everyone cheered, and there was cake.

Merriment ensued.

I slipped away, stepped outside in the cool air, hailed a cab and went home.

Ugochukwu Agwu was born a year later.

The boy's first name, the one which will be used by his parents, means "Eagle, given to me by God." The naming ceremony was a traditional affair. Once again, the Ibo men came in their handsome suits, and the women came in their big bright dresses. There were pots of joloff rice and fufu by the stove, and there was egwusi soup, and there were bottles of malt, and soft drinks, and palm wine.

Little Ugo slept blissfully as the women passed him around the apartment. An elder, Michael Mordi, happened to be visiting. He was the oldest man in the room and so, ordinarily, he would have led the ceremony by himself. But he graciously shared his duty with Emmanuel Amibor.

Mr. Mordi took Ugochukwu from one of the women, and he held the baby as if he was afraid of crushing him or dropping him, and so the cradle of his arms was equally tense and tender.

The elements of the ceremony – salt, sugar, honey, smoked fish, palm oil, kola nut and alligator pepper – were brought forth and placed on a table in the living room, and everyone was happy.

Emmanuel said, "We will start. There will be no noise. If anybody interrupts, that person will pay a fine." And there was much laughter, and then there was much silence.

Emmanuel said, "This child is a gift to all of us." And so it began. Michael took a piece of kola nut and passed it over the baby's lips, and Emmanuel said, "This is so, when your parents call you, you will listen to them and respect them." Ugochukwu, asleep, pursed his lips.

And so it went: salt was brought to his mouth, so he will savour life; honey, so he will know the sweetness of life; sugar, so that others will hear the sweetness of his words when he speaks; palm oil, so that he will obey his parents; alligator pepper, so he will have success; and smoked fish, which adds a depth of flavour to so many Ibo dishes, so that he might enjoy his culture. Ugochukwu, who was surprisingly still asleep, wrinkled his nose at the fish. Someone said, "Oh, look. He is a Canadian. He doesn't like smoked fish." And everyone laughed. But not Leo, and not Joy. They just looked proud.

A large bowl of cool water was placed on the table, and Ugochukwu got a sprinkling. Emmanuel said this would make him a cool guy, and I think he meant Ugo would not be hot-headed or impulsive.

The smoked fish was passed around the room then, and it was smoky and salty and chewy. And there were morsels of kola nut for everyone, and also the hard sharp berries of alligator pepper.

Michael smiled and held the boy tightly. Emmanuel stood up and addressed the room. "Now, this is my special appeal: if any of you has a name to give this child . . ."

And this is how it went: if anyone had a name to give the baby, he placed some money – usually a twenty-dollar bill, or sometimes two of them, or more – in the bowl of cool water, and he spoke the name he gave, and he explained why he was giving that name, and then forever after that man would have the right to call the boy that name. And the names were several and various, and they were recorded in a book:

Ugochukwunyem, or eagle, the great gift from God; Chukwufun-Nanya, or God loves me; John Frederic; Tobe Chukwu, or glorify God; Uzo Chikwa, or God's way; Ogechukwunyem, or the time given to me by God; Azuka, or I am not alone; Ugobueze, or the eagle is king; Chiedu, or God is my guide; Ashionye-Edue, or he who is ruled by his destiny; Ilobabaechine, or my father's line will continue; Joseph; Aka Olisa, or the hand of God; Ife Ncho, or what I want from God is what I was given; Olisazimuwa, or God sent me to the world; and finally, Ikechukwu, or God's power.

Ugo, for short.

And by the time the naming was finished, the bowl was filled with wet money, and it was taken away, and the money was removed and dried off. You might like to know that I am the one who will call the boy Joseph. And so it was recorded in the book.

Once again, merriment ensued.

THIRTEEN

I have always yearned to go to Gold Mountain.
But instead it was hell, full of hardships.
I was detained in prison and tears rolled down my cheeks.
My wife at home is longing for my letter.
Who can tell when I will be able to return home?
I cannot sleep because my heart is filled with hate.
When I think of the foreign barbarians
My anger will rise sky high.
They put me in jail and make me suffer this misery.
I will moan until the early dawn,
But who will console me here.

– lines said to have been carved into the wall of an immigration building
in Victoria, B.C., 1919; quoted by Richard Thomas Wright,
In a Strange Land: A Pictorial Record of the Chinese in Canada, 1788–1923

A couple of years ago, I was on a pleasantly vague mission in a used bookstore, Contact Editions. I wasn't looking for anything specific. I merely happened to be in the neighbourhood and decided to pass the time in the hope of spotting a Greg Clark or a W.W.E. Ross or something by the neglected Raymond Knister. No such luck.

Out of habit, I prowled the cookbook shelves. The truth is, I have too many cookbooks; more than three hundred at last count. But Edward Giobbi's *Italian Family Cooking* is long out of print and impossible to find, and I live in hope.

On the shelves that day: Got it. Got it. Don't want it. Wouldn't take it home if you gave it to me for free. Wait a minute.

I noticed a cord-sewn spine with a soft cloth cover. It seemed handmade, and was unlike anything else on the shelf. Not a book in the usual sense. I walked on. And yet . . .

What if these were the last handwritten scribbles of the late Mme Benoit? I turned back and took it from the shelf. The title, handwritten on the front cover in black ink block letters: "Cook Book by Lee Sew, Toronto, Ontario, Canada." There was another title, written in Chinese characters.

Inside, the pages were blue-lined and lamb-soft and yellow with age at the edges. The lettering was neat, if spidery, written with a fine-tipped fountain pen. Not just a cookbook, this was a soup-to-nuts collection of recipes for continental and Chinese cuisine, with an index at the back. From Apples to Veal stock.

All the recipes were sophisticated. Silesian Sauce, never heard of it. Soubise Sauce, heard of it but never had it. Planked Steak, who does that these days; salmon is more likely now. Steak à la Henriette, Steak à la Chiron, Steak à la Mirabeau. Turtle soup? The real, not the mock. This was classic hotel food of the finest style, quaint and out of date and meant to be served on silver platters.

But who was Lee Sew? And why would he take the time and trouble to compile all these recipes? I noted that he had made a separate index for Chinese dishes, including various Chow Meins, Foo Youngs, and several dishes in the Cantonese style.

One of these caught my eye: Sai Woo Soo Guy. I'd eaten that dish at Sai Woo, many years ago – the restaurant, in

Chinatown, famous in its day. We ate plates of Soo Guy – some kind of chicken, I think – to celebrate the arrival of someone's student loan.

A curiosity, this book. The price? Fifty bucks. Yikes. I put it back on the shelf and walked away. And I got four steps away and had another one of those prickly thoughts: You'll regret it if you don't go back and get it.

When I took it off the shelf a second time, a sheet of paper slipped out. A note in ballpoint; hmm. Someone else had been intrigued and had jotted down a couple of thoughtful suppositions: "Lee Sew is Cantonese; he might have worked in a private home; the English word *lemon* is written with the Chinese characters for 'le' and 'mon.' The Chinese title is translated as *Chinese Western Cookbook Compass*."

The bookseller, Wes Begg, is an astute man with a deep love for books. He couldn't recall where he bought this one, but he took my money with a slightly sheepish grin, and I left the store with a fifty-dollar question: Who was Lee Sew? Why did he write this book? Where did he learn these recipes? Is he still alive? Was he married? How did he get here? What's the story? Okay, that's seven questions. I had more. Was there a way of finding out for sure? Was this book a piece of the history of the Chinese community in Toronto? Where to start?

I called Bill Wen.

An obvious choice. At the time, Bill was the ranking Chinese restaurateur in Toronto. He'd been in the business forever. More importantly his restaurant, Sai Woo – it has since closed, and he has died – was named for one of the recipes in my little book.

Mr. Wen returned my call, and he asked me to meet him at his restaurant. He said he'd be glad to look at the book.

A red-vested waiter brought me tea. It had been years since I'd been in the place. The same fan-shaped watercolours hung on the pale green walls, the same tasselled lanterns dangling; even the big-bellied, blue-shirted city cops who waddled in for takeout looked familiar.

Bill Wen arrived wearing a blue suit with his Order of Canada pin subtly placed in the lapel. He hesitated. I invited him to sit, and I poured him a cup of his own tea; a courtesy to him who has shown courtesy to generations of us. I showed him the curious book and asked if perhaps he knew Lee Sew.

He took the book and held it gently. He didn't say anything. He looked through the pages. He was silent a long time. And then he said no, he didn't know Lee Sew. Could he tell me anything about the book, or the recipes it contains?

"Typical old Chinese binding," he said pointing to the cord sewn into the spine. "Long ago, even commercial books were bound like this." He continued flipping through the pages, and then he stopped flipping.

He raised an eyebrow.

"We have these dishes on our menu."

First and foremost, he meant Sai Woo Soo Guy. A slice of chicken, dipped in batter, deep-fried, then sliced on the bias and served with a thick red sweet-and-sour sauce made with dried fruit. "It could be any kind of fruit, pineapple, cherry, as long as it's dried."

This was the answer to a question I had never even thought to ask before. Sai Woo, maybe the most famous Chinese restaurant in the city, had been named for a sauce. It was worth the trip to see Bill Wen's face when he saw Lee Sew's Sai Woo Soo Guy.

Any idea how old the book might be?

"Twenties, maybe thirties."

Beyond that, he couldn't say. Did he know who else might be able to help me? Mr. Wen paused and stared at the mysterious book.

It was cool and dark and quiet in the restaurant. A young couple had just finished an early supper. The boy was skinny, with greasy dark hair, a black T-shirt and pale white skin. The girl was heavy, with stringy hair and tight jeans. They used their chopsticks with unexpected ease; she was a lefty. They were casually intimate. They'd eaten here before.

The boy leaned back in his chair, took some tea and swirled it around in his mouth. He pushed his plate away – a residue of red sauce in swirls, along with leaves of garnish – and lit a smoke. You could do that then, light up in a restaurant. She laid her chopsticks neatly down. He gestured for the bill.

"The man you want to see is Bill Wong," said Bill Wen. "He is the former head of Chinese cuisine at George Brown. He will be able to tell you something. I will call him. He will call you."

Bill Wong was in his mid-sixties then, with steely grey hair and a gathered, observant manner. He took the book in hand, took a deep breath, released it slowly and said, "I'm retired now, but I tell you, if I was still working, I'd give you a thousand dollars for this book."

We were sitting at a table in the cafeteria of the Hospitality Building of George Brown College where, until recently, he'd taught Chinese cuisine. There is a smell of soup in the air, a warm and humid saltiness.

Mr. Wong had agreed to supply me with some forensic intelligence; he is a chef, he speaks Cantonese and he knows the community. He turned the pages of my little book with care, as if it were an heirloom Bible.

"By the look of the writing, I'd say Lee Sew was a young man when he wrote this; the strokes of the Chinese characters are stable, which means he did not get tired easily. He was also a real old-timer; otherwise, he'd have written his name 'Sew

Lee.' If he was alive today, I say he would be in his eighties, maybe his nineties. Now, take a look at this recipe."

It is the first one in the book. The ingredients, in English: 2 cups coffee, 20 cups boiling water, 2 eggs, and ½ teaspoon salt; followed by fifteen lines of instructions in densely written Chinese.

"You see, in the old days, they made coffee with whole egg; the white to settle it, the shell to make it clear and the yolk to give it a nice orange-brown colour." His smile broadened as he read more.

"I tell you, this is a gold mine. Lee Sew has got it all; canapés, soup garnishes. Oh, and lobster scallops, not many people do that now.

"I'd say he worked in a hotel, maybe in a private club – otherwise, it would not be possible to learn continental cuisine. He has all the names, *à la Hollandaise*, *au gratin*; and all the techniques. This is a smart person. I think he is very clever." He paused and, as if he were talking about a revered old ancestor, he said, "I admire him very much."

Bill Wong, highly respected, a successful chef and a teacher, was quiet for a moment. He was thinking about the old days, about Chinatown, about the life of Lee Sew. I sensed a particular kinship, not just one of race, but of craft and inclination; they probably had the same scars, the same calluses on their hands.

He shivered himself into the present and drew my attention to a Chinese character on one of the pages; one of his fingers was missing half the nail, a chef's injury. "Lee Sew was Cantonese, I'm sure of it. This word, *nam*, means tender, like braised meat is tender. It is a word that exists only in Cantonese."

Bill Wong closed the book and folded his hands in front of him. "Here's what I think happened. Lee Sew would have left his village and gone to Hong Kong, and from there he would have taken a freighter to Vancouver. Judging from the age of the book, he left China when he was very young. He was probably not married.

"He'd have learned to cook in a big hotel when he arrived. The staff in the kitchen, many of them were Chinese. Then he'd have moved to Toronto, probably as a result of his hotel connections. I'd say this book was a record of the recipes he learned. Of course, this is just supposition on my part."

This was a great leap forward.

Bill smiled modestly and said, "A man who knows more is Leo Chen. He is the director of operations for the Mandarin restaurants. I'll call him. We'll arrange to meet. We'll have something to eat."

A few days later, over a plate of barbecued ribs, beef with scallions, and batter-fried shrimp, Leo Chen agreed to play detective. Mr. Chen is a busy man; he had to excuse himself from the table frequently to tidy up a business arrangement, or to take a call, or to greet a party of important clients. But he was mine alone when I showed him Lee Sew's book.

"There is something familiar about this," he said with a smile.

We were sitting at a table covered with pastel napery, in a room filled with the ladies – also in pastel – who lunch. Leo was oblivious to everything around him as he began to read. I ate. He did not.

He immediately discerned a series of facts plain to him but hidden from me. "The book is old, so I'd say Lee Sew came to Canada sometime before 1911." Why then?

"Because after that date, the Exclusion Act made it hard for any Chinese to enter the country. He was single."

How can you be sure? "Chinese men could not bring their wives, and there were very few Chinese women here to marry."

Why was that? "Because back then, Canada wanted workers, not men with families. He died here. I'd say he died unmarried and without children."

How can you be sure he was single? "Because you have his book; if he'd had a family, they'd have kept it, they would have passed it on, handed it down. This raises a question – the goal of Chinese immigrants was to save money, to return to the village and buy a little piece of land and build a house. Why did he not go back? He had a steady income. To go home with no money would have been a disgrace. So I'm going to say he was a gambler. He had his job and this book which was his treasure, he could not gamble with it. Lee Sew had good English for the time, good enough to speak but not good enough to write complex sentences. That's why he lists the ingredients in English, but the more complicated instructions are in Chinese."

I had long since stopped eating.

"At this time, the time of writing this book, I would say he worked in a private home, not a hotel. Here he has recipes for children's food, cookies and such – and we have assumed he had no children of his own. So I think he must have been working for a wealthy family who entertained, because he has recorded all these recipes for canapés.

"Lee Sew was not a well-educated man. Here is devil's food cake; but he writes 'black devil,' not chocolate; in fact, all the chocolate recipes in the book use that phrase, 'black devil.' Here's another one; game stuffing, but he writes '*yiu hay*,' game in the sense of play.

"I'll say Lee Sew was from Canton; I will go further and say he is from Taishan county. It's a feeling I have because of how he uses the language. Now I will tell you something you could not guess.

"In 1986, I was shown this very same book by Terry McRae;

her husband was president of Simpson's department store. Lovely people; they have both since passed away. I remember telling Mrs. Terry McRae what I am telling you.

"I think she may have inherited this book from her mother. It might have been a wedding present, a reminder of a faithful old servant, I'm not sure. But this book is a piece of history, I'm sure of that."

After lunch, Leo Chen excused himself and went off to a meeting, and I thanked him and walked home with a nagging question: did Lee Sew work for Terry McRae, and could I prove it?

I called Wes Begg at Contact Editions.

Yes, he remembered buying some books from the McRae estate; now that you mention it, he said, there had been a curious little cookbook. He gave me a phone number.

I called Terry McRae's daughter; perhaps she remembered a faithful old servant? Alas, she said her mother never had servants; her grandmother's family was not well off. But Terry McRae did like to scour antique stores, and she loved all things Chinese, so perhaps she rescued Lee Sew's book from some antique shop, some jumble sale, some junk store. I'd hit a dead end. But there was just one thing left to know.

Shirley Lum answered the call; she is a Chinese Mary Poppins with a red coat and a big umbrella who leads walking tours of Chinatown. I filled her in. She said that if Lee Sew was as old as my sources suspected, then he was likely buried in Mount Pleasant Cemetery.

I called there. I put the question. I got a cold answer.

"I'm sorry, but we have no Lee Sew in our database." Hmm; but what if his name was recorded the other way, Sew Lee.

"In that case, we have two."

An unexpected complication, a kind of coin toss.

Can you tell me where they are buried? "Yes, easily. Would
you like Sew Lee, who died September 28, 1973, aged eighty-
five? He's buried in the Lee family plot." Not my man, not if
he was in a family plot.

"Well then, we have a Sew Lee who died on March 15, 1967,
at the age of eighty-one. He was born in China. He died of
cerebral thrombosis. He was buried in the adult common
ground by his son, Henry Chang."

A son?

I went to the cemetery and talked to the sexton. If I had to
choose, it would clearly be the man in the pauper's grave,
according to the assumptions of my sources and informants.
But a son, Henry Chang? How is this possible? "I don't know
that," said the sexton. "I do know that you will find him in
Section 33, Lot 755 #1."

Where is that?

"Over there."

I was told this with a vague wave of the hand. I was given a
photocopy of a map. I can't read maps, and the numbering
system of Mount Pleasant defies logic. I walked helplessly for
two hours among the gravestones under a light, cold rain. A
groundskeeper came by. I asked where the grave might be. He
pointed more or less to where I was standing.

No marker.

Sew Lee, I have been trying to find you for a month and now
you are somewhere here. How is it that you had a son named
Henry Chang? Was he a friend, or a social worker? The under-
taker must have asked if you were related. Henry must have
replied, with kindness and respect. "Lee Sew was my father."
I'll never know.

Henry Chang is dead now, too.

My shoes were soaked, my jacket was wet, my hair was plastered to my forehead. Lee Sew, wherever you are, this is what I believe:

You left the Taishan county of Canton a few years before 1911 and came to Canada. After that, the Exclusion Act made it difficult for Chinese men to immigrate. You came alone.

You arrived in Vancouver and found a job in a hotel. Someone put you to work scrubbing pots and sweeping floors. When he saw you were quick, he taught you to prepare the *mise en place*, the sauces, and then the simple dishes, and the complex ones. You learned English as you went along.

Later, because someone knew someone, you were offered work in Toronto. You headed east on the train. You were met at the train station, and you were taken to a private home and hired.

The family had some status. They entertained, so you made fancy canapés. They had children, and therefore children's birthday parties, and so you made cakes and cookies. They were good to you, and you were loyal to them. "Lee, that was wonderful soup; next time, perhaps you can make it with more cream."

You kept careful notes in ink; you developed your notes into a cookbook. You were lonely; you went to Chinatown to seek the friendship of the other men from Canton; you gambled in the dark houses which were later bulldozed to make way for the new City Hall. You used the excitement of gambling to escape your loneliness.

You never returned to China the way you thought you would. And when you died, you left nothing but a few clothes and your book of recipes. And now I have found you here.

Section 33, Lot 755 #1 of the Mount Pleasant Cemetery; an unmarked stretch of grass next to a bird feeder between this new maple and that old oak. I pressed a pine cone into the soft ground.

Lee Sew is who we used to be, and he is what we have become. I gave his book to the Ontario Historical Society.

FOURTEEN

If you're born in a city like London or Paris, you know you were born to one of the oldest cultures of the world. If you were born in New York, you know you were born to be one of the kings of the world. But if you're born in Toronto – that's destiny.

– Moses Znaimer, 1984

I have heard this said about Toronto from those who don't live here: Our needs impede your wants; our size gets in your way; our haste upsets your rhythms; our self-regard is earned at your expense; our bright lights lure your children; we strip your towns of talent and we use it for our glory; you are the poorer for it.

You're wrong.

The men and women who move to this town are from Lahore, Saigon, Lagos. They came here because they wanted more. They ran toward an opportunity. They are here because they want what we have.

Those of us who came from Cranbrook and Corner Brook came for the same reasons. It's a Canadian thing. Some of us leave home, and some of us stay behind. Off to the Big Smoke? What's the matter? This town too small to hold you?

That's just sour grapes, and it is as Canadian as a sheaf of wheat, a cord of birch, a crate of apples, a barrel of fish, a stack of hides, a bucket of ore, a tray of butter tarts, a hockey stick.

But in all envy is a hint of sadness, and the lingering fear that those who leave do not come back. Toronto is not a whirlpool, pulling you in against your will. Stay home if you want to. It does not do to dwell on the past. The best come here because there is no place else to go; even we know this. If you want to do well, we'll make room for you. If you do good, we all do better.

Here's a secret: We are not just like you.

We are you.

I came here for the hell of it, the way you head for the big city when you are young and from a small town: Get me out of here, I can't breathe.

I worked in the bush on a survey crew a hundred miles west of Thunder Bay in 1967. That year I saw plenty of kids my age hitchhiking, cycling, walking, jogging and roller-skating across the country: see the country, a Centennial project.

I saw kids heading west at the start of the summer and I saw them again as they dragged their tired asses east in the fall. They covered the country. I covered a ten-mile stretch of road. But when the highway was finally paved and I got my last pay-cheque, I also did a Centennial thing. I left for Toronto.

No choice, really. I am a Northern Ontario boy. A kid from a small town has a practical turn of mind. I did not want to visit some place and spend all my money and come back with nothing to show for it but a bag of souvenirs. I wanted to escape.

We drove. I mean, I didn't drive. I can now, although I choose not to; I mean I didn't drive then. Poets don't. I thought of myself as one. But I had not mastered the art of stillness at high speed. You ought not to stare into space sitting behind the wheel. My brother drove.

He had had nice things when he was flying high: good clothes, polished shoes, razor creases in his trousers. His hair was slicked into an elaborate wave which caught the light. He wore a pinkie ring. The car was clean and dark and green and sleek and fast.

He was wild then, although it wasn't clear that his oats would be the wildly sown habit of a lifetime, nor was it clear that his habits would lead him a long way to his death years later.

He was flying high then, and the arc was downward. He'd lost his job. Not the first time. His view? He hadn't been fired, he'd quit. Another view? He was caught drinking on the job. Ah, but he had optimism then. There was nothing he couldn't do. He needed work, and if there were no more jobs for him at home – too many bridges burned – then at least there was an opening down east.

The clerks at Manpower agreed to finance the trip – the cash, not up front, but promised if and when he got to Hamilton; arrival there was proof that he was on his way, and halfway there.

I was ready to go with him. I had a duffle bag full of books, a pair of cowboy boots and a wad of cash: keys to unlock the door of my teenaged small-town prison hell. The car broke down in Wawa.

My brother couldn't collect his money if he didn't arrive in Hamilton. And I could not get to Toronto. So I paid for the parts, the repairs, the motel. It looked like a safe investment. But now I was broke.

We arrived in Hamilton on a Thursday afternoon. There was a delay in the Manpower office, some misunderstanding, a crucial bit of paperwork lost, whatever. We had to wait until Monday for the money. We took a single room in a rooming house and promised to pay when the money came in. My brother, the slick talker.

We had no food, not enough nerve to beg and too much pride to go to the Sally Ann. But we were not too proud to pick cigarette butts off the street and strip them for the tobacco. I carried rolling papers then. We sat in the room and we smoked.

You get tired when you don't eat. You can't think clearly. You stay tired all the time. You play cards. You play stupidly. You quit playing cards. You flip cards into a wastebasket. You get tired of gathering the cards off the floor. You know you can't stay in your room forever. The room starts to smell. You need to get some air. You go out for a walk, but you can't walk far if you haven't eaten much.

I found a horse chestnut on a lawn – don't you ever try to eat one – which is why, years later, I knew that the old lady gathering nuts on the neighbour's lawn was not hungry, but was driven by some other need.

My brother got the money on Monday. Not as much as he'd hoped, but enough for the next leg of the journey. We bought breakfast in a restaurant across from city hall. I ordered like a guy who'd just got out of jail: waffles and ham, and pancakes and bacon, sausages and eggs, and keep the coffee coming. I left food on the plate. I felt rich.

We smoked tailor-made cigarettes afterward; brothers on the road, away from home, caught up in the adventure. We never paid for breakfast. We finished the last of the coffee. I walked out into the sunlight. He followed me, thinking I'd paid. No one, including the guy who ran the restaurant, was the wiser. We hopped in the car and sped out of town before anyone could stop us, a tax on the city of Hamilton.

We rewarded ourselves with a trip to Niagara Falls. I was old enough to drink on the American side. We took a room in a motel, got the key . . . and called the manager to come and change the wet and bloody sheets on the beds. He laughed; we're all men here.

"I guess they were flagging. Or maybe she was on the rag."

Was there ever any flagging in Fort William? We got drunk that night in a crowded bar. My brother got up to take a leak and took his drink with him. I, half-drunk, looked up and wondered where he was. I saw him on the other side of the room, a sheepish look on his face, shrugging, gesturing with his hands. His hands were shaking when he came back to the table. He'd bumped into a biker on the way to the can, and he'd spilled his beer down the biker's belly. He'd talked his way out of a beating by buying drinks.

The trip into Toronto the next night was the only time I ever saw my brother really scared. Too many lanes of traffic in the darkness going in too many directions too fast. We were pulled over on the highway for going too slow.

We stayed that night with a pal of mine. In the morning my brother said he'd pay me back for the repairs, and then for good measure he borrowed some money from my friend, and he promised to pay that back, too, when he got settled down. He hit the road and left me penniless.

He never settled down.

My friend – I'd gone to school with him, we'd played football together, his father and my father were mailmen – had an apartment in a half-finished high-rise on the lower lip of downtown.

A sweet deal – the builder needed cash so he rented finished apartments to students while the rest of the building was being completed. I slept, I think, on a couch.

There were plenty of girls in the building. They, too, were saving on rent. I was shy and shy was good, and in my case it was not an act. There was sleeping on various couches.

It took six weeks to find a job, a long six weeks of not holding up my end, not stocking the larder, not paying my way.

And then suddenly I had a choice of jobs.

I'd taken a bank exam; the woman who interviewed me afterward said she'd never seen a score so . . . she left the sentence unfinished because it weakened her position. She offered me work then and there.

I knew Raymond Souster worked in a bank. This meant banks were safe for poets. I told her I'd think about it over the weekend. At the same time, I was offered a job as an office boy in an ad agency. I took the agency job at fifty dollars a week. It seemed the more creative choice.

The money was a fortune; that is to say, sufficient to allow me to pay back what I owed, and to pay my share of the rent, and to go to the movies on the weekend or buy a mickey of rye whenever anyone old enough was going to the liquor store; one or the other, not both.

My first day on the job I was not exactly drunk.

My father was passing through town early on his way to Cleveland. He was going to see his sister – his vacation was a way of giving my mother a break. I knew he was coming through. He phoned during a layover at the bus station. I brought him to the apartment for a cup of coffee.

He'd brought a shoebox full of cupcakes that my mother had made the day before. He pulled half a bottle of gin out of the pocket of his trench coat. We put gin in the coffee and ate the cupcakes.

I poured him back on the bus two hours later, and I poured myself on the subway; he on his way to Cleveland, me on my way to work.

I learned later the people who ran the agency thought I was a confident young man. In truth I was a small-town boy with a snootful who had no confidence at all.

The small-town disease: I thought everyone else was smarter than me. I didn't go to the Riverboat or the Bohemian Embassy or Grossman's, not because I wasn't old enough. I thought I stank of the bush. I thought people would make fun of me. I was desperate not to be embarrassed.

A curiosity: Hippie kids begged. I had pride. I was raised to work.

Kids were flooding into Yorkville on the weekends. All that spare change spent in joints, on joints. The smell of dope was sweet. The cops harassed the kids. Rising to their defence, fresh out of law school and keen to make his civil-libertarian bones, was Clayton Ruby.

Now we have squeegee kids and tribes of punks who sleep in ditches or under bridges with their girlfriends and their dogs. They don't beg in the strict sense of the word. They offer to clean your windshield with dirty water for money. Or they glare at you from behind their begging bowls, or rather their paper coffee cups. The cops harass them. They are defenceless. *Où sont les rubis d'antan?*

I rode the subway every day to work at Yonge and Eglinton. All the girls in town wore miniskirts. To pass by the tower on the southwest corner – that tower is still there – was to look up the glass façade and see the long legs of the young girls in their short skirts riding up the escalator, and when the escalator got high enough you could see Paris, France, and underpants. It didn't do to linger, but it was a brief pleasure, a momentary thrill; there was nothing like this at home.

Where is home?

Between your ears.

At the agency, a dilemma: J., a tall, willowy New Zealander, made a play for me. She was twenty-seven. I was nineteen. The difference in age seemed huge. She was a woman. I was a boy. She was sophisticated. She also used to ambush me in the stationery cabinet, and she'd put her hands on me and make me hard. I didn't know what would happen if I resisted. Not that I was interested in resisting . . .

At the same time, a man named Doc made a play of his own. He was tall, slim, an account executive with a shock of blond hair; he was devilish, à la Vincent Price. He was older than J. He, too, used to put a hand on my waist. He let me know, in so many words, what he wanted when he touched me. I didn't think I could tell him to fuck off. I thought if I did, I might have been fired. Times change, huh? I resisted with what I thought was tact.

I did not resist J. She invited me to her place on a Friday night, to get to know me better. She met me at the door of her apartment in a silky green pyjama suit. I think I brought flowers; how sweet. She grilled lamb chops for breakfast.

Not long after that, Doc invited himself to my apartment. I still don't know how that happened. I warned my roommate not to go out, and I explained why. He shook hands with Doc, stayed for a drink, decided on his own that everything was fine and he left me alone with the wolf.

Doc flirted and cajoled. He took my hand and said he'd like to read my palm. He traced his finger over my skin. Here was a line I did not wish to cross.

In the north, I would have smashed his face.

I tried to remember what it was that the girls said to me when they turned me down. I told him I had a headache, said I got migraines, said they came on suddenly, said they made me ill, said I had one now, said I thought I was going to be sick.

Doc, bless him, went home.

We never spoke of it again, nor did he try to pay another visit. He kept his hands to himself from then on. On occasion, at the office, he smiled at me as if we shared a wistful secret.

There were mornings on the weekend when, in the absence of roommates who'd gotten lucky and hadn't yet come home, I had the apartment to myself. On those mornings I would head for Kensington Market.

I bought Portuguese sausages, bagels and fresh eggs, and on the way home I bought the weekend papers. I made fat breakfasts and I read the news, and I put rye in my coffee and smoked cigarettes and felt like I'd arrived. I wish I could feel like that again.

The market was a souk, an agora, a bazaar of used clothes, fresh fish, cheap pots and pans, spices and oranges, jokes and insults, live ducks and rabbits. One morning when the air was cool and the streets were wet and fresh and the bloody water in the gutters hadn't started to stink in the heat, a woman waved. I looked around to see who she was waving at. She said, "Are you Jewish? You look Jewish. A nice boy like you, are you married? I've got just the girl for you!"

I was flattered that she thought I was a Jew.

The city was filled with Union Jacks that year, and there were cakes and ales in all the shops and birds in miniskirts and jerks wearing mod clothes who faked English accents in order to get laid, and some of them were English, and they had MGs and they did get laid. British Week. I never understood it. I thought the city had been duped. I still do.

One night, alone in the apartment, I heard voices. I heard them so clearly I went through the apartment room by room. The voices stopped.

Then they started again.

I went out for a walk. The streets were dark; midnight. The people on the sidewalks looked like so many ghouls. I went to

Sam the Record Man; ghouls pawing over the discs. I went into a bookstore; ghouls poring over the books. I dreaded going home, in case the voices were still talking.

I passed by the wrought-iron fence in front of Osgoode Hall. A ghoul lurched out of the darkness with a knife in his hand. The ghoul was drunk. The knife shone in the darkness. I still have no idea if the ghoul was real. But I kept an eye on the knife, and on him, and I kept on walking; when I passed the point of danger, I ran home, fearful that the voices would still be there; mercifully quiet.

I have had cabin fever since then. You don't get it from cabins.

Sutton Place opened that year; a luxe hotel. On the first night, a low-level thug named Meyer Kahane had his bed blown up underneath him as he slept in the penthouse; a mob hit – Kahane, ka-boom – except he survived.

I knew I was in the big city then. The only things that got blown up in Northern Ontario were rocks; and there were no penthouses anywhere between Toronto and Winnipeg.

I left to work in the bush where the money was better.

It took me thirty years to get back, by way of Gillam, Ibiza, Fort William, Iqaluit, Regina and Montreal; you know what they say: The way to Toronto is Toronto.

Sorry, Catherine of Siena. No, not very.

FIFTEEN

A crime may not be the whole story of a human life.

– EDWARD L. GREENSPAN, *Greenspan: The Case for the Defence*, 1987

Dan Guilford was wearing an orange jumpsuit when he walked into the prisoners' side of the visitors' room in the Metro West Detention Centre. He sat on a bench in front of a long low window and picked up the phone on the desk.

The guard closed the door.

Dan smiled. His youngest sister, Josephine, was on the other side of the glass. Dan has a helluva smile. He lights up a room. He's missing a front tooth. Josephine picked up the phone.

She said, "Daniel."

He pressed the phone to his ear. The phones are no good in jail. You can't hear a thing. Nobody cares. If you wanted to use the phone, you should have stayed out of jail.

Dan said, "I hear I'm going in the morning. I also hear I'm going maybe late at night. I just don't know. I don't know anything."

Josephine was upset. She tried not to let it show. Dan was about to be deported. He'd been picked up by Immigration a week earlier. There was nothing his sister or anybody else could do. He was headed for Guyana. Dan is no more Guyanese than I am.

His story is particular to the city:

He came to Canada as a boy. His father preferred cold rum to hard work, so his mother did what women do. She fled with the kids and came to Toronto. She wanted a new life. She did not get a long new life. On arrival she took a job keeping house for a lawyer and within a year she died; cancer.

Little Dan was in deep water then, cut loose from any mooring. He had no one to help him; no mum, no dad, no one he could talk to.

His oldest sister gathered him and the other kids, and she moved everyone to Regent Park. She tried to keep the family together. Dan was in shock. "I felt different from the other kids. I didn't know why."

It's not hard to figure out why: He was a black kid in a strange country with a dead mother, a drunk father and an older sister out of her depth.

Dan went to school. He made new friends. Some of his new friends drank and smoked so Dan began to drink and smoke. He grew up fast and hard. He learned to shoplift. He learned the ins and outs of break and enter. He wasn't very good. He got caught. He did it again. He got caught again. He said, "My older sister tried to discipline me. She was really strict. She wanted me in at eight or nine at night, when it was still light." That was never going to work.

And then she did what she felt she had to do. She got married. "Her husband used to beat me. He used his fists, his belt, whatever. He treated me different. If I was five minutes late, they'd lock me out."

A kid in his teens on his own in Regent Park?

"I'd roam the street at night. I'd sleep in cars or in stairways. Sometimes a friend would take me home and feed me. I didn't want anyone to know my situation. I'd walk my friends home and pretend everything was okay, but I'd spend the night on the street. Who else was I going to meet but prostitutes and drug dealers?"

He got kicked out of school. He began to break into houses at night and naturally he got caught. He started to use drugs. He learned when to follow the postman, and how to pluck the new credit cards out of the mailboxes, and what he had to do in order to activate the cards, and how to fence the things he bought with the hot credit cards to get money for drugs. He also figured out how to get handguns, and he used them to knock off corner stores to get more money for drugs.

He isn't proud of any of that. He can't undo it.

And he knows it doesn't count for much that he never shot anyone. He paid for what he did with hard time. He did his time without complaint. He does not feel sorry for himself. He rues what he did to others. When we met, he was thirty-two years old, and he'd spent eighteen of those years in jail.

Somewhere along the line, someone figured out that Dan was not a Canadian citizen. His mother – she clearly had other things on her mind – had died of cancer before she could arrange it. Dan didn't know he wasn't a citizen; he had no way of knowing and no reason to guess.

Even if he had known, he wouldn't have been able to figure out what to do. He was either too young, or too busy trying to stay alive, or too messed up, or too locked up.

He'd made plenty of mistakes since he came to Toronto – when I saw him in jail, it was not the first time he'd worn orange, although it was the first time he was behind bars for a sin of omission, as opposed to one of commission. But his debts were long since paid, and he had kicked his habit nicely.

He cleaned up in jail, and he got normal in a halfway house in Brampton. He had to board a bus and come into Toronto dutifully on Friday mornings. When he got to the corner of

Keele and Dundas West, he'd stop for fruit juice in a neigh-bourhood coffee shop. The juice helped; as soon as he felt the urge for a washroom, he would walk over to the government building on the corner.

The building houses a peculiar and unlikely mix of tenants: postal workers, therapists, criminologists on the lower floor; and on the top floor are sex offenders who are trying to re-enter life in the community. Once inside, Dan would take a specimen bottle from a clerk and go to the washroom to prove that he was clean.

Dan was a dilemma.

For better or for worse, he was one of us. We made him what he was, and we spent plenty of time and money cleaning him up, turning him around and making him a Canadian. He picked up a trade in jail. He became a mechanic. He had a job, off the books, in a garage in Brampton. He was working hard. He was sticking with his program. Rehab looked good on him. But he was not a citizen, so he had no business here.

There are no methadone programs in Guyana. The doctor who helped him beat heroin was not given any time to wean Dan off methadone, you can't quit that stuff cold, and Dan could not fly to Guyana with a stash of the drug and a needle in his kit. He'd be a marked man.

He did not know what would happen to him once the plane touched down. He gave in just a bit and said, "I'm going to a life of misery."

He gave Josephine some instructions over the phone: "Go to the halfway house. I want my boots. They cost four hundred dollars. They gotta come with me. And get my teeth. They're in a drawer. That's it: the boots and the teeth. And I want to bring my bike. I'll take it on the plane. My bike. It's mine. The rest, we'll see when I get settled – my tools and such. Immigration has my car keys and my ID. You'll have to sell my car. It's worth three thousand dollars." He ran out of words.

Josephine said, "You have to be positive and strong."

Dan's voice broke then. He said, "People are trying to help me. It's beautiful. I'm seeing support I never had in my life."

Josephine said, "I think there's a family who'll take you in down there. Maybe they can help you with a job. We're looking into that."

Dan wiped his eyes. His voice got harsh. "I'm going to be almost dead. I can't go to people I don't know and be sick in their house. I'll be puking for six months." That's what it's like, kicking methadone cold.

Josephine said, "I'll get you some shampoo, Tylenol, tooth-brushes, some gum and cigarettes. We already got some of your clothes, they're being laundered now. Think of it as an adventure." He smiled.

She said, "We have to learn to take it and turn it around. Don't have dark thoughts. If it's happening, it's because it's a test. It's Daniel in the lion's den. You may even like it down there. It's not a done deal that it's going to go bad."

"It's fear of the unknown," said Dan.

The guard came. Dan stood up and tried a smile. Josephine watched him go. She would see him at the airport. A small bit of grace. At least he was not deported in an orange jumpsuit.

You probably get too much of Toronto's news where you live. I don't disagree. Our hard copy is easy copy, available on the wire services to fill out your local rag. Our stories are sensational. We happily supply the photos.

The big city is the outside world for those who are trapped in small towns with no radio stations, no daily papers, no bookstores.

And so the world is smaller than it used to be. Don't blame us. And don't get us wrong. Our own air is rank with the stink of big money, big politics, big celebs. We're fed up, too. But if you think you know us through big crime, you're dead wrong.

The College Park Courts is where petty crime runs headlong into petty punishment like an all-day highway pileup: bang, bang, bang. That's entertainment. I go to this court now and then because I like to take my lessons from the smaller stories.

Behind the bench one day sat a solid, no-nonsense judge with short thick yellow hair. She was crisp and direct, and she had a full docket. On the day I watched her work, it was obvious she saw that her duty was to clear the cases that came before her.

The quality of her mercy would not be strained; she might drop it like the gentle rain from heaven, and now and then she might drop it like a hammer. She was reading documents in a file when a court cop led three women to the prisoners' box.

The box is narrow and the walls are Plexiglass. The women were wide through the hips. As they entered it looked like they were holding hands. They were not. They were cuffed together at the wrist. To enter the box, they had to do an impromptu, sidelong shuffle; not unlike the sight of a Motown girl group rehearsing a tricky dance step.

Girl One, a sullen blonde teen, pleaded guilty to a breach of probation, the breach not her first. The details? She was picked up in a stolen car at 3:35 a.m. At the time of her apprehension she was subject to a 10:00 p.m.–7:00 a.m. court-ordered curfew. She was given ten days, plus probation. She smirked; ten days, the merest inconvenience.

Girl Two was held over because some paperwork related to her case was missing; the lawyers on both sides had a variety of reasons why this was so; blah, blah, my honourable friend, blah, blah. At the sound of which, Girl Two half-turned and mouthed a theatrical, "Oh, fuck."

Girl Three was ready to plead to a charge of causing a disturbance when she, too, was held over for administrative reasons.

The women were re-cuffed and led away.

As she left the court, Girl Three smiled saucily at her boyfriend. He had been seated in the audience, watching, fretting. She mouthed, "Don't worry." He smiled at her. He was worried.

We are all worried here. What will become of us, what will happen to our daughters and our sons and ourselves?

Then came a sleepy-eyed hooker with a chip on her shoulder. A chippy chippy, she had been drinking in a bar when the police arrested two drunk men, friends of hers. She took umbrage and swore at the cops; was advised to stop; did not.

As the rest of the details were read out, she turned her head and mouthed a silent "Bullshit." And she pleaded guilty. You hurt me, but you can't make me cry.

She got a fine of two hundred dollars, more money than she generally earns for the slick use of her tongue. She was given six months to pay; she could earn that in a night. She was given probation for a year, an irrelevancy if she is not caught bending to give someone comfort in the night for cash. And because she happened to be three months pregnant, she was given a caution by the judge to deal with her drinking problem. Want to bet she won't?

What will become of her child?

Next up was a crack addict whose day job was installing carpets. He was picked up one night while lurking behind a house with a kitful of tools not usually associated with the installation of broadloom: a flashlight, a pair of tin snips, a screwdriver and some sidecutters. In a way, he was going to work when he was caught.

He was charged with breach of probation, possession of burglar's tools, and also two separate counts of theft under five thousand dollars. One of the thefts involved a bag of women's clothing that had been taken from a Zellers store; the clothes were in his truck. I love my wife, too; but not enough to steal from Zellers.

I imagine he was going to sell the clothes and buy fresh crack. The judge asked if he had anything to say. He said, "I want to beat all my problems and stuff." I'm sure he does.

He got five months in jail, two years' probation, an order to keep the peace and another to seek drug counselling. He was also banned from Zellers, where I presume any Club Zed points he might have had were automatically voided.

Next in line was a sprinkler installer who stole a bicycle and pawned it for fifty bucks. He had a knife in his pocket when he was nabbed. He, too, is sorry. He got a day in jail, probation for a year, and an order to make restitution for the bike, and he had to surrender his knife so it could be destroyed.

So it went: This man was charged with assault; that woman was drunk and disorderly; the next man agreed to own or possess no guns, crossbows or explosives, a useful precaution because he has anger-management problems and he happened to be in the midst of a sticky divorce.

Then came an oddly compelling case: A homeless man, charged with theft under five thousand dollars, and possession of burglar's tools. Which is to say, he was nabbed with six dollars in his pockets, the money all in coins; and in his hand, he had a single bristle from a city street sweeper.

It was revealed to the court that some of Toronto's more enterprising homeless are able to open city parking meters with those bristles; although, as the judge pointed out, if this man had been really enterprising, he would not have tried to do so under the watchful eye of an official from the parking authority.

Alas, we have few parking meters left now; they have been replaced, at least downtown, by solar-powered obelisks, one per block, which eat money and dispense receipts. So far, no one has figured out how to crack them open.

We live in hope.

In addition to being homeless, the man who cracked the parking meter and took the coins said he had a personality disorder. He told the judge he had not seen his psychiatrist recently. "Not since the Harris cuts."

The judge with the bright yellow hair was moved, perhaps by such astute political analysis, to give the man a day in jail, two years' probation, an order to seek psychiatric counselling and another to reside in a place approved by his probation officer.

She smiled and said the latter judgement was predicated on the assumption that the man's probation officer would help him find a suitable place to stay. Justice done. And seen to be done.

Up yours, Mikey Six-Toes.

Harris hurt us deeply. One person who knew better than most how badly we got hurt was, improbably, a former fashion model.

The Honourable Hilary Weston, the lieutenant-governor of Ontario, owner of Holt Renfrew, and wife of billionaire grocer Galen Weston, was charged in her official role with cutting all the ribbons and attending all the openings, not just cultural.

She took it upon herself to attend every soup-kitchen social function and to show up at every street-level, volunteer-run social services storefront bunfest. She shook all the grimy hands, and the men and women who were hungry, who were crazed, who had lost hope, would line up to see her as if she were a rock star, to beg her: "Help us."

At first she seemed horrified.

She is of that class which is so wealthy it is above all class. I covered a few of these affairs. I saw the experience change her over time; her shock was gradually replaced by compassion.

I know of one instance when the director of a shelter for homeless kids was on the verge of giving up his job because there was not enough grant money to balance the books; he could cut the cleaning staff, or he could cut some of the programming, or he could sacrifice his salary. I have it on good authority that the Honourable Hilary coughed up a large sum of her own money.

Back in College Park:

In the corridor, during a recess, I fell in with a man wearing clean jeans, a neat shirt and cowboy boots. He was in good shape, tanned and muscled like a farmer; his wrists, thick as his forearms.

He looked out of place amid the pale hookers, the lawyers with bad haircuts, and the skinny junkies on the nod. "Fucking court. I think it's a waste of fucking time."

He was not utterly wrong. Sometimes court is nothing more than show up now and come back later. I asked him why he'd come, and he said he was going to defend himself on a charge of assault.

I raised an eyebrow.

"My neighbour, one day he comes running at me like he wants to fight, so I grab him by the hair and throw him on the ground. And he gets up and calls the cops."

"Why did he come after you?"

"My neighbour has a yippy little dog, it's got some internal problems, pancreas or something; it shits all over the yard behind the rooming house, and he don't clean it up. It stinks really bad. I can't barbecue back there or nothing. So I called the city."

"And?"

"The city comes, and he gets a ticket for not cleaning up after the dog. The ticket was thirty-five bucks or whatever, he's not too happy about that. So the next time I see him, he comes at me like he wants a fight. So I threw him on the ground."

"Why throw him down?"

"I couldn't wait to let him hit me. See this? I got wires and mesh all through here, my cheek and my forehead. I can't get into any fights. I get hit in the face, I'm done."

"How'd that happen?"

"A tractor fell on my head."

"A tractor?"

"My old man's farm in Cape Breton. I went back to help him out. I was changing a tire, and it tipped over. I almost died."

"A tractor on your head? I guess you'd almost die. It must have hurt."

"I don't remember it much. I remember thinking I was gonna die. They got me to the hospital and rebuilt my face. I crushed my esophagus, but they couldn't do nothing about that."

There was a lull. He remembered the tractor. I considered what that might be like, face down in the dirt, tractor on your head.

"You working?"

"No, I can't work. Hell, I can't even eat, not solid food."

"So what do you eat?"

"Ensure."

"That's all? A protein drink? How much do you drink?"

"They give me twenty-five cases a month, but it's not enough. I can go through a case of that stuff in a day; sometimes more."

"How many cans in a case?"

"Twelve."

"I guess you drink it cold."

"It's gotta be cold, but not too cold or it hurts my throat."

"What's the best flavour?"

"Strawberry."

"Do you miss solid food? How long has it been since . . . ?"

"Coupla months. I thought I would miss food but I don't, really. Well, I really miss moose. I could eat a moose steak this big."

"Not too many moose here. Where'd you grow up?"

"Regent Park."

"Rough?"

"Not really. I mean, yeah, it was rough. But if you had to fight it was one guy against one guy, come on, show me what you got. Now it's all gangs."

"Think you'll go back to the Maritimes when you get done with this court stuff?"

"Ah, nah. I don't get along with my old man. I'm home from the hospital a week, my throat's all crushed, he says he wants me in the bush cutting wood. I don't think so."

"How's the court case going?"

"I'm waiting to get disclosure or something; some papers or something. Then I gotta come back here and get another court date. I'm gonna beat it, no problem."

"What about your throat? Can they fix it?"

"I'm gonna have an operation. They're going to stick something down there, it'll widen my esophagus if it works. I have to sign some kind of waiver. I guess if it goes wrong, they don't want to end up in court."

Who does?

Regent Park is rough but no neighbourhood is safe.

We all worry about our kids. Life's not what it used to be. It is not just the core of the city that is difficult.

The houses around East York Collegiate are built, for the most part, in the early 1940s; stolid, square, two-storey Toronto houses with walls of mottled brick: tan, brown and orange. The front yards, uniformly neat; monkey-puzzle trees on most lawns.

There is a lawn bowling club nearby, and a library and tennis courts; the Christmas concert at the church down the street was called "The Wondrous Story." Stabbings don't happen in a neighbourhood like this. Things change.

A kid named Dru Stewart died in a doorway in front of a little Thai restaurant near East York Collegiate. He was swarmed and beaten and stabbed to death because he stepped forward and stood up for a girl who was being hassled by a crowd.

There was a floating vigil afterward, clusters of kids coming and going from class, chips on their shoulders, smokes in hand, blocking the entrance to the restaurant. The kids milled around and listened to some pop dirge on a boom box, hugging each other and scowling. Their friend was dead.

A mound of tributes had piled up in the doorway – guttering candles, wilting flowers, tins of pop and bags of candies; a few meat patties in their paper sacks, and a Styrofoam burger container because he liked meat patties and he liked burgers.

Across Coxwell Avenue, a shopkeeper watched idly from his front window. "This is a nice neighbourhood. Oh, sure, a few years ago the kids from the school were throwing snowballs at passing cars. But it's gotten harder around here lately. Drugs creep in. The kids smoke on the street, in broad daylight. Some days, you walk by, the smell is so thick."

That's life here now.

An older lady wearing a yellow ski jacket said, as she walked past, "This is a hard time for young people. There are so many temptations. It makes you frightened for your children." There was a soft burr in her voice, the trace of a childhood spent in Scotland. That burr, the sound of old Toronto.

New Toronto is Emmanuel Manolakakis. He runs a martial arts school on Coxwell. He lives nearby. "This is a great neighbourhood. I have a young family. But the kids from the school at lunchtime, they hang out. You can feel the tension. It seems as if it's been building for the past six months." The tension had now exploded in the worst possible way.

Someone had sprayed "RIP Dr. Dru" in black paint on the side of the wall of a small dental clinic nearby. There was a hand-lettered sign taped to a wall near the doorway where Andrew died. The sign read, in part: "We cannot tell what may happen to us in the strange medley of life. But we can decide what happens in us. How we can take it, what we do with it and that is what really counts in the end. How to take the raw stuff of life and make it a thing of worth and beauty. That is the test of living."

It is a test, I suppose. But when the raw stuff of life is the blood and the guts of your friend, the real test was whether those who knew the killers would come forward.

The kids eventually passed the test.

Inside the Thai Fusion restaurant, Csilli Klungphutsa and her cousin, May Rojcharoenkul, sat helplessly in the afternoon, watching the crowd of sullen mourning teens who blocked their doorway.

Csilli and May came here two years ago from Bangkok. They opened the restaurant five months ago. On an average day, they might have served a couple of dozen lunches. On this day they made three lunches to go, and they served one plate of pad thai to a diner who was bold enough to push his way past the crowd of kids and come inside.

Of the kids, May said, "We can't ask them to leave. We don't want to hurt their feelings. Right now, they are sad."

Csilli said, "I saw the boy after he came here. I was downstairs. I heard something happen. I came up. May said, 'Don't look, a lot of blood!' I don't like to look, but I don't believe her and I looked. I was dizzy when I saw the blood."

May said, "Before he fell he took off his coat. I saw his body bleeding here, and here, and here. It happened very fast. We were shocked. We can't move. I vomited. We were scared."

Csilli said, "Later on, we went to the Thai temple."

"We are Buddhists," said May. "We bring teenaged food to the temple, like pop, chips, bread and jam, chocolate, cornflakes."

Csilli said, "We bring these things to send the boy to heaven."

May said, "We pray so he can be at peace."

"I have a teenager," said Csilli. "I tell him to do right. You know how, when something happens, mothers talk. When I saw that boy, I thought of my son." We all think of our children now.

Two beat cops came into the restaurant as we were thinking about our sons. The cop with the brush cut gestured to the crowd of kids in the doorway. "Did you ask them to move?"

"No."

"They're blocking your door."

"They're sad."

"You don't need kids hanging around your door."

"It's okay," said May and Csilli.

It wasn't okay then. It isn't okay now.

Three martyrs, ascending into heaven. You know their names: Farah, Holly, Cecilia.

They are saints because they were children. They are martyrs because they were killed to slake our lust, our greed, our jealousy.

Farah Khan was five years old. Her father slashed her throat and cut her up into manageable pieces and stuffed her in a bag and dumped her by the water's edge with the help of his second wife.

He had a violent temper. He was insanely jealous of his first wife. They were married in Pakistan. She became pregnant. They separated before Farah was born.

The elders in their village – may they bow their heads in shame – awarded custody of Farah to her father; a ruling of sharia law. But Farah's father suspected that this girl was not his child. He was sure his first wife had had an affair. Farah was brought to him here in Toronto, because the law is the law. He seethed with rage and shame.

He called his daughter names: "useless child," "bastard off-spring," "child of a dog." Once, Farah asked for ten dollars to pay for a package of photos from school; she was in kindergarten. He beat her with a shoe.

She weighed thirty-five pounds at the time of her death.

After he cut her throat and butchered her – he had a set of surgical tools – he dumped her body among the rocks along the shore of a west-end lakefront park. When he was arrested, he told police that Farah had committed suicide. He is in prison for life.

We hung our heads. This was some village thing, some dark medieval ignorance; this was not ours, yet the shame of it was ours, if only because Farah was slaughtered here.

Nothing human is alien to me.

Holly Jones was ten years old.

A mere four years after Farah died, while the smell of her death still lingered in the air, Holly was abducted, raped and strangled, cut up with a handsaw and stored briefly in a refrigerator before her body was stuffed into bags. The killer dumped the bags in the water off Ward's Island. There were dumbbells in the bags to help them sink.

The cops found her body the next day.

They knew that the killer had hauled her limbs and torso in a gym bag onto the subway, and from there out to the island on the ferry.

They searched Holly's neighbourhood thoroughly. They asked men who lived on the nearby streets to provide DNA samples by means of swabs. An unemployed computer programmer – a man who lived alone – was sympathetic. He said he hoped police caught the killer. He refused to give a swab. Detectives noticed a fresh smell in his apartment; they noticed new carpet on the floor.

They tailed the man for days. If he knew he was being followed, he was careless. He tossed a pop can in the trash. The cops seized the pop can and matched his DNA to that found under Holly's fingernails. He confessed quickly.

He is in jail for life.

Nothing human is alien to me.

Cecilia Zhang was nine years old.

One night, a few scant months after Holly died, Cecilia was abducted from her bed as she slept. Her family was stunned. The rest of us were sickened. The police were furious; they were also baffled.

Cecilia had been taken from the house by way of a second-floor window. The kidnapper clearly knew the layout; knew that her grandfather was in town visiting; knew Cecilia had given up her bed and was sleeping in a guest room.

No one in the house heard a thing.

There was no ransom demand.

Cecilia's father struggled with grief during the press conferences. He was handsome, young and well-to-do. His lank dark hair, his delicate features, his stylish leather jacket. He appealed to the kidnappers; his grief, his aching eloquence.

We held our breath.

The city smothered in silence; daily stories in the news; no news, no news. We looked inward; who among us did this? Grief counsellors in Cecilia's school; yellow ribbons on neighbourhood trees.

Her body was found five months later in a ravine near a river by a hiker. It does not do to dwell on the natural history of her remains.

Police think she was killed three days after she was taken; that's a guess. They arrested a man, a visa student; there are rumours that he had gambling debts.

Cecilia loved stuffed animals. She was good in school. She wanted to be a veterinarian when she grew up. She was exemplary in her selflessness. Near the ravine where her body was found is the Church of the Croatian Martyrs. We made pilgrimages there; we left a mound of cute stuffed animals; the flowers, the candles, the hand-printed cards of condolence.

Her memorial service was Pentecostal, lavish and uncomfortable; the church was packed with clergy, cops, politicians, family and friends; tear-streaked faces turned toward the light; the arms of weepers and mourners raised high.

Nothing human is alien to me.

There are memorials, scholarships and annual remembrances for each of these children. Holly's face is reproduced as a garish mural on the side of a wall in a park in the west end; her eyes big. I don't know why the mural is in this park. She did not play here. She was not taken from here. The mural frightens some of the children.

We all bear the shame. These murders happened here. We watch our children carefully. We teach them fear.

There ought to be a public memorial, not in any park but at city hall. Or perhaps at police headquarters. A stained-glass window; a triptych. The three martyrs. Or a stone pillar, with the names of our young dead.

There are many more children in this town who have died of neglect, who have fallen out of windows or from balconies, who were starved, or left unattended, or who were shaken to death.

We are haunted, baffled, fearful.

You can smell it in the air; these lives, these deaths are a part of the landscape of here, like a carpet of dry leaves on the ground in the fall.

Nothing human is alien to me.

Nor alien to you.

SIXTEEN

"I'll give you a nickel!"

– AN APOCRYPHAL DEPRESSION-ERA IMMIGRANT,
fresh from Europe and used to haggling,
when informed by the driver that a ride
on a Toronto streetcar cost ten cents

Fares for public transit are high, and ridership is low and getting lower; we drape our streetcars with full-bodied ads; our subway stations have been turned into giant indoor billboards; the revenue we get for this is peanuts; the cost is the loss of our brand name. Ride the Red Rocket? Your ad here.

I like the streetcar although it is slow and it is hell on other traffic; it stops, everything stops; it breaks down and nothing moves. But it is a civilizer of cars. We likely would not build a streetcar line today; there is no vision now. This is a driver's town.

Public transit is not for everyone. It takes thirty-eight minutes to get downtown from my place on public transit; the same distance takes eight minutes by car on the expressway. When traffic is moving.

But, in spite of the coughers and the wheezers and the guys who wipe their runny noses with their hands and then hold on to the handrail, I continue to take public transit. It gives me time to think.

A byline is a privilege. Writing is a pleasure. Time to think is the one true luxury of the newspaper man.

I don't pay much attention to the other papers.

I own the land-speed record for most newspapers worked for in the least amount of time. I do what I do. It gets me hired.

I try not to read the other columnists. Some days, it's unavoidable. One day Peter Worthington's daughter – he is a *Toronto Sun* columnist – was very nearly pushed off the platform in the bowels of a subway station, and into the path of an oncoming train. The pusher did not succeed.

Peter went on in his column about how dangerous it was around here these days. True enough, but it is dangerous precisely because our streets are sprinkled with the delusional, thanks to the triumph of the right-wing knife artists who slashed all those holes in the social safety net.

We don't have the money to look after people properly. We turn them loose. We expect they will find what they need in hostels, in shelters, in rooming houses. We expect they will take their meds.

That's the right wing in this town. They're nuts.

Bloor line, heading east, late in the day.

I found a wad of loose-leaf notes folded and tucked between the seat and the side wall of the subway car along with some crumpled candy wrappers. The person who wrote the notes and folded and tucked them away, and who then forgot what she had done, had also clearly nibbled and departed, lighter by the weight of a five-sheet sheaf.

I had nothing better to do, so I unfolded the notes, dusted off the chocolate-bar crumbs, and I read.

The notes may have been rough, and the handwriting may have been childish, but the notes told an eloquent story. I have edited for length, changed the names and left the spelling and grammar intact.

The writer is apparently a student of social work. She had been doing fieldwork:

Nick is a sing. father of 4 children. Lost wife 2 years ago. Thomas 9 Kerree 7 Nina 5 Sam 3 Nick 42 Grandmam 62. They live in town house located at Missussaga with 3 bed room 1 bathroom, kitchen, living room and basment with him lives his mother-in-law who help care for the children she is also an older lady who is not in good health she can not speak write or even understand how to use the telephone.

As a result of Nick's great demands he works full time job and his mother-in-law is left home care for the 4 children Nick is having a heavy work load there are many things go unoticed. My great concern is to childproof this hous.

As I look at the house room by room how has been kept you will understand my concern.

Kitchen: for such a big family the kitchen is very small as I look around. First I look at the old stove the knobs do not have much or any marking high, low, med. The fridges is small it doesn't work well water is leaking from it and leftovers are not stored properly which there are lot of that in there. Sink with dirty dishes. Toaster is very old doesn't pop up on it own with out manual power it burns and causes lot of smoke. sharp knife in lower drawer.

As a mother one thing I know is young children like to try new thing. This children could open the fridge and eat foods which is spoild, turn the stove and the bathroom tub is very dangers for young children, Dad's shaver hair dryer they could turn it on and hurt them selfs. Detergent. bleach. Sharp kneif could cut them.

Nick is a good friend of mine who is open to new ideas. Therfore I ask permision to do this assesment on his home and also allow me to take the safty measures in his home. It is all up to me to reduce these hazars in the house.

First the Grandmom is to old and not able to communate well withe the toddle who is in her care all day long. I have arange for the toddle to taken to a pre-school programe two days a week. In the mean time Grandmom goes to a senior group where she meets people who speaks both her mother tounge along withe English.

I also programe the most imporant numbers on the phone and lable them by colour's. Colour red emergency. Blue Nick's work. Yellow the next door person who speak her launge.

Kitchen safety measures are stove doesn't work have written temture on the high, low, medium mark on the knobs. So I had new knobs replaced on the stove. I also had him get a biger fridge in working condetion. I got bowls with lids to store all leftover in seprately. I arrange to have the two older kids help to wash dishes. The toaster is in the process of been repaired. I also had a fire distwicher placed in the kitchen.

Bathroom safety measures. All the taps that was driping had new washer replaced in the taps in both the sink taps and tub taps. On medican cabnet I put a lock. Also the hair dryer and eletric shaver are pluged out when they are not in use and stored in the bed room closet.

Bedroom: Dad has occupied one bedrom alone while Grandmom has the other and all four kids were on other, but what I have done put the girls in the master bedroom with Grandmom Nick now has the smallest bedroom by himself. The two boys are in the second largest. Most interesting everyone's belonging are kept in their own bed room, that includ toys, book, clothes, ect.

Laundry: I had all the unwanted stuff throw away. Nick build a cupboard in the laundry room to store deturgent and amniour. Nowe the laundry room is a total safe place even for the youngest child to go in and out off.

There was more.

But it is more of the same, and I could not bear to read it all. I folded the notes and stuck them in my pocket. I was thinking of Nick and the kids and the grandmam when I got off at my stop.

You think you know Toronto?

This is who we are.

Two young punks sat in the back of the Jane bus mouthing off, their gangsta talk making other passengers uncomfortable.

A young man asked them to keep it down. The punks pulled a gun and shot him, and a stray bullet wounded a young girl who was with her mother up at the front of the bus.

The police were looking for two young black men dressed in dark clothes. And this was what it was like on the Jane bus, the day after a shooting:

A young man ate fried rice with chopsticks; a middle-aged woman carried an armful of dry cleaning; a load of students carried stacks of books; and a couple of mothers had babies in prams.

There were no punks with guns, at least, none you could see; nor was there the easy laughter of strangers rubbing shoulders with each other at the end of the day. The working people of Toronto, tired and sad and thoughtful, were riding home in silence: past the pizza joints, the drugstores and the hair salons.

The mood was sombre, and the talk was of the shooting.

I sat next to a young black man who was dressed in dark clothes. He said, "There's a lot of ignorant people on this bus. You never know when something's going to happen." He looked sad. He said, "There's a lot of ignorant people."

It is a good thing not all of them are armed.

When the bus pulled up at Wilson Avenue, a young girl swivelled in her seat. She was wearing a fluffy pink parka that covered her head, but, oddly, did not cover her midriff. She gaped and pointed and said, "This is where the shooting happened."

No, dear, this was where the bus driver pulled to a stop with two people seriously wounded; this was where the driver did what he could to save two lives; and this was where some forty passengers – no, witnesses – scattered. I got off.

Two teenaged girls stood waiting in the shelter. They said, "We talked about the shooting a lot in class today. We're terrified it could happen around here. We don't know guys with guns. What were they doing with guns on a bus?" A strand of police tape fluttered in the grass nearby, a remnant of the shooting, or some other crime.

Two young black men in dark baggy clothes were waiting near the shelter. Jason said they ride the Jane bus every day. Sean said, in a voice which carried the sweet soft accent of St. Lucia, "I hope it don't happen when I'm on the bus." And Jason said, "It's one of the most messed-up things." It is, it is.

What is it like to be young black men on a day when the police are looking hard at young black men? Jason said, "People look at you, both black and white." Sean said, "I figure from the way they're looking, they're thinking about it and they are looking at you. I just feel sorry for the girl. Whoever did this should be dealt with justly."

I noticed a young boy sitting by himself on a nearby bench. He was reading the newspaper. He said his name was Meshach, so-called after the chum of Shadrack and Abednigo. He said he was thirteen years old.

"I think that shooting is horrible. Why would a big man shoot a young girl? Why did he have a gun in the first place? He shouldn't have no weapons," Meshach shook his head.

He said, "It's sad to think it could happen. I ride this bus every day. It could have been me." And then, quietly and directly, "My cousin was thirteen when he got shot in the head."

I fairly gasped.

Meshach pointed to his temple, and then to the bridge of his nose. "The bullet came through here, it went through here. My cousin, he lost his eye. That was four years ago."

No wonder he is worried about guns.

And what of the people who were witnesses to the shooting? Did he think they should come forward, spill the beans, rat if they had to? Meshach said, "People are scared right now. They think of what might happen if the guy with the gun comes to get them. But I say somebody should say something." He's right.

Someone should come forward.

So far, no one has.

And then Meshach stood up and folded his paper because his bus was coming and he said, "I pray sometimes when I go to bed. I'll say a little prayer for that girl tonight." And he got on the Jane bus and he took his paper with him.

I hope Meshach includes the bus driver in his prayers. The driver is a hero who tried to save two lives. The driver had to take leave from work because the scene kept coming back to him, the shock of it, the blood of two people on the floor of the Jane bus.

A few days later, John Rowell picked up a stubby piece of chalk, double-checked his notes and wrote some questions on the blackboard. He teaches English to new Canadians at Emery Adult Learning Centre. This was his second class of the day.

The sound of the chalk on the blackboard was soft. The students were from Asia, the Middle East, Africa and Jamaica. The questions were provocative.

Mr. Rowell wiped the dust from his hands and referred to the shooting on the bus. The questions: If you had been on the bus, what would you do now? How do you feel about co-operating with the police? Have you been a victim or a witness of violence? Has your experience with the police been good or bad? What can you do to improve the safety of your area?

Welcome to the big city.

The students broke into groups and began to talk among themselves. Joysie said, "I go to school, I go to work, I come home at midnight. My community is safe. But I suppose people should co-operate with the police."

Margaret said, "I'm at Jane and Finch. The young people are restless. They don't have enough to do. They feel left out. They want to make a name for themselves. We need role models to help them, to talk with them." The others in her group nodded.

She said, "When you see children by themselves, you don't know what they're thinking. Father working, mother working, no one coming home – television is training those kids!"

More nodding of more heads.

Jeff said, "I've been around Jane and Finch a long time. There's everything – drugs, guns, gangs, a lot of violence. A young child shouldn't keep late hours. Parents should be strict with curfew. Females should be more careful, maybe take a taxi at a late hour."

Eunice said, "People need to be co-operative with the police, and maybe we need more security cameras." I think she meant we needed cameras on buses, as well as cameras on the street.

Margaret could have used a camera in her hallway recently. She said, "I had an incident at my home. I was awakened around 3:00 a.m. A young man was standing outside my room. I said, 'Who are you?' He said, 'I'm looking for the chain man.' I didn't know what he meant, unless it's that my son sometimes repairs bikes. I said, 'Get out of here!' He said, 'Can I have some water?'"

This seemed odd to Margaret, too.

She said, "He took some water and rode his bike away. I called the police. On the way over they saw a boy on a bike with a bag full of stuff he stole from some car, so they caught him. It was not the boy in my house, but they did catch one. Me, I would co-operate with the police."

And then Mr. Rowell brought the whole class back together. He focussed the discussion and asked how many of the people in his class had seen or been a victim of some kind of violence.

A few hands went up.

He asked what they would do if they saw anything.

One woman said that, if she'd been on the Jane bus, she wouldn't have been able to talk because she'd have been in shock. Another said she would have taken notes and given them to the police.

And a young woman said she'd been at a basement party one night when someone started shooting. Her friend was struck by a bullet. He died in her arms. She didn't see the shooter. She said when the police came they treated her as if she were a

criminal; she was handcuffed and thrown in the back of a
police car.

She didn't trust the police.

A woman with children at home wondered about the roots
of violence. "The law in Canada causes kids to be bad. If you
take your kids in hand," – she meant, if you spank them when
they're young – "the Children's Aid is going to step in." She
added, "I have five kids – two are rotten, three are good." Rueful
smiles at this; most parents know it's the luck of the draw.

Another woman put up her hand and said, "In Nigeria, marriage is forever, so both parents are with the children. Marriage
is not a bed of roses. But beating your kids, that's bad."

At this, the class broke into applause, although it was not
clear to me what they were applauding for – the sanctity of
marriage, or the right to swat a brat; perhaps they were endors-
ing both.

And then a young man stood and said he didn't trust the
police because he'd been stopped once, just for walking down
the street one night with his hood up when it was cold.

In the end, about half the students said they'd co-operate
if they saw a shooting or a stabbing, while the other half said
they would be afraid to say anything for fear of retaliation.
And then the bell rang, and Mr. Rowell's students went off to
their next class. There is no Toronto but the one we make
together every day.

In the centre of town the rich ride north-south, and the poor
ride east-west. That's true as far as it goes. It goes pretty far.
Don't look at your map. Listen:

Two women heading home late after a long day's work,
sitting side by side, swaying gently, half asleep, heading east,

leaning on each other's shoulders, rocking with the rhythm of the train.

They passed the time with gentle talk, their voices low, no hurry now. The first woman said she lived in Scarborough but she went to work each day in Islington, at the other end of the subway line. In order to arrive on time she had to get up early in the morning, long before her children were awake. She tended another woman's house. She came home late five nights a week, long after her own kids had eaten supper.

The second woman said, Oh, my dear, I know what you mean.

The first woman said she couldn't afford to move from one side of the city to the other in order to be closer to her job, and she couldn't take the time to find a decent job closer to home. The second woman said, Oh my, that's hard, what are you going to do?

If it weren't for the Bloor line . . .

The north-south story is a little different.

A once-proud press lord – oh, how he blackened his name – told me that he phoned the mayor one morning after a snowstorm. Seems the press lord couldn't get his car out of the driveway. "And as you know," he said, "I have a very long driveway."

Yeah, me too; almost too long to shovel.

He said he had an important meeting downtown, he was going to be late, millions at stake, etc. Mel Lastman, the mayor of the day – yes, sir, right away, sir – sent a snowplow on the double.

That's what mayors do, is it not?

Did the press lord get a ride downtown? Nothing like it; turns out the driver of the plow dropped the press lord at the

nearest subway station, where the great man didn't have sufficient coin to purchase entry.

I doubt he knew the price. In any case, the price was no
impediment. He extracted his billfold, thrust a crisp hundred-
dollar bill through the wicket and said, "You're doing a fine
job, my good man. Keep the change!" Then he puffed up his
chest and burst through the turnstile, boarded a southbound
train and made it downtown in time for his meeting; disaster
averted. If it weren't for the University line . . .

I'm still a bit in awe of this city.

I'm not quite sure how I got here, even now. But I know how
to get around. If I leave the house with the daily paper under
my arm and a token in hand, I don't just feel well-heeled. I feel
like I belong.

The subway token is my ticket of entry, my passport, my
most valuable coin. I keep my tokens in a slim blue plastic
holder. I am the only guy I know who owns such a thing. I buy
tokens ten at a time. The holder has room for eight. This is an
annoyance up with which I put. If they ever do away with
tokens – I've heard those rumours – I will feel deprived.

I once saw Stuart McLean on the subway during the supper-
hour rush. He had a store-bought apple pie in hand. He
looked vaguely uncomfortable. He held the pie the way a
waiter holds a tray; he held the pie eye-high. I have no idea
why. It didn't matter. It just looked right. As if he'd stepped
out of *The Vinyl Café*.

And once, in the distant past, I saw the journalist Gordon
Sinclair waiting for a train on the platform in the St. Clair
station. It was a visual pun – Sinclair, St. Clair – and I wanted
to call across the tracks and tell him so but he looked too fierce,

as if he'd only just discovered that the station wasn't really named for him.

I half-laughed in his direction.

Middle-aged anger was funny in those days.

Not any more, it isn't.

I dislike depth as much as height, but I went underground when they built the Sheppard line. I spent an afternoon in the tunnel borer. It looked like a giant pop tin turned on its side, with a giant rotary slicer where the pull-tab would have been.

The slicer cut away the earth as the borer crept forward, and the loose earth passed through the guts of the borer and out the other end like so much excrement. When I ride the Sheppard line, I remember this with peculiar fondness.

It ain't all smiles on the subway.

I hate the squeal of the wheels when the train takes a curve, and the screech of the brakes when it stops; it hurts my ears. I don't like the punks who sprawl across two seats, or the yobbos who put their feet up. I hate all the litter on the floor.

And of course I hate the ads.

I once asked the transit boss if he were planning to wrap my subway trains in ads to make a few bucks. He looked at me with disapproval. I said they are my trains, dammit. I pay taxes; the trains are public property. He smiled painfully. He said nothing. He never said he wouldn't. He's done it now. We do that here. We sell ourselves too cheaply.

Remember the Luminous Veil?

An advertising company sponsored a portion of the cost of the veil, in order to get the rights to mount a massive video screen for the purpose of informing commuters about shampoo. Somehow, that idea never made it through council.

And what follows now is a subway story in the same way that *Moby-Dick* is a story about fisherpersons with artificial limbs. On the subject of which, I know a woman who taught the hoary old whale tome to her creative-writing class, and the student persons dismissed it out of hand because the hero was "bad to the environment."

How the mind wanders, wind-tossed, on such seas.

I was in a hurry, but a man on a train is a captive and so I succumbed to a kind of enforced leisure with a copy of the *New York Times*. I do not buy this paper every day, but it is a pleasure for its coverage of the Yankees and also for the excellence of its crossword puzzle, which is better than the puzzle in my own paper, and which increases in difficulty as the week progresses. I had the Friday edition. My brows were knit.

5 down: Ab __ (from the beginning).

As any schoolboy with a smattering of high-school Latin knows – or remembers sooner or later; later in my case – the answer is "*ab initio*." I was filling this in when a tall slim young man with the posture of a question mark got on board.

He sloped toward me as the train pulled away. I was only vaguely aware of him, but I was quite aware that others around me were looking at him guardedly. There were not many seats left. He aimed himself in my direction and sat down by my side.

I suppose I must have seemed unguarded.

He was carrying one of those free newspapers, many copies of which were strewn on the floor of the subway car because a leviathan-sized segment of the population here is every bit as bad for the environment as peg-legged Ishmael.

The young man looked at me. I looked at him. I could see why the others were guarded. He was retarded or developmentally delayed or whatever the hell he was; certainly he did not seem as reserved or restrained or repressed as the rest of us.

He looked away from me, and he bent low over the cross-word in his paper. And then he looked up at me again, out of the corner of his eye, as if letting me in on the secret.

I gave him the smile of brotherhood – yes, sir, we are all in this together – and tended to my *Times*. He seemed to focus harder on his puzzle then, and he gripped his pencil and he did that thing with his tongue that kids do when they're thinking.

I continued thinking about my puzzle, not his.

He gave a little shiver of impatient concentration, and he made a show of holding his pencil over an unfinished clue. He looked sideways at me again with half a smile and then he frowned once more.

I don't always get the obvious clues.

He wanted help.

I forget what the word was, and I had no idea of the extent of his disability, but I remember leaning over and reading the clue aloud. It was fairly easy. I gave him the first letter. He filled that letter in. He wasn't sure about the rest of the word, so I told him what it was and he wrote the letters in the empty spaces, and the people around us were watching us and the train lurched forward again.

I was about to return to my *Times* when he did that little shiver of concentration again – there was just one word left for him – for us – to finish. We finished it. I congratulated him.

I thought we were done, but he quickly flipped a page and found another puzzle and he gave me his little routine once more.

The train pulled into my station then, and I got up and wished him luck and said I had to leave.

He smiled wordlessly.

I was making my way out the door of the train when I noticed him turn to a young woman sitting nearby. He held his paper tightly in his hands. He bent over and did that little frown-then-grin, and he stuck his tongue out and he looked at her. She sort of gasped.

I wondered if he did this daily, riding the subway with his paper and his pencil, posing a quick little puzzle for the rest of us. I wrote about him in my column. And I got a dozen notes from readers who said they'd helped him, too.

The long hard walls of the corridors make the Finch station a good place to hear a busker. All chords carom pleasantly here, but on this day my mind was on other things. It took a minute for the tune to register; a trite little ditty, the singer wishing he was homeward bound. The song, never one of my favourites. Stay or go, is what I say; yearning is a waste of time.

But a stray chord lifts your step, and the text of this song has subtext because, sooner or later on the subway, homeward is where all of us are bound. Ahead of me, a skinny gangly kid loped toward his destination. When he drew even with the busker, he stopped and, with a gesture, posed a silent question. The busker did not miss a beat. And so the kid chimed in on harmony.

For a moment I heard their voices twinned and intertwining. And then, after a verse and chorus, the kid loped off. A few steps more and I, too, drew near.

"That happen lots?"

"Not lots, but sometimes, sure, some people stop and sing along."

"He any good?"

"He'd have been more comfortable in G. I was in A."

There was something familiar in his voice. I couldn't quite place it. I was in a hurry, but I decided to keep the conversation going for a moment.

"You gig around a lot?"

"I did the Harvest Festival in Cobourg. I did Bancroft in the spring."

"Where are you from?"

"I was born in England. I came to Canada in '57. I used to be in a band. Maybe you know it. Edward Bear."

It took me a moment.

"Edward Bear, um, oh, Edward Bear. You had that monster hit, it was huge, it was, um . . ."

"The Last Song."

Sic public transit gloria.

SEVENTEEN

In Toronto – in Canada – it's frustrating sometimes to find that people ease up on ambition, that there isn't the same drive to make things happen. But while there isn't that sense of aggressive ambition here in Canada generally, there is . . . a sense of decency, a sense of fair play that makes it one of the nicest places in the world.

– AL WAXMAN, quoted in *TV Guide*, July 18, 1987

I was on holiday in Charlottetown the summer after Toronto's big snowstorm. I bumped into a guy on the street. We chatted idly, the way you do. He said he'd been to Toronto. I said oh, yeah, when?

Turns out he came here to drive one of the snowplows.

I said people made fun of us because we called in the army. He said well, it was a real mess. He said he worked around the clock.

He said the city treated him and the other volunteers very well. He got free tickets to see a Leafs game, and everyone applauded when the volunteers were introduced and that was a nice moment. He said there really was a lot of snow and he was glad to help.

He said Toronto was a nice town.

We don't laugh when the army fights your forest fires. We don't laugh when the army builds your sandbag dikes. Calling

JOE FIORITO

in the army was the best thing Mel Lastman did. Oh. You don't know Mel?

He was perhaps our most memorable mayor. To know him is to know us. How best to describe him:

Savvy? He came of age selling bruised fruit in Kensington Market, and then he made a fortune selling furniture and appliances on credit. He sold cheap, but the interest more than made up for what he lost on sales.

Cocky? He had not one but two sons by a woman who worked in his store. He kept the news from his wife. He paid his mistress to keep her mouth shut. He got a bargain. She got a one-time payment; peanuts.

Stupid? Mel's sons lived high on the hog, while his little bastards starved. They grew up and got mad and they sued. They lost, but we all now know that one of those boys looks more like his father than the real sons do.

Unlucky? He was hurt in the tainted blood scandal. He got Hep-C.

Opportunistic? On certain occasions, when he misspoke himself, his handlers blamed it on his medication.

Pushy? He threatened harm to a reporter who asked about his wife, who had been caught shoplifting a pair of pants.

Dumb? He fretted over the notion of a trip to Africa; he told a reporter he thought he might get boiled in a pot.

We elected him twice.

So who's stupid?

Mel came back to Kensington when a statue of Al Waxman was unveiled in a little park just off the Market. His driver pulled up in a limo. Mel sat, half in and half out of the back seat, his collar undone, his tie askew. He looked tired and emotional.

His speech was a mess. He stumbled and he squinted. He thanked everyone in the crowd. He thanked Al's lovely wife,

Sara. He thanked Al's lovely son Adam. He thanked Al's daughter, Tammhaba. Huh?

He blinked. He squinted. He was puzzled. Someone in the crowd called out, "Tobaron." That is Al's daughter's name.

Tobaron was absent. There was an uncomfortable silence. Mel looked up from his notes like a dog who hears a far-off noise. He looked down at his notes and he tried again. "Al's daughter, Tammhaba."

Someone called out loudly once again: "Tobaron."

Mel shrugged and laughed. "You said it, I didn't." And he continued with his speech. A good thing Tammhaba wasn't there. She might have cleaned Mel's clock.

When it was all over and he made his vague way off to some other engagement, you could see people digging each other in the ribs: "That's our Mel, you gotta love him."

No, you don't.

Al Waxman's statue represents a not-quite life-sized Al. Cracked a wag, "Everything in the Market is 20 per cent off!"

King of Kensington? Check the opening shot in reruns. He was eating peanuts. Solly Stern – he's the son in Max and Son Butchers – said, "He used to come into the butcher shop and study people. He'd buy a bag of nuts from the store on the corner and sit in that chair over there and watch the people." Al ate the peanuts. He watched the people. He got the character. He used the nuts in the opening montage.

A guy named Perry Rosemond created the series, although he demurred about the lead character: "I didn't create 'King.' I wrote a couple of pages. Al created 'King.'"

The idea for the show?

"It came out of the north Winnipeg gambling clubs. People go to church separately, but they'll gamble with anybody. It had to be multicultural. We made it a gambling club, we put it in

King's basement. Over time, the gambling disappeared. King was a maven. He could fix anybody's problem."

Al was not available to shoot the pilot, so the part was first played by the actor Paul Hecht. When the pilot was picked up, Al was there, and the part was never not his.

Rosemond reminisced: "I always had Al in mind. We were struggling actors together. In 1958, I shared a room at the Dentists' Fraternity House with Gordon Pinsent. We used to have acting workshops on Saturday mornings. That's where I met Al. He had taken lessons with Uta Hagen. Pretty soon, he was directing the workshops. After we finished, Gordon would paint portraits of the dentistry students for twenty dollars, and I would go sell shoes at Benny James' shoe store. But Al would go and get himself a shave." He was a star from the start.

Prior to the unveiling, I noticed two bums eating soup-kitchen sandwiches at a picnic table. Quebeckers, by their accent. One of them walked over to the still-wrapped statue and peered at the marker. His face lit up. He called to his hung-over pal. "Al Waxman! Y'a une ceremonie aujourd'hui." The clochards knew the King.

And the kid in the doorway across the street from the park? Michael Lin never heard of the King until they started preparing the site, but you could say he knows Al, and he gets the spirit of Al, as well as the rest of us.

Michael is in his teens. He came here with his family from Fuzhou, China. He speaks Mandarin, Cantonese, English and Fukinese. He wants to be a lawyer. Now, and for as long as he lives at home, the first thing he will see in the morning when he steps outside to go to school is Al.

If the King were alive today, he'd find the market mostly unchanged. Still for sale in the little shops are peanuts, pine-apples, rubber boots, tube socks, rayon shirts, cheap luggage, bedroom sets, oranges, coffee, empanadas. There are more bums than there used to be. There are more Chinese. Here's something which has not changed at all:

Michael Lin's father is a delivery man. His mother works in a restaurant. They had just bought their house. They were working hard to make ends meet. That's what families did in the old days. That's what they do now. They try to make a better life.

Michael watched the gathering crowd and said, "People are nice here. They help me out a lot. We borrow a Frisbee from the neighbour. Canada is a peace and freedom country. People have good manners. They are polite. If you bump into them, they say 'Sorry!'" Yes, we do.

Down the street from the Lins is the Jesus family. Julio Jesus was sitting on his porch, watching the unveiling. He has lived in the neighbourhood for forty years. He watched proudly. "I still see *King of Kensington* on TV. It's a very good show, even though it was made a long time ago. It's a natural, real-life show. Al Waxman was a nice guy. I used to see him in the neighbourhood. You could say he was a nice Jewish man."

There was something about Julio's accent. He laughed, "I'm Portuguese, but I speak with a Jewish accent. I know good Jewish men. I worked for years at the Haymishe Bagel Shop." Which means I have eaten the bagels of Jesus.

A pal of mine once saw Al Waxman at a country fair; Al, in a lull, was not above working a small stage. My pal and his pal, stoned and sitting at a picnic table, were far too fully aware of the irony of Al's presence not to giggle when they saw him walking across the field, smiling at everyone. Al waved at them and said, "Don't get too high on life, kids." The King would have said that, too.

Another thing about Al: he flourished early and flowered late but he never escaped Larry King. The King never wore a black shirt with a black suit jacket over a pair of designer jeans. No mineral water, no blue martinis for him. He was big, he was big-hearted, he was corny and sentimental. He was us. You could count on him when it mattered. He made some curious choices, but he put bread on the table. He never forgot who he was or where he came from.

Old Toronto, new Toronto.

Tom Mihalik raised the money for the statue. A fair chunk of the final tally came from his own pockets. He shrugged. He smiled. He said it was good for business.

I was talking to Tom in his clothing store one day. Tom sells job lots of designer clothes. He interrupted our talk to take a phone call. I heard his end of the conversation.

"Yes, my friend, how are you? I have everything you need. The suit, very nice, and two shirts. I'll throw in some nice ties. Don't worry – whenever you want I'll have them ready, my friend." Hmm. Movers buy Tom's suits; ditto shakers. I thought the caller must have been someone important. I nudged Tom.

He said, "That was a fellow who's been out of work a year. He has a job interview coming up. He should look nice. He has no money now. He'll pay me when he can." That's good for business.

When the merchants of the Market met to work out a plan for the statue, there was all kinds of business talk at first. Morris Leider was there. He runs European Sausage, a quaint old store with the sawdust on the floor and the coppery smell of cold flesh in the air and plenty of loud and happy butchers cutting and slicing and asking who's next; it is a front for Leider's giant sausage factory in the suburbs.

"I just signed a deal with the Turks. They want sixty metric tonnes of back bacon, smoked. It's a Muslim country. It's for the hotels."

Morris buys one hundred thousand pounds of meat and turns it into four hundred thousand sausages every month. At that moment, he was working on a deal to sell sausage to Korea. "I also ship hot dogs, ground beef and steaks to Cuba. I ship smoked hams to Jamaica at Christmas. I ship steak and sausage to Antigua, to the hotels. All over the world." Not bad for a kid who came from Ukraine to Kensington as a teenager with nothing but a hole in his pocket.

Frances Borg, who runs Sanci Tropical Fruits in Kensington Market, breezed into the restaurant, took off her coat and smiled at Tom; these two have known each other forever. Frances said, "I remember the day Tom got off the boat. He had such a beautiful blue suit." Tom was a boy when he got off the boat. He said, "The suit came later; when I got off the boat, I was lucky to have shoes."

Tom and Frances and half a dozen others observed that you can't say Al Waxman without thinking of the Market, and you can't say Kensington without thinking of the King.

And the King was dead. So what should we do?

Tom sat at the head of the table. He was just about to speak up when the owner of the café served coffee and cracked, "So, Tom – is this where you jump up and say you're the Prince?"

"No way," said Tom.

"He can't be the Prince," said Morris Leider. "I'll be the Prince – I was here before him!" Sensing the moment, Mike Colle called the meeting to order. He is the MP for Eglinton-Lawrence. He grew up in Little Italy, but he has Kensington roots – his mama used to bring him to the Market when he was a boy. He said, "Al Waxman through his art embodied the Market. We have to roll up our sleeves and commemorate his contribution. Where better than here? This was Al's home, his church, his synagogue."

Tom added, "This is really Mike's idea. We have to grab the opportunity to thank Al for those wonderful shows. Al was Kensington Market. He carried greatness with him, he was a superstar, a true Canadian – King of Kensington, that tells you everything."

At the far end of the table, someone said: "People come to Toronto from all over the world and because of Al – he was such an ambassador – they say, 'Where is this Kensington?'"

Ping Chiu, owner of Cheese Magic, is a man of few words. His roots may not run as deep in the Market as some, but he understands the Market, and the people of the Market, implicitly. During a pause, he said: "Al Waxman Park."

Morris Leider nodded his head. "I was thinking the same thing." Danny Zimmerman, of Zimmerman's, added, "The park, what's it called, Bellevue Square? If you can't change the name, maybe you could make a garden in the park and plant it with nice flowers, in Al's name."

"How big is the park?"

"Half a square block."

"Oh, the size of European Meats!"

"Ha, ha!"

Frances asked if there would be a statue of Al, or if there would be a bust, and someone said, "I don't figure Al for a bust. Al was not a bust man. He was a full-figure guy, if you know what I mean!"

Everyone knew what he meant.

EIGHTEEN

You're too old now, my dear.
And I'm too old too, my dear.
Our faces are full of flaws.
The truth bites into our beauty.

– ELIZABETH SMART

Milan and Dagny Mijovic have a lap dog, Timmy, a Maltese-Yorkie cross. The tiny dog is named, not for the Dickens character, but for the coffee shop in the Manulife Centre, where the three of them go every day for cakes and cappuccino.

This is not Europe and the Manulife Centre is not a piazza. But Milan and Dagny are elegant and charming, Old World and old school, and Timmy, who perches alertly beside them on his own chair, is no less *raffiné*. You smile to see them together.

Most days, they take their cakes with Ruth Cohen, who has an apartment in the building. Ruth brings her perky Maltese, Kelly. One recent Christmas their pleasant afternoons were threatened by a gang of security guards. The three old friends offered to tell me the story over a nice cappuccino. I am from the old school, where cappuccino is served as a breakfast drink. I took an espresso.

Dagny said, "We had almost finished. I was taking cups to the counter when I saw two security guards pacing back and forth. One of them I know; he is always saying, 'How is Tim?'

But this time he came to me and said I can't bring Timmy in here any more, no more dogs are allowed in the mall." I said, 'How about I carry him?' He said, 'No. You can walk, but you can't stop in any stores.'

"I have been coming here four and a half years. Everyone knows Timmy. The coffee shop, they give him water to drink. They always ask, 'Is your baby okay?' But now I can't come in any stores."

I said it seemed harsh.

Dagny said, "I called Ruth right away."

Ruth lowered her eyes modestly. She would not blow her own horn, but she is the kind of woman you can call when there's trouble. Ruth did a little sleuthing.

"What happened was, a woman got bit by someone's dog near the market." At the mention of the bite, Timmy and Kelly averted their doggy eyes. "The woman was warned not to touch the dog," said Ruth, "but as it happens, she didn't understand English. The response of the security firm was to banish all dogs from the Manulife Centre. People with dogs were refused entry –" and here she got non-denominationally indignant, "– at Christmas time."

Milan set his coffee aside, reached into the pocket of his coat, and fed little Timmy a doggie treat. Dagny said, "Timmy doesn't eat this stuff at home. He only eats it when we are out. At home he eats steamed beef, breast of chicken. We are vegetarians for twenty-two years, but we want him to get his vitamins." It's a dog's life.

The dog eats as well as I do.

The banishment sent a ripple of shock throughout the building.

Ruth said, "We got a petition going. Every single store in the upper and lower mall signed. They were furious." Dagny said, by way of justification, "We spend, I would say, two hundred dollars a month at Timothy's on cakes." Ruth took the petition to building management.

What started as a tempest in a tiny teacup might easily have escalated into a tornado, but such is the power of a woman on a mission for her friends that management spoke to security and the ban was lifted.

The big brave security guards did not have the nerve to tell Dagny and Milan. One of them persuaded another resident to approach Ruth with the news. The incident lasted ten days from start to finish. It was a victory for the little guys and the little dogs.

The head of security declined to comment; said it was policy not to talk; referred me to building management, who likewise declined comment; referred me to head office.

I declined to call head office.

My policy?

Woof.

You can get on fairly well in this town if you are old and have a dog and a pension and friends. The climate here also seems unusually good for certain older writers, which fact gives me courage.

Gwen Beer made her fictional debut recently with a short novel, *Two Brides from Trochu*. It is a classic prairie romance. The first edition sold out within a few days. Such brisk sales do not happen often in this country; she leaves Alice, Mavis, Peggy in her dust.

Gwen agreed to an interview, and over the phone she gave me directions to her apartment. She lives in a modest seniors' building near Overlea and Don Mills Road.

I arrived an hour early, or perhaps I was a few minutes late – some small confusion on my part, not the first time. I shared the elevator with an old gent. He was one of those survivors of the greatest generation; you could tell as much by his ramrod bearing.

I asked him how things were going. He said things were going fine. He asked if things were fine with me. I said any day I was upright was a good day. He agreed. I could tell he was tipsy and pretending not to be. I was with him in spirit, if not in spirits. He got out of the elevator with a salute.

As I peered down the wide corridors of Gwen's floor, looking for the right direction, I noticed an old woman primping some flowers on a table in the corridor; she primped, and then looked to see if anyone was watching, and she did not notice me, and she plucked the flowers from the vase and walked away with her stolen bouquet as quickly as she could into her apartment. I have a hunch she does this all the time. Who can blame her?

I found Gwen's address and knocked tentatively on her door. Writers can be touchy; I feared that if I was late she might have gotten bored and gone out; or perhaps if I'd come too early, she might be in the shower, wet-hen mad as a result of the interruption.

I heard a cheery voice.

"Come in!"

The door was locked.

"Wait a second. I'll be right there."

Gwen Beer is a tiny woman with fierce bright eyes, a firm handshake, and a straightforward manner. She led me inside and sat in her armchair. She'd been playing patience on a small table; winning, by the look of it. "Pull up that chair and sit across from me," she said.

I did as instructed. The last cold light of a grey day shone through her living-room window. She wasted no time. She pointed behind me and said, "There's a bottle of Bristol Cream in the cabinet." I poured two tiny glasses of sherry. She admonished me. "Fill them right up," she said. "You're a big boy."

She didn't have to tell me twice.

She said, "Ever since I was eight years old, I wanted to write a book. I made a little note in my autograph book that I was going to write one before I died."

For the record, Gwen Beer is ninety-six years old. She may have gotten a late start, but she isn't wasting any time. She is now well into her second novel, and she has some solid notions for a third.

"This first book is about two families, with two girls growing up on separate ranch farms. It's the story of their lives."

A saga, then.

The opening paragraph:

"Pauline Watson stood and looked at herself in the mirror. A sweet young face looked back at her, soft shining hair of red gold, eyes a beautiful violet blue and a mouth that turned up at the corners. It looked very kissable." I'd say that's a grabby lead.

I won't cite any more for fear of spoiling it, just in case you run across a copy, or should there be a second edition.

"I sold sixty copies the first day. I set up a table in the sitting room downstairs. Everybody who's read it said they loved it." She took a sip of sherry. "One lady said I should have put in more description."

Ah, the critics are relentless.

"I printed it myself," said Gwen. "It cost me $1,541 to have one hundred copies printed. It sells for $14.95." She took another sip. "I covered all but a few of my expenses."

And that is as succinct an outline as any of the sad economics of the writing trade. You take a bit of a loss, and the critics say there isn't enough description. And this is why some writers drink harder stuff than sherry. But oh, a book, and your name on it.

The writer's roots?

"I was born in 1908. I grew up on Bathurst Street, opposite Olive Avenue. I've gone back to see the house. It's an old antique. We had the top floor. My father died when I was two months old. I had an older sister and an older brother. There was no widows' compensation. My mother was the most courageous lady. The family wanted to split us up but she wouldn't hear of it. She raised us on twenty dollars a month."

As soon as they were old enough, Gwen and her brother and her sister took jobs in order to help out. She recalls working at the old *Toronto Telegram* as a young woman. "I was a little toad in a big pool. I was selling advertising. I was there when the little dynamo was there, Frank Tumpane." The columnist Tumpane; still a legend among Toronto writers after all these years.

Dynamo? Takes one to know one.

Little toad? Never Gwen.

Of her writing habits, she said, "I write here. I have a table and an armchair. I can fold the table down when I want to. I write in longhand, on ruled paper." And if she looks up in mid-sentence she can see the corner of a nearby church, and the park in the distance.

She remembers a winter morning when the first light of day hit the windows so hard, and the powdery snow on the ground swirled in the wind like so much smoke, that she thought the church was on fire and she called 9-1-1 and the fire trucks came quickly.

And then they went away again.

She'd done the right thing.

"I'm one hundred and thirteen pages into my second book," said Gwen. "It will be called *The Fisherman*, or maybe I'll call it *Down By the River*. I haven't decided. The first chapter? There's a young man sitting on a dock at night with a huge fishing pole. There's a net on the end of his line. He feels a tug on his rod. He pulls up the net. 'Jumping Jehoshaphat, there's a naked woman in my net.' It takes off after that."

I bet it does.

"I was going to print two hundred copies. I don't want to be stuck with them. I'm not a gambler. But maybe I'll print two hundred copies."

Her fans will demand more.

Not all the elderly find their calling late in life.

Some find their calling early, and if they are lucky, they drift into retirement with a few comforts and many memories.

But the drifting is not always smooth.

Alfie Kopman sat on a bench in the lobby of his apartment building, coat on and cap in hand. Alfie is a gent of a certain age. Children, take note: a gent does not wear his cap indoors.

Alfie's cap was white, a souvenir of the racetrack. Alfie was big on harness racing in the old days. "I used to own horses, and parts of horses." He means the tails. He did not mean the noses.

He was not going to the track on this day. He was going to the supermarket. A special yellow bus had been hired to take him there. The bus is a good story. No, it isn't. Yes, it is. Finally, it is not.

Alfie used to shop for groceries in a pleasant supermarket in a nice mall across the street from his apartment building. Shopping was an outing, a pleasant bit of exercise. That was good. But the supermarket closed for renovations. That was bad.

Alfie said, "I think half the people in my building are older than seventy. I call them senior seniors." Alfie is one of these in age but not in attitude.

There are no other supermarkets nearby, which meant that when the supermarket closed, the seniors – and the senior seniors; and Alfie – were left high and dry, as well as hungry and thirsty.

This was a problem for old couples with no cars, and for men who'd given up their driver's licences, and for women who were unable to manage alone on public transit; and it was a problem for anyone else who didn't want to impose on their families because their sons are so busy at work, and their daughters work so hard, and the grandchildren have to be driven to music lessons or hockey practice.

Alfie said, "I gave up my car two years ago. That was tough."

The supermarket was pressed into providing a service so the old ones could get their groceries: A bus driver was hired to come around and pick people up. He helped them board. He drove them to a distant market. He waited while they shopped. He loaded their groceries onto the bus and brought them home again. This, twice a week.

Alfie had played a small but pivotal role in making the supermarket chain aware of the problem, and in getting them to hire the bus, and in having the bus pull up at the door in front of their apartment buildings. He tapped his forehead. "I may be old, but I still got it up here. I'm sharp as a tack. Business did that, not education. I worked since I was thirteen years old." Alfie was eighty-six when he said that.

We waited patiently for the bus. He told me he'd been in showbiz when he was a kid. He ushered, and he managed theatres; after the war he went into nuts and bolts, and after he'd had his fill of nuts and bolts he went into automotive; but mostly he was in plumbing.

As he told the story, a woman began to clean the lobby windows. Alfie greeted her. He greets everyone. The outside world gleamed when the woman put her rag away. She smiled at him.

Alfie pointed out the windows. He said, "You see all these apartment buildings around here? We sold the bathtubs." He paused to remember selling all those tubs. "Don't get me wrong. I'm not a plumber. I couldn't fix a tap." Me, neither, Alf.

He was shopping for one. His needs were simple. That's the way life goes – if you live long enough, you end up on your own; and if you love well enough, you end up with a broken heart.

"I don't need much. A brown bread, a milk, some bologna, some bananas." Just then, a neighbour came out of the elevator. She was nicely dressed. She, too, was going shopping on the bus. Alfie gave her the eye. She was pulling one of those little carts on wheels.

He said, "Don't overdo it." She said she wouldn't. He watched her step outside. He watched the way she moved; it is a mystery, even to an old man, the way a woman moves. Alfie said, "The first time I went on the bus, I overdid it. I got too much. I could hardly carry it home. You can't overdo it."

The bus arrived. He got up from his bench and walked outside. He let others get on ahead of him in line. By the time he boarded, the bus was SRO. The driver asked Alfie to get off and said he'd come back shortly. Alfie made his way back to the lobby with a gallant shrug. No rush.

He passed the time telling stories.

He didn't notice the bus when it came back half an hour later. The driver didn't notice him. Alfie watched as the bus pulled away. He shrugged again. "It's a pain. But don't worry. I can improvise. I got canned stuff. I got some fruit up there." There would be another bus, another day. Here's what's wrong:

We have built this city to serve people who have cars. We do not plan neighbourhoods with little markets and corner stores.

Alfie has lived in his apartment for nearly thirty years. He should move at his age? A simple circumstance – the closure of his supermarket – turned him into a hostage in a tall tower.

When I need a pork chop, I go for a walk. I can fill my daily needs two blocks away. I'm one of the lucky ones.

Irene is not so lucky. She lives in Alderwood, a pleasant neighbourhood in south Etobicoke, about as far from Alfie as you can get on a city map.

Alderwood, lost in time: little old houses on big city lots. The homeowners tend to be of an age; because men die younger than women, there are many widows. Irene said that when her supermarket closed she, too, was stranded.

Public transit? Not easy to use when you are older and burdened with bags of the weekly mince and broccoli; harder still when the trip requires a transfer from one bus to another.

Taxi? A round trip in a cab would blow her budget – it's ten bucks each way to the nearest supermarket, on top of which she'd have to pay the driver two bits a bag to load her groceries.

Getting her grub on-line is out of the question – the minimum order is too pricey, and there is a charge to deliver, and not everyone has a computer.

I asked how she got her groceries.

Storefront Humber, a multi-purpose seniors' centre, has a bus. Brian Davies is the driver. He's technically only supposed to pick up seniors and drop them off at clinics, which is all the centre has funding for. But once a week – shh, don't tell – Brian takes seniors for groceries.

It's simple pragmatism: we've all got to eat, and there are plenty of seniors in South Etobicoke who'd have to give up their houses and move into nursing homes if they couldn't do the shopping.

I tagged along with Irene one day.

Some eighteen people had called ahead to book a ride. Brian had them arranged in five groups. "By the time I drop the last group at the supermarket, the first group is ready to go home again." The radio played oldies as he drove. The shoppers were women of a certain era. Their husbands were more or less dead. They were of that generation of women who get dressed up to go out. They'd done their hair. They were happy to see each other, like kids at recess.

They said, "Oh, Brian, you've got a lot of old fogies today." And when he dropped them off at the Kipling-Queensway Mall, they said, "I'll see you in my dreams, dear."

Irene was in the third group.

She's seventy, a relative youngster. Most of the others were in their eighties. Brian helped them off the bus. They scattered with their bundle buggies. Irene went inside and took a shopping cart.

"I was born in London, England. Every neighbourhood had its own market. My mother shopped every day. When I moved to Alderwood, everything I needed was there on Brown's Line."

Brown's Line is deader than a doornail now that the mall has closed down. Irene uses Brian and the bus once every two weeks; five bucks a trip. She said, "Fresh vegetables are a problem but I have a freezer at home. So one week, I'll have fresh, and the next week, I'll have frozen."

Her shopping list? Apples, potatoes, mayo, milk in bags, three loaves of bread, and cereal. She'll freeze the milk and bread, and she'll thaw them as she needs to.

When her cart was full, she and her old girlfriends waited for Brian in the mall. They sat together on a bench. They said, "You can't call your neighbours to take you shopping all the time." "The Queensway bus doesn't run on weekends." "How could you take all this on the bus?"

Funny, how we brag about this town. We are a city of neighbourhoods, our planners are cutting-edge, and so on.

Here are some plain questions:

Why don't planners study what's happening in the suburbs? Who says malls are good for everyone? Why do some people have to move into retirement homes just because they don't have cars? And why, at the end of a lifetime of hard work, must Irene and her friends rely on the brilliant charity of others in order to shop for groceries?

Take it easy. It's Toronto, Jake.

Time passes quickly here. We do best when we stay busy.

Paule Belmonte perched on a high stool in front of an open window at the downtown bus terminal. She clicked her ballpoint pen, straightened her clipboard, clasped her hands and waited. She is a volunteer for Travellers' Aid. For the past fourteen years it has been her job, twice a week, to lighten the burdens of the weary and lift the hopes of anyone who is fretful on the long road from Here to There.

This was her last shift.

Greyhound Canada. Through-Coach Service: New York City for St. Catharines; Niagara Falls; Casino Niagara; Buffalo; Rochester; Ithaca; Binghamton; and New York City. Platform Nine.

The litany of place names is a comfort to Paule, but it did not comfort everyone. A Japanese girl with a big new backpack approached the window. She looked uncertain.

"Niagara Falls, yes? The bus, where?"

Paule oriented the girl in a manner which was at once helpful, clear and confident. You would expect clear confidence from her – she had been a nurse in the Emergency room of the Toronto General Hospital, responding to the bloody, the immediate, the imperative.

The merely interrogative? Piece of cake.

"I wanted to keep busy after I retired," said Paule. "I like the diversity, meeting so many people. I have even made a few friends. One Iranian gentleman I met at our window at the airport. He later became a roomer in my apartment. He recently went back to Europe. He will come back with a bride. He just phoned me from Denmark."

The strangest question she's ever had?

Paule, who came to Toronto more than forty years ago, replies in an accent which reveals her Belgian-French roots. "I could not believe that someone would ask, 'How far is it by bus from Toronto to Paris?' At first I thought Paris, Ontario. But they meant Paris, France. I thought they were joking. They were not."

She savours the memory, and then trumps it.

"And then there was a lady who asked me how to get down-town. She wanted to go to rue Ste Catherine. The poor woman thought she was in Montreal."

Most people merely want to know the price of tickets, or where they can find luggage tags. But there are always a few souls who are stuck for cash. As you would expect in an organization that helps half a million travellers a year, there is a system. "I tell them first they have to go to the headquarters in Union Station. We can give a bit of money. But we have a book we keep. Anyone who has been helped financially, their names go in the book. If their name is in there, they can't get money, not a second time."

A tall man with a German accent and a bland and neutral smile approached the window. He said, "Excuse me. To go to the Chinese neighbourhood, is it okay now?" This was in the aftermath of SARS. Paule assured him that it had always been okay, and she gave him clear directions, and he strode bravely off.

In his wake, a young woman with blonde hair and flushed cheeks stepped up and asked for the time of day. She said, breathlessly, "I'm travelling to Newfoundland. I'm not from there. My boyfriend is from there. I can't tell time. I just get nervous." Paule told her it was 12:20 p.m., and she said so without a trace of curiosity about how a young woman might have grown up without knowing how to tell time.

The young woman paused and said, "I don't like travelling. My boyfriend is staying in Kitchener. He wants to make some more money. It's so dirty here. Well, I'll just go for a walk. I'm so nervous."

She was going to Newfoundland, and her boyfriend was not. She shouldered a large black hockey equipment bag and said, as she wandered off, "It's very heavy. It cuts into my shoulders. It's my boyfriend's. He gave it to me. I'm just nervous."

After a few moments, Paule said, "That was a little strange. People say the strangest things. I think it's kind of relieving, to talk. Not too long ago, there was a lady with a handbag full of jewellery. I don't know what quality. She was going to pass the winter in Florida. She should not have been travelling alone. She, too, was nervous."

On her last day, Paule helped fifty-two travellers.

Just before the end of her shift, two pigeons fluttered in through the open doors of the bus station and landed in a puddle of sunlight on the floor. Paule blinked. She has been losing her eyesight slowly for the past six years. "There's nothing to be done," she said. And so now she was leaving Toronto to go to live near her son in British Columbia.

She was not going by bus.

Dora De Pédery-Hunt goes nowhere by bus. On the night of her ninetieth birthday she swept into the Arts and Letters Club on the arms of two handsome young men. She was wearing a long white gown adorned with the medallion of the Order of Canada. We applauded her entry. The Rakoscy March played. And Dora looked around the room with a wry and imperial smile.

"I only invited people I can stand."

There were some sixty people she could stand that night.

Dora is a sculptor. To be precise, she is the most important medal maker in Canada. Odds are you own her work if you have any pocket change – flip a coin until it comes up heads; if the head is wearing a tiara, that's Dora's work, and it is the merest of her achievements.

What's it like to be ninety?

She rolled her eyes and said, "I think it is quite all right, but I would love to be less." Don't get the wrong impression. She continues to make art hand over fist. "I get up at 4:00 a.m. every day. I get in shape. Then at 5:00 a.m. I am working."

She lives and works in a tiny downtown apartment crowded with books, photos, flowers, maquettes, drawings, correspondence, awards. Alas, she has no studio. She works in her kitchen, on the counters and at the sink; where you keep condiments, she keeps chemicals; where you keep cutlery, she keeps tools. Her apron is covered with plaster.

She made a terrific birthday speech. She recalled her first birthday. "I was born in Budapest in 1913. My father was at the opera. My mother was with lady friends at a party. She felt perhaps the coffee was not agreeing with her. It was not the coffee, it was me. I was born in the middle of the party. The pictures show I was two pounds. They found an old shoebox and put me in it. My father came from the opera and baptized me. He called me 'Dorothea,' the gift of the gods. I was Sunday's child, who could talk to the birds and understand the flowers. I could not shake that name – the shoebox baby."

The shoebox baby came to Canada in 1948 as a refugee. When she stepped off the plane in Montreal, she met an official who had some forms to fill in. "He asked, 'What is your trade?' I told him I was a sculptor. He asked, 'Please, how do you spell it?'"

Dora paused a beat. "And I wondered, 'What kind of country is this?' Well, I spelled the word for him. He seemed puzzled, so I explained that I carved small animals from wood. He said, 'Lambs?' I said, 'Lambs, too.' He said, 'Welcome to Canada.'"

While she was waiting for the train to Toronto, Dora wanted to freshen up. After all, she'd just spent three years in a postwar transit camp. The washroom cost a nickel. She was a nickel short. She approached a policeman and asked him for the money. "He reached into his pocket slowly. He didn't give the nickel to me. He said, 'I will come.' We walked over. When I came out, it was obvious I had cleaned up. The policeman shook my hand. He said, 'Welcome to Canada.'"

What colours both stories is this – Dora was, and is, a stunner. I think the official was dazzled into befuddlement. I think the cop didn't want to let her out of his sight.

Dora established herself quickly in Toronto. She met A.Y. Jackson, and he gave her a key to his studio. He also gave her some sheets because, she said, "He slept on bearskins."

Charles Staffer is president of the Hungarian Visual Artists of Canada. During the party he set down his martini, touched the knot in his tie and said, almost bashfully, "We first met twenty-five years ago. I adore her very much. I brought her a little Rembrandt etching, a small one. I have fifteen medals of hers. I love her, really – it's a funny thing to say, since I'm married fifty years." Move over, Charles. All men love Dora.

Art critic Kay Kritzwiser was at the party. She wore a pink beret. Of Dora's rise to prominence during the sixties, Kay said, "She made culture seem respectable. She gave artists confidence."

Del Newbigging is a medallist and a friend of Dora's. He was an art teacher for many years. He grew up on a small farm and taught himself to sculpt from a book. He was Dora's student in the sixties. He said, "I remember when I decided to make my first medal. I took my usual approach. I wanted to find a book, so I asked Dora which one. She said, 'I am the book.'" She is chapter, she is verse.

When consulted about birthday gifts – what do you get a woman of ninety? – Dora's niece, Ildiko Hencz, had this recommendation: "Rye whiskey. Or perhaps brandy. At every family function, Dora's contribution is a large jug of excellent manhattans."

There were birthday greetings from the Governor General of Canada; from the Roman Catholic Archbishop of Toronto; from the curator of Coins and Medals at the British Museum; from the Hungarian ambassador; and many others.

There was shrimp. There was champagne. There were grapes. There were also sixty chocolate birthday cakes, one for everybody, each lit with a single blazing candle, each inscribed "Dora" in flowing white icing. The cakes, small and round, not unlike medals.

Dora lives near Maple Leaf Gardens, in a subsidized seniors' building. A friend had the adjacent apartment. The friend moved out. Dora used the apartment next door as a studio. Management found out. Dora lost the studio.

We still can't spell "sculptor."

Eventually, we all come to live in an imaginary city navigated with the help of an invisible map only we can see. Soon, a young man will ask an old man for directions, and the old man will say, "Roncesvalles, south of Fern, near Danny's shoe shop." The young man will look at the old man as if he's nuts. "Shoe shop? There's no shoe shop."

But oh, there was once.

The sign in the window was quietly eloquent.

"Attention to all customers. After 52 yrs. in business we are closing the store on Jan. 31/04. Please come in as soon as possible to pick up your stuff. Thank you. Store management."

Store management is Dan Pefhany and his wife, Ermiony; everyone in the neighbourhood calls her Ellen. He tacks no more heels now. She buffs no more boots. Why did they pack it in? Dan shrugged.

"I'm eighty."

Reason enough.

Everything in the cobbler's shop – lasts, stitchers, stretchers, sanders, buffers, cutters, boxes of heel guards, sheets of leather, thousands of bright eyelets and little sharp nails – will be packed up and shipped off to Africa. Ellen said, "I'm going to send it all to the poor countries for free. We're going to help people who need help."

And so the map of the neighbourhood changes.

An old lady with a pair of tight grey loafers breezed through the door with a flourish. "Hello, my darling," said Ellen.

The old lady squinted at the sign. When she finished reading, she said, "Lots of people will be crying. You was very handy, and good prices." Ellen cut two new leather insoles for the woman; handy, and good prices.

How does a man come to spend his life before the last?

Dan's father was a miner in Cape Breton years ago. A chunk of rock fell on his head; so much for the life of the mined.

When the old man got out of the hospital, he bought a shoe shop. Dan learned his trade by watching his father work. When the war came, they got a contract repairing shoes for soldiers.

Dan moved to Toronto after the war. He married Ellen not long after. It was one of those things. Dan was single, and his family knew a family in Greece. She was encouraged to come. It wasn't easy at first. She hadn't planned to be in shoes.

They've worked together ever since.

She winked and pointed to her noggin. "I learn here." She meant she learned by watching Dan. "He does the work, I do the refinish. If I don't like the work, it goes back to him. We are side by side together, all these years, all work to be done properly."

She picked up a woman's black half-boot and pointed to the leather above the ankle. "I do fine work, delicate work. This boot, I open up the stitches. I go in. I make it small. I put it together and I stitch it like it was." Dan looked up and said, "She does some things better than me."

He held a woman's dress shoe; black suede, with a wobbly heel. He peeled away the insole, then pinched and pulled some small nails with a pair of nippers. His hands were still strong. He put the shoe on the last.

The last was made of metal, shaped vaguely like a foot. It glowed dully in the light, buffed by every shoe he'd placed on it for the past fifty-two years. Dan tacked new nails, securing the heel for a city sidewalk or for one last dance. He gave it to his wife. Ellen gripped and twisted the heel. "That's good." Dan set it aside. He said, deadpan, "Sometimes I use my last first, and sometimes I use my last last."

Ellen moved lightly behind the counter. She shined an old brown shoe and hauled out an old memory.

"A few years back, this lady came to pick up a pair of shoes. She took off the ones she was wearing and said, 'Fix these.' Then she put the fixed ones on and she went. She left her purse behind. Ten minutes later she comes back. 'Mrs., I forgot my life in your store!' I gave her the purse. I said, 'Here's your life.' She said, 'Inside is seven thousand dollars!' Later, she sent me a gift basket – honey, tea, everything."

Dan turned over a tired black lace-up. He said, "Everything inside is cardboard and plastic. You know all those oil spills? They scrape up the oil and dry it out and make shoes with it." He pointed to the sole. "I grind this, it turns to liquid from the heat."

Not like the old days, when prudent stylish men bought good leather shoes. Not like the old days, when Dan re-soled fifteen or twenty pairs a day; for the past few years, he'd been lucky to re-sole one pair a week.

Dan said, also deadpan, "One day a man comes in. He asks how I'm doing. I tell him I'm still saving soles. Waiting over there was a priest from up the street. He said, 'Hey, that's my job!'"

Dan said, "There used to be eight cobblers on the street." At the end of the month there will be one cobbler left. I have been in that store; and the cobbler is younger than Dan, and he declines to do small jobs, such as stitching straps or working with dyes.

Ellen has no use for him.

What will the shoemaker and his wife do now? They had already made plans to rent the shop to a man who wanted to sell bicycles. Ellen said, "We don't know nothing else but work.

We've never been places. The first thing, we'll see how the bicycle guy does." And then she brightened. "I said to my grandson, 'From February, I'm yours.' He put his hands to his face. 'Oh, Grandma, you mean it?'"

Old, my dear; not too old.

NINETEEN

The poorer you are, the less healthy you are likely to be, over a shortened lifetime. This is one of the most neglected facts in Canadian health care.

– NICHOLAS REGUSH, *Condition Critical*, 1987

I don't know her name, and I don't know where she came from, nor do I have any idea of her immigration status. All I know is that at the time, for official purposes, she wasn't here legally. And all you need to know is that she had no money, no resources, no job, and a baby.

One night, the baby had an asthma attack, a bad one. Because the woman was here without permission, she had no medical coverage. She had no job. She couldn't pay for a doctor. She hoped the attack would pass. It did not.

The gasps continued, and the child began to weaken, and the woman couldn't wait any longer. She did what you would do, alone in a strange land with a sick baby.

She rushed to the Emergency room at Scarborough Grace Hospital.

They told her on arrival that, because she had no health card, she would be billed $235 for the privilege of being admitted; in addition, when the doctor examined her baby, she would be billed $300 more, all fees exclusive of any medicines prescribed.

Put yourself in the woman's shoes: you can barely speak the language, you have no family or friends nearby, and you are not just broke, you have no hope of earning any money.

She sat in the cool of the waiting room and soothed her baby, and she counted the cost. The money might as well have been a million dollars. But after a time, in the thin dry medicinal air of the hospital, the crisis passed; the child calmed down and began to breathe easily.

The woman got up quietly and took her baby home.

Not long afterward, she got a bill in the mail. She stared at the bill blankly. It was as she feared. No, it was worse. The hospital wanted an impossible sum for granting her the privilege of sitting in the Emergency room for a brief time with her sick child.

She showed the bill, helplessly, to her public health nurse, a handsome woman named Jennifer D'Andrade.

Jennifer, who had come for a routine check on the baby, knew that the mother didn't have a hope in hell of paying. She told the woman not to worry. But Jennifer was worried as she considered the situation: dozens of cases like this in Scarborough: sick kids, frantic parents, similar bills, the situation getting worse.

It isn't just that Toronto gets one-third of Canada's immigrants, and Scarborough gets the half of these; there are also, at any given moment, hundreds of men, women, and children who are here illegally. They hide in flea-bitten motels, or they are crammed into tiny rooms in illegal rooming houses, or they live three or four families to a house.

These are the desperate ones.

They come, and they continue to come, because they are willing to risk their lives for blue jeans, television, a place to pray, plenty of food, the right to vote, clean water in unlimited quantities, an absence of roving squads of executioners, the presence of electric lights and good schools for the kids; they want all the things we take for granted, all that is banal and glorious on this planet.

They spend their savings to buy their way out. They risk their lives to stow away on ships or planes. They destroy their identification in the hope that, if no one knows who they are, then they can't be sent away.

We don't think about these people very much.

They are invisible. We are in a hurry, we can't see them, we have our own concerns; if you stand still here, you lose your place. Scarborough had at that time just a single public health clinic for a population of more than half a million people. The rich don't know and the poor don't need to be told.

Who says there is no caste system here?

The woman was lucky, in a way. She had Jennifer D'Andrade. And Jennifer snapped into action. She went to the Scarborough Hospital and walked into the office of Yasmin Vali, the director of patient care. She slapped the bill on the desk.

"What are we going to do about this?"

Yasmin Vali is a woman of deep gravitas. The women talked. Yasmin waived the bill, and she and Jennifer went to work. They made some phone calls. They talked to some doctors. They set up some meetings. They discussed some strategies, twisted some arms and cut some red tape.

Dr. Paul Caulford wrote an editorial in the hospital newspaper; in it, he put a rhetorical question: If one of those immigrant motels on Kingston Road was burning, would we demand payment for sending in the fire trucks? Why is health care any different?

And then things started to happen fast, and it wasn't exactly like one of those old movies – you get the drug companies to donate medicine, and I'll get some volunteers, and we'll find a place to work – but it wasn't unlike that, either.

They set up a free clinic in an east-end community centre.

I tagged along with Jennifer one evening. She packed a couple of oversized fishing tackle boxes with medicine, stowed them in her truck and drove to the Warden Woods Community Centre.

The clinic is a computer room by day.

Here, two nights a week, people with no health insurance come for care. How many come? One hundred people a month, more or less, from twenty-two different countries and counting, people who speak all the languages of the world. Jennifer does the intake. I sat with her one evening and took notes. This evening's patients were typical:

A shy young woman from Indonesia who had applied for health care but was told there would be a waiting period of three months. Her coverage hadn't kicked in yet. She had no family doctor. She needed a TB test and various vaccinations so she could take a job as a home-care worker; by which she meant she hoped to get work as a nanny. She was twenty-six years old. She was living with her sister. For the moment, she was okay for food and rent. Jennifer sent her to see the doctor.

The next patient was a woman from Granada. Her skin was luminously black. She was twenty-nine years old, and single. In a sweet, slow voice, she said she had just had surgery to remove a fibroid tumour. She said the tumour was the size of a lemon, and it had been pressing against her bladder. The operation to remove the tumour left her with a four-thousand-dollar debt, and a lingering tenderness. She said she was supposed to wear a catheter for two months. The catheter kept slipping out. Every time she went to the hospital to get the catheter put back in, it cost her $250. A nurse from the hospital sent her to this clinic.

She said she had been earning $150 a week as a nanny, and she was baby-sitting for someone on the side, and she was doing some cleaning of houses, and she was studying typing on her one free evening. But she could not work or study while she was recovering from the operation.

She said she had been living with her brother to save money. She was singing as a soloist in her church choir. She had been in Canada for seven years. She had applied for landed immigrant status. Her immigration hearing was coming up. Her lawyer wanted three thousand dollars to process her claim.

After the operation, she moved in with friends. That wasn't practical; not much privacy. She was renting a room in a basement. The room cost her $250 a month. She was trying to send money home to her mother and her sister in Grenada. Her employer helped her pay for the operation. Her employer wanted to be paid back.

She was in debt so deep she could not see daylight. The pain was visible in her face, audible in her voice, apparent in her ginger movements. She began to weep. Jennifer comforted her and sent her to see the doctor.

Next, a young couple.

She was an angular beauty from Siberia, proud of her youth, proud of her swollen belly, proud to be here, proud of her husband. He was tall, slim, fiercely happy, dark, a landed immigrant from Afghanistan. He was working in a box factory. He was the one who sponsored her. She was seven months pregnant. They met seven months ago. "It had something to do with the war," she laughed.

War may be hell, but this was love at first sight. They held hands. You have never seen a more handsome couple. Their child will set a new standard of beauty in a city of children whose beauty is exotic and unprecedented in the world.

The couple shared a one-bedroom apartment with his brother, an arrangement which was barely tolerable and would soon become intolerable for all when the baby arrived.

The Siberian girl was twenty-two years old. She had not had a prenatal checkup – no blood work, no AIDS test, her anti-bodies had not been checked, her blood pressure was unknown. If she had the baby in a hospital, without medical coverage, the birth would cost two thousand dollars.

Off they went to see the doctor, smiling.

Next, an elderly couple from Tanzania.

They, too, held hands. This was their fourth visit. They had high-blood pressure, which fact they discovered when they walked into a drugstore one day and used a free blood-pressure machine – and now you know who uses those things.

They had driven in from Mississauga. There is no free clinic in Mississauga. This was not exactly a free clinic for them, either – it's a long drive, gas costs money, and they were too old to work.

"We live with my sister," he said. "She helps us buy the med-ication." How were they feeling? "We feel better," they said. "But every time we check our blood pressure it is not coming down." Off they went to see the doctor, perhaps this time to try some new medication.

Then came a young guy, an all-Canadian boy whose pros-pects had been temporarily squandered. His life was on hold. He had lost his wallet, his health card, his social insurance card, everything.

He needed an inhaler.

He had been out on the West Coast. He said he was robbed. He was embarrassed about having been robbed. Or maybe he was lying. He had been staying with his sister. He had been using her inhaler. He said he was not staying with her any more. He did not say she kicked him out, but you get the drift. He was renting a room for $125 a week; shared kitchen, shared bath. He did not say what he did to earn the money. He said, "It's pretty much a rundown shit-hole. There are six guys staying in the house. We all pay the same, $125 a week." Do the math: the landlord is making three thousand dollars a month renting single rooms to hapless men.

The young man did not have a driver's licence. "The things you do when you're sixteen," he said. He means he lost his licence driving drunk when he was out West. "I can't work at my trade." He meant he can't be bonded. He said he was an alarm-system installer.

He said he works casual. He meant he worked off the books. He said he owed money to another hospital because he hurt himself when he came back from the oil fields. He started not to like Jennifer's questions.

"Look, I just came in for an inhaler."

She told him where to go to get new identification, which he could then use to get a new health card.

The last patient of the evening was a landed immigrant from China.

He was thirty-nine years old. His health card was on the way. He, too, looked tired. It was the middle of the evening. That was not why he was tired.

"I have an infection in my ear. I can't bear the pain."

He said, "I am a software developer. I brought some money with me. I have three job offers in the States, but I couldn't get a green card. I am accepted as an immigrant here, but I can't find work here." That's not to say he was idle. He was working in a factory. That's not just Toronto. That's how it goes in Canada.

More than thirty doctors, nurses, dentists and other special-
ists donate their time and their after-hours expertise to this
clinic; several of the drug companies give free medication; a
couple of labs do the X-rays and the blood work free of charge.
This is a band-aid solution.

It is also a miracle.

Incidentally, the baby who started this whole thing recently
entered school, and his mother got her citizenship, and she
found a job and now she is paying taxes and building a life just
like the rest of us.

Toronto is cold, impersonal, indifferent?

I don't think so.

This is a city of conjunctions, connections, intersections.

Dr. Shabbir Alibhai works at the Toronto General Hospital.
He is a Muslim. Yo'av Kaplun is a medical staffing specialist, also
at the General. He is a Jew. The hospital is a big and busy place.

No reason for them to meet.

And then Yo'av's father became ill, and the illness took a turn.
Yo'av feared the worst. He brought his father to Emergency. It
looked like he'd have to stay for tests. The first words Dr. Alibhai
spoke to Yo'av: "Will your father require a kosher meal?"

A Muslim asking a Jew about a kosher meal?

It was more than kindness in a crisis. The question took
Yo'av's breath away. This is one of those Toronto stories,
beginning long ago and far away:

Yo'av: "My father was born in 1927, in Odessa, on the shores
of the Black Sea. His mother was murdered by the Nazis
during the Holocaust. He made his way to Israel, on his own,
as a teen. It took him five years.

"When he got to Israel, he worked in a kibbutz. Then he went
into military service. He would have been a pilot but he was

only five-foot-two." Instead, he became an aircraft technician.

"After his military service, he joined El Al. He worked for them until 1968. Then he emigrated. He wanted peace – both inner, and around him – so he came to Canada."

Shabbir: "I came to Canada from Tanzania when I was six years old. I don't remember Tanzania, not a bit. When they left, my parents had a choice. Toronto versus England. We had relatives here, so my father chose Canada. I knew I wanted to be a doctor from the time I was in Grade Five. I went to medical school at the University of Toronto."

Yo'av: "At home we began to notice that my father couldn't eat lettuce, he couldn't stand cheese. This was unusual because he was in good health. A doctor's dream, he walked four kilometres a day, he did yoga, he was extremely self-disciplined. We couldn't understand why he was deteriorating.

"He had an appointment with a doctor but it was a month away. I said, 'You're going to wait a month?' He said he wasn't worried. Am I a good son? I made him an appointment with a specialist."

Shabbir: "The specialist found multiple masses in the liver. That raised suspicions of cancer – not necessarily in the liver, but that's where the hunt began."

Mr. Kaplun was sent home and told to rest, in order to prepare for a series of rigorous tests. But it seemed as if the cancer became enraged upon discovery.

Yo'av: "My dad was getting weaker and weaker. It was happening so fast. I knew he should be admitted. There was no time. We brought him to Emergency."

Shabbir: "My team was on call. My residents saw him first."

Yo'av: "That's when we met."

And that's when the doctor asked the question.

Shabbir: "As soon as I know someone's faith, I want to know

how that will be involved with the treatment not just of the disease, but of the patient. I am familiar with many faiths. I don't want to rob people of those beliefs."

And here is where medical and religious ethics began to intersect.

Shabbir: "Mr. Kaplun began lapsing in and out of consciousness. We weren't sure where the cancer was. We didn't think he could handle the tests. So we decided to manage the symptoms."

Yo'av: "My father was in pain but he refused medication. It made him delirious."

Shabbir: "Often Holocaust survivors refuse pain medication because they feel a kind of identification with the victims."

Yo'av: "It was happening very quickly. You want to do everything you can. But toward the end – I only found this out later – he whispered in Hebrew, '*Ani rotze la'mut*.' 'I want to die.'"

Shabbir: "It's not that different in Arabic."

The two men paused. The memory is sharp.

Shabbir: "In the Jewish tradition there is the concept of the *goses* – the dying host. It refers to the difference between someone who is struggling to live, and someone who is dying. The important thing is you are not supposed to reduce the level of care.

"Mr. Kaplun was having trouble breathing. We gave him oxygen through nasal prongs, but his breathing was still laboured. I gave him a mask. But I could tell the mask made him uncomfortable. So if I take the mask away, am I reducing the level of care?"

Yo'av: "My feeling was to maintain the level of care."

Shabbir: "Other questions arose. There was a cancer with no clear primary cause. It soon became clear that we were not going to get an answer in life. Would there be a possibility of getting an answer in death? I know there are strong religious restrictions to autopsies. But if it was colon cancer, there could be issues for the other members of the family."

Yo'av: "It was an issue for four people – myself, my brother and our sons. We needed to make a decision. I called my rabbi. He said, 'It's not a fishing expedition?'"

Shabbir: "I was sure we could do a limited autopsy to minimize the harm done to the body."

Yo'av: "When my father died, we had to act. The rabbi had said if it was for the preservation of life . . . I spoke with my mother. She agreed."

Afterward, when the solace of ritual had comforted the grieving family, Yo'av found he couldn't stop thinking about the Muslim doctor with the intimate knowledge of Jewish tradition. He learned that Shabbir Alibhai, in addition to being a devout Muslim, had been exposed to religious ethics very early in his training.

Yo'av seized an opportunity. He established what he hopes will be an annual lecture in his father's name: "Ethical Issues in End-of-Life Care: The Approaches of Judaism, Catholicism and Islam."

It might easily be called, "Will your father require a kosher meal?"

He had a cold and a dog's bark of a cough. He was one of those wiry guys who looked like he could walk all day fuelled by nothing more than the fumes from a bowl of soup. But not today. He was bone-tired, sore of chest. He'd come to the church on the corner of Sherbourne and Dundas. He couldn't take it any more. He wanted to see a Street Health nurse.

Street Health is what you think it is: a team of nurses who deliver medical care to people on the street. The wiry guy scribbled his name on the sign-up sheet. Coughed. Took a folding chair. Coughed. And waited for the nurse to call his name. He sat down amid the card players, the smokers, the coffee drinkers, the poorly clothed, the poorly fed, the poorly housed. He could not stop coughing.

He stared at the red and gold light leaking through the stained-glass windows of the church. The sky was partly cloudy; now and then the light was muted, and now and then the colours were so rich it looked as if the floor of the church was awash in blood and piss.

Four nurses arrived at noon. Barb Craig has a short thatch of thick blonde hair and an air of utter calm. She set up her station behind a screen along one wall of the church. No running water. Not much privacy.

But good enough for men who won't always go to a hospital.

On Barb's table was a plastic tray with the usual medical jumble: thermometer, blood-pressure cuff, gauze pads, rolls of tape, antiseptic creams, soaps, tweezers, scissors, toenail clippers, corn and callus removers, rubber gloves.

She wore a stethoscope the way most nurses do.

She called the coughing man.

He slumped in a chair next to Barb. She pulled his file. She read and he said, "I've been coughing. Since yesterday afternoon. Non-stop."

"Are you taking anything?"

"No. I haven't. I'm coughing. Too much."

"Do you have a health card?"

The key question. The man lives in a shelter. Cards get lost or stolen. If a man has no card, Barb might steer him to another corner of the church, where some nice young people are helping old men get the two pieces of ID needed to get a card.

They help some five thousand people a year get ID.

"Yes, I have one."

"Got a doctor's appointment?"

"Three days from now."

"Nothing sooner?"

He shakes his head.

She purses her lips.

"Where are you staying?"

"In a shelter. Last night I was coughing so hard and sweating so bad I went through three T-shirts. Pisses me off. People were mad at me because of the coughing. Nobody could sleep."

Including him. He'd have fallen asleep in the chair, but he couldn't stop coughing long enough to nod off. Barb put her stethoscope on his chest, checked his temperature, asked a few routine questions, gave him some cough medicine, told him to get some rest, stay warm, drink plenty of fluids. They shared a rueful look. A man who sleeps on a pallet in the midst of other pallets rarely gets any rest.

Another nurse came by and handed the man a cookie. She always brings cookies; today, chocolate chip.

The man said, "Is it hard?" Barb shot him a quick look. He said, "I got no teeth." He took a swig of cough medicine and rose stiffly, cookie in hand; not hard.

Barb's next patient was a woman, shy and slow of foot. You did not need to be a nurse to know she had a headache. Her face was grey, her voice was low, her eyes hurt in the light. She told Barb she'd had the headache for more than a day, had not eaten breakfast or lunch, had eaten a bit of shepherd's pie the night before; just a bite.

She said she lived by herself in a small rented room. In the jargon of the psych trade, she had a mild developmental handicap. Barb had seen her before, had taken her to the dentist, the doctor, the pharmacist; she had done these things on her day off because she is a good nurse, and because this kind of care is also medicine.

Barb said, "The illnesses we see aren't simple any more. They're chronic. Colds last longer. Clients are getting younger."

A young mother in need of a check-up arrived with her infant in a bundle. The other nurses came by to coo and fuss; cute kid. The woman said, "She's getting big, eh? She sleeps with me. This morning she didn't even cry or wake me. She crawled up on my chest all by herself and started feeding."

A bleary man at the next table sat waiting to have a dark knot of stitches cut from the bridge of his nose. He glanced over. There is no privacy in the clinic, save for the natural discretion of the poor.

The man's voice was thick. "My brother never had a boy until he had three girls." He reached for the infant's hand. The mother tensed. The man drew back. He said, with a hint of self-pity, "That baby's more important than me." A nurse looked at him flatly. She said, "Everyone's important here."

Barb's next patient was an older fellow with a big round ball of belly and a gruff but pleasant manner. He said he used to worship in this church as a boy. Said his family had money. Said he hadn't come to worship today, wasn't here for psalms.

Barb soaked his feet in a basin of warm water, dried him with a towel, clipped his toenails, rubbed his feet with skin lotion. He purred and said, "When I was a kid, we sang a canon from a symphony. Today, nobody knows who Strauss is."

Street Health runs six clinics a week across the city with a staff of seven and a budget of half a million dollars; nurses treat some five thousand patients a year.

Barb treated a few more colds and gave solace to those who had the flu, and then a brown-eyed handsome juicehead hobbled in. He was limping because, in a fit of temper over a spilled drink, he had kicked a frying pan; there was a deep gash on his instep.

Barb didn't press him for details. She removed his dressing. It was stiff. His foot was salty-smelling. Barb disinfected the wound. He flinched. He said he lived in a nearby rooming house with his grandfather, who also drinks. He asked for some shampoo, toothpaste, and a bit of laundry soap because the old man "has his accidents."

Barb finished dressing his foot. He got up and began to limp away. She offered him socks. He looked back with a grin. "Thanks, but I got plenty of socks, and the old man doesn't need 'em; no feet."

Every day I talk to people I don't know. I'm a stranger here myself. I ask questions; my job, my habit, my inclination. Most people are kind and will tell you what life is like here and now if you ask.

A young man was sitting in a wheelchair in the sun. He had turned his face up to the warmth. The day was cloudless, and the chair was older than the man.

He'd had a stroke, or perhaps he had been sideswiped by a fluke of genetics; one of his arms was lifeless and the other fluttered, and his head lolled. That did not mean he would not talk.

And so I said hello.

He didn't say a word in reply. He reached out with his soft left hand. Normal is as normal does. I took his hand, and we shook left-handed.

I was in St. James Town then, trolling the edges of a great sea of social housing. I asked the man a question to warm him up. He made an impatient, guttural sound. He rummaged for something behind his back. He pulled out what I thought at first was an old placemat printed with the letters of the alphabet.

It was not a placemat. He stabbed at the letters one at a time with a careful finger. H. E. L. L. O. I stabbed a greeting back. He stabbed his name. I stabbed mine. And I spelled out my question.

He didn't have the information I needed. Oh, well, nothing ventured; I was about to leave when for some reason, perhaps as a way of continuing our digital conversation, he stabbed out his age; thirty-nine in December. And I might have been mistaken about what happened next. He reached out and grabbed me.

He grabbed me where one man ought not to grab another. Or, rather, he grabbed me in the place some men seek when they reach out for other men.

I thought for an instant it was a motor-skills thing. I did not want to be rude. I was standing. He was sitting. What he held of me was at a level with his hand. It could have been an accident.

And then he squeezed. His motor skills were not a problem then. I know when I'm being squeezed down there, and I know when I'm being squeezed, not just with intent, but with care. I stepped back, not so much shocked as disappointed.

I looked at him. His mouth was open. His eyes were rolled back in his head. He turned away. Or maybe he didn't turn away at all; maybe he was pretending to loll. I thought of stabbing a quick and declarative remark on his alphabet board. I did not. I merely waved him off and walked away.

Every man has urges. I don't think he had been sitting there waiting for me to come along. I was the one who reached out to him; perhaps he misunderstood. Or perhaps I still do.

All I am sure of is this: We are human. We need to reach out to others. A man who cannot speak must have an awful time being discreet when it comes to the expression of his urges.

As I walked away, I noticed a guy leaning against a concrete wall nearby. He was smoking a handmade cigarette. He wore dark shades, a cloth cap, a red shirt, a black vest, jeans. He had a backpack slung over his shoulder. An urban hipster.

I still needed an answer to my question. I walked over, showed him my business card and put my question to him. He pointed to his ear in silence. Oh. I see. What are the odds?

I'd just caromed off a guy who couldn't speak and bumped into a guy who couldn't hear. He reached into his backpack and pulled out a small white eraser board and a green felt marker, urged them on me, miming a gesture – go on, write.

I wrote a single word with a question mark, and so began a conversation. I'd write. He'd erase my answer with a tissue and he'd write back. He had some of the information I needed, but not enough to be fully useful. I wasn't sure what to do next. We exchanged a few one- and two-word pleasantries, and then he cleaned the board and scribbled one more question.

"Married?"

"Yes. You?"

"Alone."

He did not write "no," or "unmarried," or "never married," or "still single"; he did not write "widowed" or "divorced," nor did he write about how hard it was to meet women when you can't hear or speak. He was more than eloquent. He wrote one word.

Alone.

The sadness of that word seemed infinite.

What would I have said if we'd been two guys just shooting the breeze at work, or chewing the fat over glasses of beer after work? I cleaned the board with a tissue and scribbled this:

"Better alone?"

The best I could do, an idle male pleasantry, shorthand for, "Oh, well, you know women; can't live with them, can't live without them."

He took the board back and cleaned it off. He wrote down one more word: "Yes." I doubt that he meant it. We shook hands.

I wandered off without a word.

I like to think I write for a living but here was a man – two men – who really do write for a living. No idea if they knew each other. For some reason I still do not understand, I was unable to ask the question, perhaps because I was unwilling to hear the answer.

The death of George Katsouleas is a mystery. He did not have a heart attack or stroke. There were no signs of an aneurysm. He was thirty-eight years old. He had some slight mental-health problems. He died in his room, alone.

Well, we all die alone.

I know of another man who moved here from Mumbai and found a room in public housing. He had been looking for a job. He did not know a soul in town. He died in his room at his desk. He was not found for months; no one missed him.

And I know of a woman who lived in public housing. She was so big she could not move about. She paid an alkie on her floor to get her groceries; he took the money, got free food from the food bank, spent her money on booze and gave her what groceries he could collect. He was the only one who missed her. But he kept his mouth shut. She'd been dead six months by the time anyone else noticed.

A man in that same building died around the same time. He was an artist, he was old, he kept to himself. His friends were used to his absence. He was not missed. He, too, was stricken, fell down, bloated, rotted and dried up before he was discovered in an apartment that was stacked floor to ceiling with his paintings, drawings, sketches.

I suppose it happens elsewhere: bachelors die on prairie farms, old men die in outport shanties, loners die in cabins in the bush.

And while we are alive, we wonder: Who would miss us?

George Katsouleas lay in the morgue six weeks while authorities tried to find his next of kin. Those who knew George knew this: his parents and his sister died when he was young. He had no next of kin.

His coffin was plain. The lid was closed. Low music played in a side room in a downtown funeral home. A dozen social workers came to mourn. They spoke in turn.

Barb Craig, the Street Health nurse, took care of George from time to time. "He had a great big smiling face; when he was happy, he just beamed." Someone said he liked sports. He was a football fan who rooted for the underdog, perhaps because he was an underdog.

For a time, George worked as a lighting technician. He was good at his job and he liked to work, but now and then he would get sick. He couldn't take the stress. He'd get aggressive, and that was no good. He'd take his meds, and they'd slow him down so badly that he couldn't work, and that was no good, either.

He hated taking pogey. He hated getting benefits. He wanted to earn his way. Eventually, he had no choice. He went on welfare. He lived in residences and shelters, but he was not one of the broken-down, beaten-up, hard-core homeless.

There was something about George.

Toby Mullally drives a rescue van for Central Neighbourhood House. He said, "When you looked at him, you saw a light. He was Greek, that was one of the first things you learned about him. He reminded me of the Romantic poets."

Eventually, after much discussion with his nurses and his social workers, George applied for a disability pension. It took some doing – these things take time – but his application was approved. With the prospect of some start-up money coming in, George took a room on his own. He found a dresser and some bits of furniture. Toby found him a bed and helped him move.

And then the public service went on strike.

George never got his start-up money. One of his friends, Maurice Adongo of Street Health, asked for some welfare money on George's behalf. But because disability payments had been promised, the answer was, "Sorry, no can do."

It looked like George would lose his room.

He got depressed. His depression spiralled. Maurice said, "He felt as if the whole world had turned against him." George dropped out of sight. No one saw him for a week. He slipped through the cracks. His landlady was worried. She called the police. They came and opened his door. He hadn't wanted to leave his room. He never left it alive.

A priest read from the Bible: "'In my father's home, there are many rooms.'" That may be so, but George could not afford to keep his room here. The priest read from Psalm 40: "'He made my footing more secure.'" Maybe so, but here on earth, George slipped.

On the lid of the coffin, someone had poured fine blond sand in the shape of a cross. There was a single rose, sent by one of the shelters where George had stayed. And there were tributes.

Barb Craig said, "When he got his teeth fixed, his grin was perfect. He had more energy than anyone I know."

Wayne Skinner of the Centre for Addiction and Mental Health said, "We were his family for too short and too long a time." Maurice Adongo said, "Work was the most beautiful thing for him."

We hang on by the slenderest of threads.

The thread snaps.

The city could not afford to slip George a few bucks to tide him over, but the city paid for his coffin. He was buried in Beechwood Cemetery. There are marsh grasses and bulrushes, and there is a small black ash tree nearby; in time, the tree will grow tall and provide his grave with evening shade.

The shade will be his headstone.

TWENTY

But our good times are all gone. And I'm bound for movin' on.
I'll look for you if I'm ever back this way.

– IAN TYSON, "Four Strong Winds," 1963

You don't expect to find a midway at the mall in the middle of a Friday afternoon, but there it was: a merry-go-round, a whack-a-mole and a ferris wheel on the pavement in an east-end parking lot.

It was quiet, just after lunch – no calliope, no salt smell of popping corn, no "Step right up!" Not yet. The kids were still in school. I had the place to myself.

The carnies, loose-limbed men with push brooms, blue tattoos and smokes were sweeping up, greasing up and stocking up; they loped around the lot with sleepy eyes and knowing smiles.

Working in a suburban mall for a few weeks in late spring gives them a jump on the summer season, a chance to blow off winter's dust and make some early, easy money.

Over by the Berry-Go-Round – it is just what you think it is – an old woman on her way home with a single bag of groceries stopped and stared at one of the giant red berries. It had seats inside to hold four kids as it whirled. To hell with the kids. With a berry that big, she could make pots of jam from here to kingdom come.

Next to the Berry-Go-Round, a woman named Darlene was tending the String Pull. It's a child's game; pull a string, win a prize. She shared the booth with her grinning baby boy; what boy in a playpen wouldn't grin if his mom were midway mistress of the String Pull?

"What'll you do when he's old enough to go to school?"

Darlene lifted her son and gave him a hug. "He's not going to go to school. He'll go to circus school. He'll get a better education, and he'll make more money." I raised an eyebrow. She said, "No, when they travel with the circus, they only miss two months of school."

Over at the shooting gallery, a sleepy carnie poured a load of lead shot into the butt end of a pneumatic machine gun. School was out now, and a knot of wet-haired high-school boys crept near. They elbowed each other in the ribs. The alpha kid stroked the stock of a gun with his palm; a high-school gun slaughter in Alberta was fresh in mind.

"Hey, man, how much does this cost?"

"$380.00," said the carnie.

"Can I have one?"

"Are you gonna be like a crazy student and shoot your peers?"

"I'll fucking shoot them before they fucking shoot me."

"Clear off," said the carnie.

The giant midway generator kicked in then, as if it had started on his command. The kids were startled as the rides and the lights and the music came up; some tough punks, if they were scared by organ music.

The Kentucky Derby barker tested his mike: "Shoot 'em up, shoot 'em in, shoot 'em any way you want to win. Rolla balla, balla, ball."

Roll a ball, your horse darts forward down the track.

Two old mall dolls in tight jeans, slingbacks and sleeveless tops gave him the once-over. The barker pretended not to notice. He worked on his spiel.

"Come on in, we'll get you one; roll a ball, you win, you won!"

The mall dolls giggled and wiggled onto dainty stools; they lit their smokes, adjusted their bra straps, handed over their money and soon they were having the time of their lives.

"Rolla balla, balla, ball!" says the barker.

The older woman with the longer hair did not roll her ball; she was hypnotized by her horse. Her short-haired companion rolled her balls assiduously and won the race.

"She did it, she done it, she won it!"

Her prize, a plush palomino.

I wandered off.

Some old grandpa was standing alone, apart; his skin, pink, pale and freckled, as if it had been freshly scrubbed.

"Gonna go for a ride yourself, gonna play a game?"

He said, "Not me. I got the grandkids. I've been here half an hour and it's cost me thirty bucks already. Oh, well. As long as the kids are happy, I don't give a damn."

The kids were twelve and five years old, and they were very happy waiting for the Himalaya, a big-time speed ride worth half a million U.S. dollars. It goes really fast. Grandpa did not want to go anywhere fast.

Farther along, a carnie named Dennis-the-Mennis – that's what it said on his T-shirt – worked the whack-a-mole. It is an easy game, fun for the whole family: "At the sound of the bell, whack the moles as they pop up. Every time they pop up, whack them."

Nobody was whacking moles at the moment. Dennis offered me a free turn; maybe I'd draw a crowd. I picked up a mallet. Lights blinked. Music played. Moles popped up. I whacked 'em. The truth? I have mole-whacking talent. I am so good, I have a motto:

"No moles left unwhacked."

Dennis was a happy guy. Why would he not be? A little sub-urban parking lot is cleaner than most small-town fairs, the money was good, there was no hint of cow dung in the air and I was shilling for him, making it look easy.

Whack a mole. In the hole.

You see, we are not all sophisticates.

We do here what you do there, and there are nights when we just gotta sing. I was nursing a ginger ale one night at the bar of the Stargate 2000 Stardust Hotel, waiting for the karaoke crowd to arrive.

I don't sing, I listen. I love the sound of off-key yearning.

There was something familiar about the man setting up the amps on the dance floor. The way he moved, effortlessly; he tore some duct tape like it was tissue; he bent to untangle a nest of patch cords; nimble on his feet, with an athlete's ageless grace; small from the hips down, massive from the hips up. When he stood, I saw him in the spotlight. The pompadour cinched it.

Mr. Irresistible, Sweet Daddy Siki.

"Test, one-two, two-two."

Sweet Daddy had a long career: six title fights, in which he earned three draws; that's a title and a half, all told. He doesn't wrestle any more. He left the ring with his sad souvenirs – busted ribs, a broken leg, a broken ankle, a broken hand (twice) and a slight paralysis on one side of his face, where Hans Schmidt kicked him with his foot.

It hardly bothers him now.

For a time after he quit wrestling, Sweet Daddy had a band. He toured, he played little towns and big and he cut a couple of records – "Sweet Daddy Squares Off Against Country Music."

Now he has a karaoke act.

"A man's got to keep busy. I'm happy working. I'm the happiest man in the world, doing this." The bar was filling slowly; ladies' night. He talked as he worked, and the ladies watched him work.

His given name is Reginald. Sweet Daddy? "In Montreal, must have been in 1961. One night there was a woman ringside. I looked down and she said, 'Hey, sweet daddy!'" The way he said it, he drew it out the way she would have done: long and low, sweet and inviting. "After that, the ring announcer introduced me like that. I was embarrassed at first, a little bit." And that may have been the last time a wrestler was embarrassed in the ring by a hint of sexual innuendo; now, it's all suck this, fuck that and crotch grabs.

He said, "Some of those guys today, the things they say. And the women, almost naked, out to here, with those little strings up their . . ."

He paused. I could almost picture it.

"I'll tell you how it's changed. One night in Buffalo, I was being interviewed. I said I had the most perfect body in the world. Man, I'm telling you, the Church came down on me so fast, so hard, I couldn't say that any more in Buffalo."

I asked him about the modern wrestlers, if he thought they were on steroids. Sweet Daddy sipped a diet soda and shrugged his massive shoulders; his muscles were his own.

"When I was wrestling, there were Dyno-balls, pills that would give you muscles. A lot of guys took them. Some guys died from them. I won't say who. But I never took drugs, not me."

Sweet Daddy finished his sweet soda then, and took the stage; he warmed the crowd with a song. He favoured Merle: "If We Make It through December." His voice was pleasing, earnest, two parts country, one part blues. As he sang, he did a little step, dip, sidestep thing; you knew, just by looking, that you could not push him over.

Ladies' night; single mothers, with welfare cheques in the bank that day. A young woman and her friends sat at a table in the back; they were sucking longnecks, smoking cigarettes, cutting up men and working up the nerve to sing. On her way to the washroom, she stopped in front of Sweet Daddy and stood before him, hand on hip. He kept singing. She cocked her head to the side, smiled, pointed a finger and said, "I'm no big old man but I could whip your ass!"

In your dreams, child; in mine; perhaps in his.

Sweet Daddy doesn't wrestle any more, but he has trained a slab of meat called The Edge, and a kid named Joe who may, said Sweet Daddy, call himself Joe Legend in the ring.

Yeah, I know who the legend is.

Late in the year, after carnie season was over, I went to the offices of Funland Outdoor Amusements; a dull warehouse in an industrial park in Etobicoke. It is an elephant's graveyard of fun: the Hurricane was stilled, the big red Berries did not go 'round and the Roller Bowler was in pieces for repairs.

John Robertson is the one who came up with the idea of games and rides in mall parking lots in the springtime; anything to keep the money coming in. Off-season, he runs a moving company, which means a full year's work for his key operators and his drivers. He was working the phones. He waved a hand at someone. I looked around. Freaky Freddy Martin, John's lead hand, peeked around the corner and gestured for me to follow.

Freddy does all the maintenance on all the apparatus. He had news. "John's the third Robertson in the fairground business; you know that, right?" I nodded my head; of course I knew. "I was just talking to a guy in Kitchener. He owns John's grandfather's Swing Ride. He said he was willing to sell." Freddy grinned like a kid at Christmas; roots are important to the tumbleweeds of the fairground business; the Swing Ride qualified as a piece of history.

Old Jack Robertson got his start during the Depression, working as a shill, a pitchman and a master of the Texas Reader – a deck of cards shaved so that an operator could cut any card at any time. He taught young John the business; where are those cards now?

Freddy said, "The Swing Ride is chairs on chains, it swings around, it's a puker. It's probably forty or fifty years old. But these things don't wear out. They're built solid. It might take a couple of grand to buy, and ten grand to restore. But a piece like that, new, would cost sixty grand."

A bargain puker, then.

Freddy turned to the electronic innards of the Roller Bowler, which is emphatically not a puker but a simple game of skill – you roll a big black bowling ball down a humped track: too fast, you lose; too slow, you lose; just right, you win a honey bear.

Freddy flipped a switch, lit the lanes and gestured. "Go ahead, take a turn." It did not feel quite right without my sweetie by my side, but I stepped right up and rolled a ball and I lost and I lost, oh man, I can't believe I lost again. "When all the lanes are full," said Freddy, "we're making money." I rolled until I got it right. It takes a feather touch. On the fairground, at two bits a ball, it would have taken me five bucks in quarters to win a bear.

John came by then. Freddy beamed, and he told him I was a natural at the Roller Bowler, and he sprung the news about the Swing Ride. "We could sneak it into the show. Can you imagine the look on Old Jack's face when he sees it?"

John rubbed his chin; sentiment runs deep, but it doesn't clean rust off metal. "Do we know what kind of shape it's in?"

Freddy said, "The motor's still good. It's worth a trip to Kitchener to take a look."

You could see John think: a family heirloom; Freaky Freddy can fix anything; I've got men to move it; we've got all winter to do the work; it might be worth it to see the look on Old Jack's face.

"We'll see," he said. You see?

We are not so slick after all.

TWENTY-ONE

We're bigger than all of us.

– ROBERT PRIEST, 1990

Enza Anderson was taking the morning commute to Mississauga. It was too early in the day for her thigh-high supermodel's cocktail dress; no spiky heels today, no perfect makeup. Instead, she wore heavy black shoes, neat blue jeans, a white shirt with no collar and a black topcoat. Her hair was cut close to her scalp, and she wore a red baseball cap.

She looked like a dot-com boy wonder, and not a drag queen.

Except for her nails – long, brightly lacquered and startlingly red. Old ladies and young men stared. Now and then, Enza stuffed her hands in her pockets. Not to hide her nails. To protect them. She'd just had them done. That's not all she'd just had done.

Enza had implants.

She now has real, in the sense of man-made, décolletage. Nice ones. Big, round, full ones. The proudest ones money can buy.

She was on her way to Mississauga for a routine, post-surgery check-up. She invited me along for the ride. She wanted to show them off. When I picked her up at her place, she asked if I wanted to touch them. Well, what could I say?

She was almost bashful.

I was touched. And of course I touched. They were nice, in a particular, pop-cultural, let's not get all hung up on gender sort of way. She wore a sports bra under her shirt to keep from jiggling as we made our way to Mississauga.

She was still a bit tender. As we rode along, she told me about the operation; it was, she said, a piece of cake, and as she told me this the people bent their ears toward us, looking out the window all the while, or pretending to listen to their iPods.

"I was there at 7:15 in the morning. By 8:00 a.m. I was on the table. I came out of the anaesthetic around 11:00 a.m. I said, 'Wow.' I felt a sense of calmness. I wasn't worried about what people were going to think." Commuters, listening surreptitiously, kept their thoughts to themselves.

Enza has a drag act – she is the Supermodel, famous for her saucy sense of humour as much as for her gams and her little cocktail dresses – but the surgery takes her to another level. She's also been taking hormones. She has been transformed, and she is transforming.

She said, "Months before the operation, I started looking at women's breasts. I'd notice them. I'd think, 'Oh, those are a nice size. There's a nice shape.' Men were looking at them sexually. I was looking at them prosthetically." Passengers were looking at us.

As we rode along, she showed me her portfolio of photographs, the souvenirs of a career in drag. Enza Supermodel, city icon, with Irshad Manji, Moses Znaimer, Carlos Delgado, John Nunziata, Dalton McGuinty, Barbara Hall, Martin Short as Jiminy Glick, Sheila Copps, Fred Penner, Mel Lastman and Julian Fantino. For your information, Delgado had the most natural smile. Jiminy Glick appeared laughingly at ease. The rest of the pols and the celebs looked vaguely twitchy.

Enza said, "Fantino's people are nervous when I'm around.

They follow me. They tell me, 'Enza, no kissing.' Here's a photo of me kissing him." Fantino, twitchiest of all. I'd say it was an Italian thing, but Enza's Italian, too. I've always liked her. She is smart. She is also kind and clever. She deflates pomposity with wit. And she has a supermodel's keen sense of public relations. She said, "I don't kiss politicians twice. The second kiss is wasted. And I don't kiss when there's no media around. Why waste kisses?" Why, indeed? But why get tits?

"It was a treat I gave myself after the election."

She finished second in her ward during a recent municipal election. She ran against an unamused Kyle Rae, who is also gay, who got married as soon as it became legal, and who is the short-haired silverback pol of the Gay Village.

Enza said, "I'd been thinking about getting them done for a long time. I put them on my credit card. They cost seven thousand dollars. I may have a lousy credit rating, but I've got great breasts." The bus bumped along. She bumped along with it.

Commuters gulped their double-doubles and looked wide-eyed out the window – this is Toronto, mustn't be caught gawking – but they kept their ears open all the way to Mississauga.

When we got to the clinic, a nurse showed Enza to a private room, and I went with her. Dr. Hugh McLean came by and asked Enza to remove her shirt. Enza sat up straight then, and she looked at her newness proudly in the mirror.

She asked when she could wear a regular bra. "In a few days," said the doctor. "You want to avoid pushing them up at this stage. Give them time to settle in."

The doctor sat before Enza on a low stool, and Enza slipped off her bra. The doctor looked closely, he pursed his lips in appraisal, he made happy noises. His nurse seemed pleased. That is her job. She held a clipboard in front of her own breasts.

My guess is hers are real.

After the exam, Dr. McLean looked at Enza's photo album with bemusement – I don't think he'd seen anything quite like these pictures – and Enza looked in the mirror again. She turned her shoulders for a side view. She said, "All my gay friends want to touch them. I say, 'No way.'"

Dr. McLean said, "You're incorporating them into your image."

A heck of an image.

The doctor does one hundred augmentations a year. He clearly knows what he's doing. Enza's looked pretty good to me, in an abstract sort of way.

I struggle to find a question.

Is it difficult, implanting breasts in men? "It's basically the same procedure. We make a small incision. We detach the chest muscle from the rib and we create a pocket big enough for the implants."

Enza is a 36B. Big, but not too big. What will she do with her old falsies, now that she doesn't need them? "I'll keep them as a souvenir. In twenty years, when they're doing my life and times . . ."

Has this changed her life?

She seemed sad. She isn't dating anyone at the moment. It's not all parties, all the time. Life gets lonely. In drag, she is whip-smart and outgoing. Out of drag, she's shy. There are other complications.

Her mother is dead. Her father has no idea.

Last year, Enza went to the New Year's levee at City Hall. She showed up, she kissed the mayor, she swanned around, kicking up her heels, batting her eyelashes, having fun for the TV cameras.

And then she went home and changed before going to visit

her dad. He's getting on in years. The two of them were sitting together watching television after supper when the news came on. There was a clip of Enza – those legs, that wig, her smile. Her dad suspected nothing.

The image lingered, then it changed.

Fred Dunn is in his eighties. At one time, if you wanted to see him, you had to take a hike. His old address:

F. Dunn,
Foot of hill, edge of field,
Toronto, ON

I don't know the postal code.

The nurses from Street Health threw Fred a party when he turned eighty. These are the nurses who patrol the bushes with medicine and socks. They trim old men's nails in the free clinic downtown.

They love Fred. They got him a fine chocolate cake and a bottle of sparkling wine. And he walked from the foot of his hill to the corner of Sherbourne and Dundas in order to attend. That's a hike from here to the moon for an old man.

You could not and you should not ever have said Fred was homeless. He'd have bristled at the suggestion. He'd have cut you off. He'd have turned away. He wouldn't have spoken to you. He had a home.

It just happened to be a tent.

He'd lived in it for more than a dozen years. He had everything he needed or wanted there: pots, pans, jugs of water, lanterns for light, a bunk, his books, his clothes, a three-hundred-metre oval track and the log he called Dunn's Ode to Joy.

He was proud of the track. He had laid it out himself. He ran laps barefoot, all summer and all winter. He liked to carry Dunn's Ode to Joy on his shoulder when he ran. The log was heavy. I couldn't run with it on my shoulder. Neither could you.

Fred called his place Camp Goodwill. He said he was in training. He never said what he was in training for.

Maybe he was training to be eighty years old.

The nurses are in love with Fred. They came to visit him often. They listened to his stories and his poems and his songs. They brought him socks. They took care of him. Naturally, on his eightieth birthday, they blew up some balloons.

Fred walked to the party wearing sturdy shoes, a pair of camouflage pants, a hooded sweatshirt and a baseball cap. His clothes were neat and clean. His beard was trimmed. His hair is blond and grey; not salt-and-pepper but salt-and-sand. There was a "Who, me?" smile on his face when he stepped into the basement of the Street Health operation.

One of the nurses uncorked the wine while the others paraded in with the cake, and there were eight candles on the cake, and the nurses all sang, "Happy Birthday, dear Fred!" He lowered his head then, and he covered his face with his hands.

He said, "I'm disappointed."

There was a moment's puzzled silence. The nurses looked at each other. And then Fred looked up brightly and said, "I thought there would be eighty candles." Everyone laughed.

Nurse Barb Craig filled a plastic cup with fizzy wine and set it down in front of him. Fred looked at the wine and he looked at her. He said, "Take your shoe off and I'd pour champagne into it." Nurse Barb, who was wearing sneakers, replied, "I'm not taking my shoe off!"

Everyone laughed at that, too.

Eighty years takes its toll.

Fred lost an eye to cancer a while back and his remaining eye has a cataract, but he was able to see well enough to count the candles on his cake, and it's clear he still saw well enough to flirt.

The candles on the cake burned brightly.

On the subject of running barefoot Fred said, "When your feet get colder, colder, colder, you just say 'I told her, told her, told her.'" I don't know who she is. If Fred knows, he's not saying, and I can't imagine what he would have told her; something about shoes and champagne?

He gabbed a mile a minute. No time to waste.

The candles burned lower.

On the subject of his life he said, "I'm a peace activist. I'm a runner-poet-athlete. I run with a timber on my shoulder. It's a matter of building stamina." The candles flickered.

On the subject of the past, Fred said his mother died when he was young. His memory of her is dim. It is a difficult story.

His father was a wealthy man who was married and had a family of his own when he had an affair. Fred was given up to be raised by an uncle. He was a sickly boy. He lifted weights to build himself up.

He remembered seeing a photo of his mother. "She was wearing a long white gown. There was a ribbon across her breast with the word 'Peace.' She was holding a staff with a dove on the end of it." At the memory of his mother, his eyes filled with tears. And then he sang in a quavery voice. "Peace, peace, peace on earth. Peace, peace, laughter and mirth." The boy's loss impels the man to sing for peace, and the man runs with a log on his shoulder to build up the sickly boy's strength.

Fred said, "Where'd they go, eighty years? You age in your body, not your mind." On the subject of religion he said, "God is a feeling of oneness with humanity. I had some Seventh-day

Adventists come and leave me food. They said Christ was coming with a flock of angels. I said, 'Not necessarily.'"

Nurse Barb said, "Fred, your cake's going to catch on fire."

He shook himself, as if waking from a dream. He took a deep breath. Four candles with the first puff; three more puffs took care of the rest. Fred said, "I need to get my birth certificate. I want to get a passport. I'd like to take a group of singers and dancers to the United Nations. I want to sing for peace." You get the notion he'd want them to walk. You guess he wouldn't mind if they all carried logs.

And while the others ate their cake, he sang. "Shall we gather at the river, the beautiful, the beautiful river." And then he said, or perhaps he was singing, "I'm not as young as I used to be. It could happen to you. It happened to me."

Nurse Barb persuaded him to eat his cake.

He had a single forkful. He said, "I trained with weights. I was developing power. You have to have power to run the hundred metres. You need nutrition and resistance. I met Ben Johnson. He used drugs. I didn't." He said Dunn's Ode to Joy weighed eighty pounds.

"Grunt and groan, heave and strain. That's the way we lifters train."

Fred wrote that couplet in 1963. There's more, but you get the gist of it right there; the point is, power training served him well because, in the year after the party Fred had a bit of prostate trouble, and then his good eye got seriously dimmed by a cataract and finally Nurse Barb persuaded him to pack up Camp Goodwill. She found him a small apartment over a coffee shop not very far away from his old neighbourhood.

Fred's new place is not far from his old place, near the Bloor Street Viaduct. On quiet nights he might have heard the thump of the jumpers. We don't talk about the jumpers.

How did he like indoor living? I went to see him after he moved. I brought that question with me. He adjusted his eye patch – he looks as fierce as a pirate, but his voice is quite gentle – and he said without a trace of sentiment, "It's progress. It's another step in the journey. Onward, ever onward." That's not just how he talks. It's how he thinks.

The new apartment is a pocket version of the camp. Fred brought his weights with him when he moved. He also brought his heavy iron training shoes. He brought his books, his tools, an axe, his sneakers, his pictures, a brass horn, a set of tenpins, some tiki lanterns, a Christmas stocking, a dog cage, a pair of skis and poles; also his poems. The poems were the easiest to carry.

He keeps them in his head.

Soon after he moved in, he bought some nifty second-hand stuff to brighten up the place, including a gaudy ceramic rooster soup tureen and a model sailing ship with green sails that rests on an ocean of red sequins, surrounded by seashells and a starfish.

And what of Dunn's Ode to Joy?

Fred was silent for a moment. "The Board of Education used to dump their wood, their garbage, down in the valley near me. Last spring they came by with a front-end loader and cleaned up. It must have gone then." He changes the topic. He misses his timber.

But rather than dwell on the loss, he talks knowledgeably and at length about world events: the war in Vietnam, widow-burning in India, industrial pollution, and the death of a young woman who was shot by a stray bullet in a Toronto restaurant some years ago.

"Her beating heart was stilled by death, no longer will she take a breath." He stopped reciting and said, "Wasn't her life precious? If your life isn't precious, how can mine be? It doesn't

matter who you are, or your gender or the colour of your skin –
aren't we all the same?"

Would that we were all the same as Fred.

He caps one poem with another. He is a machine gun of
poems about peace. "Each person has a dignity all their own,
whether they're in a crowd or all alone." For good measure, he
throws in an analysis of the national debt during the Trudeau
years, and an outline of his dietary regime: "I don't eat much
cooked stuff. I eat cheese, eggs, wheat germ, milk and V-8
juice. Wheat germ has vitamin E. That's good for your heart,
it makes muscle work easier."

Fred has everything he needs in his new place. Among the
things he doesn't need is a television. "I'm not interested. And
I don't have a computer." He taps his head. "I have a computer
inside here, and no one can tap into it."

Not long afterward, Fred had surgery to remove the cataract
on his remaining eye. It takes guts to let someone cut into your
only eye. But the operation went well; he read the morning
headlines the next day.

Over the phone, he told me he had got one hundred yards
measured off on the street outside his apartment, and he has
another birthday coming up, and I have a hunch Fred's looking
forward to finding a new weight to put on his shoulder when
he runs; also looking forward to more champagne, this time
poured into and drunk from a particular sneaker.

The character of place is the character of people.

Albino Carreira says you should come by the house so you
can see his roses. He is being modest. No one goes to Albino's
to see the roses.

You go to see his house.

It is a fairy-tale place, covered from sidewalk to rooftop with bits of wood the size and shape of corks or spindles or dowels, varnished lovingly and individually against the elements and carefully laid onto the front, back and sides of his house in whorls and forms and patterns.

His van is like that, too, which is how we met.

The van is blanketed with tiny plastic dinosaurs, wee super-heroes, various minute figurines or tokens prized from packages of cereal or tea, or else they come from toy stores where you can buy bags of them for a buck. I gawked, we talked and he invited me to the house.

If his designs were any less complex, or if his house were any less covered, you'd be tempted to lock him up. Instead, you stand and stare in awe and admiration. The house is crazy-perfect.

The most complex of the wooden decorations are screwed onto frames and mounted, but many thousands more have been screwed directly onto the house any old place he can find a spot that looks like it needs filling in. It is impossible to tell how many wooden plugs there are because the house is a work in progress; but if you said he'd used a quarter-million screws, you would not be far wrong.

He's a Robertson man; screw-wise, not screwy.

His house is gaudy, giddy, Gaudi.

Glued here and there amid the wooden plugs or corks or dowels – I'm still not sure what to call them – there are more wee plastic critters – frogs and spiders, lobsters and snakes, sol-diers and birds.

I have seen mighty things in my time, but I was drop-jawed, trying to work out what to ask first. Albino's a pro at dealing with guys like me. He jumped in and started talking:

"I broke my neck six years ago on a construction job, taking down some scaffolding. I fell and cracked my head open. I was doing a favour for a guy who didn't like heights. He wasn't doing a good job. He was also a little drunk after his lunch. The foreman was mad at him.

"Anyway, when I fell I hit my head against the wall. I couldn't move. I was bleeding bad. Nobody could see me from below.

"One guy was smoking a cigarette up above. He threw his smoke out the window, and when he looked down, he saw me. Lucky he did, because if he didn't, I'd have bled to death.

"The doctors welded my spine together; they put in screws. They put a halo around my head to keep it straight. They put screws in my forehead." Albino leaned his head forward, lifted the collar of his shirt and invited me to look at the back of his neck.

Bend your head forward now. Feel what it's like back there. Where you and I have a protruding bone he has a shallow groove, an absence of bone, a soft trough in the skin.

He said, "After all the operations, I was sleeping on the porch where it's cool. You can't just lie there. I started to screw some wood onto my mailbox, to make a decoration. Somebody saw it and said it was beautiful, I should do more. So I did some more.

"At first I used the branches of trees. I cut them up. Pretty soon, the house was on TV. A guy sees me on TV, he works in a pool-cue factory, he came by and gave me some old pool cues, blanks; no good for him but good for me. He gave me ten thousand cues in six months, all free. I give him a bottle of cognac now and then. You see up there?"

He pointed to his roof. Just then, four visitors wandered into the yard; they just wandered in, because that's what people do at Albino's.

The visitors were a young woman, her Portuguese parents and an Episcopalian priest from Pittsburgh.

They did as Albino said; they looked up.

Albino pointed to some long strands of knobs whose gentle curvature led up to the heavens and repeated the story of his broken neck for the newcomers. He said, "You see up there? It looks like my spine. These things I make, they're like my spine. I know. I saw the X-rays."

And after some oohs and aahs from the newcomers, and the ritual round of snapshots, the Episcopalian priest gathered us all together on the porch. I hate that about Episcopalians, always gathering.

Heads were bowed, hands were held, and who was I to object when the priest said, "Lord, we thank you for Albino and his vision." Thanks, Albino. The vision is on the east side of Clinton, a couple of blocks north of Bloor. You might not notice the roses. You can't miss the house.

After the prayer, he went inside and had a glass of wine.

Mr. Harnarain Khanna does not drink. Alcohol does not touch, and has never touched, his lips. He told me this while he was holding on to the railing near the window by the western entrance of the Yorkdale Mall as the morning crowd rushed past him; hurrying to buy, hurrying to sell, hurrying. Mr. Khanna was in no hurry.

He leaned into the railing and began a set of gentle stretches. When he achieved true limberness, he breathed deeply and said, "Soon I will be ninety-five years old." The fact of his age is an astonishment to him, and a delight. But he hadn't come to the mall to talk about age and the passage of time. He came with a message.

In fact, his pocket was stuffed with messages or, more properly, with bromides, homilies and gentle exhortations printed on small brightly coloured paper squares.

For example: "One who has controlled his own mind can help others." Or, "Those who sit on the sidelines are sidelined by life."

Ah, the wisdom of the ages.

He has taken it upon himself to hand-deliver these little bits of inspiration every day to the clerks, the store managers, the shoppers and the strollers who frequent this mall. He has brought a new message every day for the past four years. I followed Mr. Khanna on his self-appointed rounds one day. He is well-known to the people of the mall.

A young man, a fast talker, approached and said, as if Mr. Khanna were not standing there in front of him, "I love this guy. He comes here every day. Give me one." And without even waiting for a reply, he plucked a daily message from Mr. Khanna's hand and read, *sotto voce*: "'Without self-discipline, it's hard to maintain a good attitude.'"

The young man nodded in agreement at this. He clutched the piece of yellow paper firmly in his hand, a keeper. To Mr. Khanna he said, "Your age? I'll never reach it. How do you do it? Take a glass of wine?"

Mr. Khanna said, "I've never had a glass of wine. Not one glass in my life."

The young man was agog. "I love this guy."

The beloved Mr. Khanna made his way through the mall. "I distribute daily, for free. This is good work I am doing." He left a slip of paper on the cash register at the Timothy's, and as he did he squinted at four men who were drinking coffee and gabbing idly.

Mr. Khanna whispered, in confidence, "Look at those old men. They are known to me."

"Hi, Harry!"

"How's it going, Harry?"

"What's the good word today, Harry?"

The men had white hair. They are retired. They come to the mall every day.

"You are all older than me," said Harry impishly. The men had a good laugh at that, and Harry handed them some yellow slips.

The men said, "We worry about him if he misses a day. Did you know he sends us all a birthday card?" Harry said, "My birthday is October 18. These men are my older brothers."

"Ha, ha," they replied.

Harry was born in Lahore, long before the Partition. He was the all-India doubles badminton champion in 1936, 1937 and 1939. It's true. He's a legend. You could look it up. He worked as a banker when he wasn't batting birds in the air. He had a house in Simla.

"That is a hill station, Simla. Do you know it? British officers in the Punjab would come there in the summer." I did not know it.

But if you are looking to explain the present with clues from the past then – aha! – Harry was a Manager of Branches for the Hindustan Commercial Bank, in the Punjab; it was his practice to write an inspirational message on a slate, and post it outside his branch every day.

Now he brings his message to the mall. He smiled at two young women who were helping shoppers at the information kiosk. He pointed to one and said, "She is very good." She beamed. "And this one is getting married soon." She, too, beamed and said he could come to the wedding.

Harry said, "They are all members of my family."

At Bikini Village, the staff room in the back has been papered with the old man's messages. Angie Skotanis pointed up high and said, "This is one of my favourites: 'True love is all about giving, it's not about giving with whining.'" Harry smiled and moved on; he was giving, not whining.

Kerry Tyrell of the Sunglass Hut said, "His messages. They're always so interesting. We use them in staff meetings. Here's one: 'Clean your own closet before you start cleaning the neighbourhood.'"

Just then Harry noticed another group of retired fellows who were power-walking briskly through the mall. He said, "These men are also known to me." The men stopped walking and shook hands with Harry.

They said, "This guy is 100 per cent. We love this guy. He makes us happy. Keep well, Harry." Harry keeps very well, indeed.

His secret? He is as disciplined as Fred Dunn, as devoted as Albino Carreira and as clever as Enza. He peered in a store mirror and said, in mock-admiration, "Look at me. I am thirty-nine, am I not?" More seriously, he said, "No meat. No whiskey. You cannot cook an egg in my house. No fish. No dairy. Only vegetables." On him, it looks good.

And then Mr. Harnarain Khanna, the former Manager of Branches for the Hindustan Commercial Bank, entered the Yorkdale branch of TD–Canada Trust. Manager Michelle Varty greeted him like a colleague and said, "He's very with-it. He knows his banking." She had a pile of Harry's messages on her desk. She said, "Here's one I like: 'The moment you say "Poor me," you're finished.'"

Of his riches Harry said, "I was born in 1908. I am soon to be ninety-five years old. My desire is to live for five more years. I pray my pension will continue." The notion of his pension continuing caused him considerable mirth, and he laughed out loud and then he went home for a nap.

He is known to me now.

AFTERWORD

And these men and women are also known to you now:

Fred Dunn hauling the Ode to Joy on his shoulder, and Abbas Khan looking for work on Cash Corner. James Bond, the oldest living homeless man in the city, and Jerzy with his cigarette-butt scars. Salma Adam with her fresh diploma, and Enza Anderson with her fresh titties. Lee Sew and his famous Sai Woo Sauce. Leo, Joy and baby Ugu. And my three Italian grandmothers, Cora, Sina and Assunta.

They are who we are here.

How do you like us now?

The ice sheet carved us up. The Family Compact carved us up. And the boys in the backroom carved us up. Our first mayor, William Lyon Mackenzie, led a rebellion and Marilyn Bell swam ashore. We won the Stanley Cup once or twice, after which we threw all the hippies in jail and built the CN Tower.

O tempora, o mores.

We're fresh out of rebels. The backroom boys are still sharpening their knives. We haven't won a Stanley Cup in years, and the lake is too dirty to swim in, but we drink the water anyway. We still throw the kids in jail – they are gangstas now, not hippies – but the kids just keep on coming.

As do the refugees.

We make room for newcomers the way others made room for us. And when there are wars in the world, the wounded from both sides come here and they do not fight any more.

We were mocked, and we mocked ourselves, as the CN Tower rose up. The damn thing turns a handsome profit. Think of us, think of it.

We tend to mind our own business; sometimes we mind yours. We work hard. We are afraid to stand still. We were frightened by SARS, but we did not panic. The lights went out shortly after the epidemic, and we stayed calm and we did not loot, perhaps because for the first time in anyone's memory, you could look up and see the stars.

You'd be like us, too, if you lived here.